'If you want to read a gossipy a[...] selling houses for the rich, the [...] delicious!'

'A hugely fun tale of how the super-rich buy their super-prime lairs – I was absolutely boggled throughout. Toto, I have a feeling we're not on Rightmove anymore . . .' **Marina Hyde**

'A gloriously entertaining glimpse behind the closed doors of the high-end house market. I never knew property could be so riveting' **Prue Leith**

'The world portrayed in the highly enjoyable *Highly Desirable* could be on another planet' *Daily Mail*, **Book of the Week**

'An engrossing beach read for anyone wanting a peak into life's VIP area' *The i Newspaper*

'This insider's glimpse into London's luxury property market is a compelling read. In Max's world, houses are snapped up for £170 million. As London's most exclusive property agent, his client list is strewn with stars. Along with his dedicated team, he's negotiated jaw-dropping deals with dukes, duchesses, renowned musicians and national treasures. In this candid book, discover the fascinating and at times shocking truth about the workings of the real-estate market for the rich' *Woman's Weekly*

'If you are as devoted to *Location, Location, Location* and Kirsty and Phil as I am, you'll be gripped' *The Oldie*

'Anonymous. Funny. Cutting. The madness of the London property market. Great for the beach' **Nicolas Wheeler**, *City A.M.*

The Secret Agent has run his own business dealing in the super-prime London market for twenty years. For five years he wrote the hugely popular weekly 'Secret Agent' column in the *Financial Times*, and now does so in *The Sunday Times*. He has an MA and MFA in Creative Writing and lives in London.

HIGHLY DESIRABLE

Tales of London's super-prime
property from
The Secret Agent

HEADLINE

First published in 2023 by
HEADLINE PUBLISHING GROUP

First published in paperback in 2024 by
HEADLINE PUBLISHING GROUP

1

Cataloguing in Publication Data is available from the British Library

ISBN: 978 1 0354 0305 9

Designed and typeset by EM&EN
Printed and bound in Great Britain by Clays Ltd, Elcograf S.p.A.

Headline's policy is to use papers that are natural, renewable and recyclable
products and made from wood grown in well-managed forests and other
controlled sources. The logging and manufacturing processes are expected
to conform to the environmental regulations of the country of origin.

HEADLINE PUBLISHING GROUP
An Hachette UK Company
Carmelite House
50 Victoria Embankment
London EC4Y 0DZ

www.headline.co.uk
www.hachette.co.uk

To my father.

And in memory of my mother.

Contents

Inevitably, I've had to obfuscate some details to protect the identities of those portrayed in this book. What I have tried to do is capture the essence of their characters and the spirit of the business.

Prologue

'Shall we go for a quick coffee?' she asks.

Those seven words are the ones I've been waiting for.

'Great, yes, that would be good,' I bumble in response.

We've just finished viewing a rather mediocre flat. I'd mapped out a suitable coffee venue in advance, hoping this could be my breakthrough moment with the Oscar Winner. We walk the two streets in a wind so blustery it's hard to hear anything. I attempt carefree conversation, enquiring after her weekend. She nods politely, gesturing at the swirling around us to indicate that I should shut up until we're safely inside. The questions I'd teed up – or rather, am desperate to ask – about the iconic films she's been in, her castmates and the inside track on A-list rumours will have to wait.

As we enter the café, I realise the inside of my jacket is vibrating non-stop. I curse that I've left my phone there, nestling against my heart, rather than tucking it into my bag where it can't assault me. I need clarity, sparkling wit, a calm mind. I need to be able to recite relevant property data: recent sales, speculative cost of refurbishment, pounds-per-square-foot value, potential swiftness of transaction, profile of the sellers. But how is this possible when I know with a sinking inevitably who is on the other end of the phone, demanding my attention?

It's the person I call 'Billionaire'. Among my circle of clients, friends and family, he is the only one to deploy such an aggressive method of communication. He has his PA call continually until I pick up. No message: just ring and repeat. I once missed forty-three calls when I had the temerity to take a forty-minute bath at 7pm. But today I need to pay him urgent attention, as we're in the midst of a deal that is hanging by a gossamer thread. It's been complicated by some legal sign-offs that Billionaire failed to get when he bought and refurbished the apartment he's now selling. He has given the other side an ultimatum: exchange by close of play today or he's withdrawing from the sale. And I know he means it. One thing he's taught me over the fifteen years we've worked together is he doesn't issue idle threats. I need to call the lawyers on both sides to work on a solution, appease the buyers and see if there is a wafer-thin possibility that I might persuade Billionaire to take a rational and reasonable approach. Unlikely. But I need to salvage the sale of his £22-million apartment. If it goes through, it will solve the cash-flow problem that COVID has created and guarantee the salaries of my team of four.

But instead of dealing with this crisis, I'm musing over organic juices and discussing the merits of a spirulina shot versus a turmeric one with the Oscar Winner. I mean, this is the stuff that lifelong friendships are built on, right? I've been looking for a flat for her for two months now. She's always polite, always on time, always (and this is my litmus test for people) greets the housekeeper. But we haven't yet broken through to that crossover point where we joke together and our conversations become something more than mere work chat. Now is my moment – and I'm about to blow it.

There's an intimacy to finding a home for someone. You need to understand them: what they want, how they choose to live, what's important to them and why. Is it an east-facing kitchen to capture the morning sun? Is it a place to entertain and break bread with loved ones? Is it a space for solitude and peace? Is it a home with perfect Palladian proportions?

This is my opportunity to start achieving some of that understanding – and I can't take it.

'I'm so sorry, I have to dash. Apologies,' I say, grovelling.

'Oh,' says Oscar Winner, with just a hint of surprise that her estate agent is the one cutting short this cleansing-juice bonding session. 'We'll chat again soon,' she adds promptly, but with only a hint of her megawatt smile.

I settle the bill while ordering a taxi, and then dash out into the gusts of wind swirling through Little Venice. I message Billionaire and say I'll call him in five minutes. It's impossible to speak in the wind. I compose myself while waiting for the Uber. This deal has to go through.

I call him as soon as I'm in the car. 'Hello, I'm sorry, I was with' – and here I drop the name; why not, it's the truth? – 'but got away as soon as I could.'

'Tell them the deal is off,' says Billionaire, unimpressed.

'Sorry?' Even as I say it, I'm distracted by Magic FM playing at full blast from the car's speakers.

'Sir, could you turn the music down a little?' I say to the Uber driver.

'What?' Billionaire barks.

'I thought we were going to give them until close of play today?' I say.

'I've changed my mind; I don't think they're serious.'

'Please. You've invested time and money in this. Let's play it out until the end of today. Humour me,' I say, with a laugh that I hope masks my desperation.

I'm met with silence.

'The thing is,' I tell Billionaire, 'the building regs are an issue, and it means they can't get financing, which they were planning to.'

'If they're too poor to afford it, screw them. They've wasted my time.'

'They're not. They haven't. They love it. It's just it makes financial sense for them to borrow money. And if we dismiss them, we'll just have to go through all this with someone else.'

'Whose side are you on?'

'Yours. Always.' That response needs to be unequivocal. *Always.*

And there's that silence again.

'How about this?' I continue. 'Why don't we give them today and if they don't exchange by the end of it, we walk. And I'll take you for lunch at the Ritz' – his favoured venue – 'and you can choose the wine. But if they *do* exchange, you take me for lunch.'

I'm gambling on the fact that he likes a gamble.

There's an agonising wait. I've learned not to fill these silences. I listen to Celine Dion faintly singing.

At last, he speaks. He says simply: 'Why not?'

'Why not indeed?' I say rapidly, jumping on this moderate affirmation.

One unexpected hurdle down, I now have a major juggling act to pull off.

'You can turn the music up again,' I say to the driver as I hang up, and Dion blasts out the chorus – 'It's all coming back, it's all coming back to me now' – as we pull into the mews where my office is.

As I walk in, the eyes of two of the team swing on to me. Natasha doesn't look up. Billionaire's PA has been calling them all on rotation.

'What's happened?' asks John.

'I've got to salvage this deal by 6pm.'

'Mate, what can we do to help?' Damien says, putting down the weights he's been lifting. He's still in gym wear, which I make a mental note to discuss at our next Monday meeting.

Natasha does not deign to avert her gaze from whatever is engrossing her.

'Right, I'll do a coffee run,' says John. 'Double espresso, for you, Max?'

'Yes please.'

'Skinny latte for me,' offers Natasha languidly. She finally looks up. 'I imagine this means we're putting off The Board for now?'

'The Board' signifies our all-important, first-thing-in-the-morning confabulation around the office whiteboard. It lists the properties we're selling, their price, the offers we've had and the clients we're looking to acquire for. We're estate agents selling properties in London in the super-prime sphere, usually off-market without any digital footprint. We also act on behalf of clients purchasing, getting them into things before anyone else, charming, cajoling and negotiating the best deals. We've been known to stretch outside London and even occasionally abroad, but our core work is centred on the most expensive boroughs of the capital. It's a people business, so we have to get on with everyone, from porters to PAs, from lawyers to laymen and their advisors.

John pauses by the door, looking at me expectantly. I'm just about to dial the number of the friendlier of the two conveyancing solicitors involved in the transaction. I look back at him with a *What?* expression.

'You know, I almost worked with her once . . . terrific audition . . . the chemistry was there all right, but the producer insisted on a name . . . Ludicrous. And, you know, the picture suffered. Sometimes I loathe the business side of my business,' he says.

'*What?*'

'The Oscar Winner,' he clarifies. 'That's who I'm talking about. She and I have history.'

'That's terrific, John. let's talk about it another time.'

*

Two hours later, I've hit a brick wall with the buyers' lawyer. He's holding firm that the building regs need to be retrospectively signed off before they'll proceed. This could take weeks or months, and may not even happen. Local councils don't respond well to pushy agents trying to get sign-off on overpriced apartments, particularly when high-handed owners have flouted the rules and bypassed due process. Billionaire's lawyer is flummoxed. We're at an impasse.

I can see my business crumbling. I imagine John performing show tunes in a tunnel linking tube lines, Damien buying a one-way ticket back to Australia and Natasha returning to her parents' crumbling estate in Northamptonshire to boss some witless old retainer around.

From the recesses of my property brain, I remember a client getting an indemnity policy, a kind of insurance policy to protect them from potential planning permission issues. Could this be a solution? I call Billionaire's lawyer to see if it might be feasible. It could be, he says.

Why didn't he come up with that solution? I wonder – but I'll save that for another time. The issue at hand is getting it signed off in the next couple of hours, and finding out how much it will cost. I don't even consider asking Billionaire to delve into his pockets. This will be on me. I race to the buyers' hotel, as I'm going to need them to 'take a view' on the indemnity and instruct their lawyer to do so as well. If they want it, I gently point out, they can instruct their lawyer to make it happen. I know they love the flat, but what Billionaire doesn't realise is that he's not always the richest guy in the room; the buyers have 'fuck you' money too. This £22-million flat will serve as their London *pied-à-terre* and will be their fourth property. It's not a passion purchase, it's one of convenience. The flat is immaculate (in the trade, we call it a 'turnkey') and that's what they require.

I apologise profusely for coming to see them in person. I explain that Billionaire is wonderful but hot-headed, and I put the indemnity proposition to them. I go into full charm mode, bordering on obsequious while maintaining a veneer of professionalism. I hope. They say they'll think about it and let me know. I don't tell them it's 4pm, the clock is ticking and that they could lose the flat – and I could lose my business – if they don't think about it quickly. It's never wise to push or appear desperate, however desperate you are. I can almost feel the relish with which Billionaire will withdraw the contract and order a fearsomely expensive bottle of wine at the Ritz, leaving me with a bill I can't afford. Doom and gloom descend on me as I cycle listlessly through Hyde Park back to our office. I rehearse how to tell the team we're looking at the end of an era. Getting off my bike, feeling the world on my shoulders, my jacket pocket vibrates. I pull out my phone, resigned to the inevitable.

It's the buyers: they'll accept the indemnity.

I call the lawyer and pay the £1,200 for the indemnity myself. At 6.42pm, after having begged the intransient lawyer to stay in his office, we've exchanged. It's done – and we'll close the year solvent.

JANUARY

2 January 2022

I spend Christmas at my father's, escaping London. It's rather a muted affair. I'm struck by a bad bout of flu and perform endless COVID tests, which fortunately come back negative. From bed, I give my best stoic-while-receiving-well-wishes performance to the younger members of the family. I offer a double-handed embrace to anyone knocking at my door, saying with mustered strength, 'You are good to come and see me.' This rapidly wears thin, as my family are the stiff-upper types.

I track various clients who've escaped to sunnier climes: Mustique (all right for some), Tulum (for the Insta-Kid, where else?), Gstaad for several. I read, listen to Audible and tell myself next year is to be a good one. On all fronts.

In work terms, the year ended better than expected, largely thanks to Billionaire's flat closing. In addition, we exchanged on another biggie. It's as good as done, though we're not paid until completion, so I'm cautious of tempting fate. What was striking about this negotiation was it was all done over Face-Time. Literally. I showed up with my iPhone and did a tour. The house in Holland Park had a ticket price of £17 million. We agreed it after a single virtual viewing. No quibbling, just a simple 'We'll take it,' as casually as picking out a sweater from Marks and Spencer. I still can't quite believe it.

I wonder, in my sickbed haze, if we could develop a reality-TV format based on buying this way; it would certainly make my life easier. The production company could find the buyers (types like the Insta-Kid, who doesn't believe anything is real unless documented on camera), and I'd play the convivial host guiding high-net-worth individuals as they whittle a selection of three properties down to one. My mind speeds to a global streaming franchise: iterations in Saint-Tropez, the Hamptons, the Greek islands. Am I overdosing on Day and Night Nurse, leading to hallucinations? My show could be *Buy It On First Sight, Millionaire Listing*. Perhaps it has legs . . .

The buyers of the Holland Park house were already familiar with the street, had Google-mapped it and perused the floorplan. And, critically, they had a seemingly satisfactory Zoom with their decorator, whom I set about charming. Not only one of the easiest deals I've ever done, but if calculated against time spent versus income made, my most lucrative. *Mazel tov.*

It seems to me that COVID has made people more decisive rather than less. It's certainly shaken things up: I know a dizzying number of couples on the rocks. We all get stuck in ruts in life, but sometimes we're too busy to notice. The pandemic has demanded we slow down and ask bigger questions, such as: who do you want to spend the rest of your days with? These musings are, of course, for the privileged, who aren't merely having to think of survival.

5 January 2022

John appears first, with a piping-hot ceramic cup in hand, humming something indistinguishable but surely a show tune. On seeing me, he bursts forth: 'You're here! Should you be? How are you?'

'I'm rested and healthy. What's with the cup?'

'Environmental – I can't bear those reusable things so I've brought my own, handcrafted by a Portuguese artisan. Chic, *non*?' John does everything with a certain flourish.

The chitchat is interrupted by Natasha and Damien – arriving together.

'Reunited!' John claps.

And so we are. Damien, our meteor of enthusiasm, a Hemsworth doppelgänger, is normally at home in Australia for the month over Christmas, but he tested positive just before departure and that put paid to that. Natasha has been in Northamptonshire with her family. Neither of the two has hit thirty: each is strikingly attractive. I can't pretend now that it wasn't a subconscious factor in their hiring.

In my defence, people like being shown properties by good-looking brokers. It's an old-fashioned model. Damien, a six-foot blond Aussie, brings a can-do attitude and brims with positivity. Natasha has thick russet hair, an aquiline nose and equine face; she possesses the classical beauty of bygone times. John, occasionally known by me affectionately as 'The Thesp' (for he is one), works his magic in a different way – which is not to say he lets us down in the looks department. All indications point to him being in his late fifties (we don't ask). He's always impeccably turned out, even if the shirts are frayed at the cuffs and collars and the cashmere jumpers have discreet patches sewn on. He graces us with his presence between curtain calls and brings us a verve atypical to estate agents, along with a terrific client list – he's known and loved by everyone.

I'm suddenly distracted by a dog peeing on the floor. Natasha bends down with some wipes.

'Umm, Natasha.'

She looks up.

'You appear to have a dog with you.'

'He's adorable,' John says. 'A miniature dachshund?'

'Yes. He's called Lord Edward; he's a Christmas present from my parents.'

I say nothing.

'I thought perhaps he could be our office dog? Our mascot? Our good-luck charm?' She looks at me and makes her case: 'I was going to leave him in the country, but we can't bear to be parted from one another. And look at that face.' She picks him up, showering him with the sort of affection I imagine she's never shown a human. John makes cooing noises, while Damien looks baffled by the tininess of the animal.

'All right,' I concede, 'but this is a strictly no-barking, no-leg-lifting zone.'

'Lord Edward is going to be like the best-brought-up Victorian child – seen and not heard,' Natasha promised.

I look at Lord Edward and am not quite sure if this will be the case.

Damien gives me a side-eye, then I catch a look between him and Natasha that has a hint of the conspiratorial. There's always been a 'will-they-won't-they?' element to their dynamic.

'Now we're all here, I thought it would be a good time to talk about strategy for the upcoming year,' I say, changing the subject.

'Absolutely,' agrees John.

'COVID will be with us for the long haul, but there's a positivity in the market. A sense of *carpe diem*, I feel. We can't count on the regularity of international buyers; we can't really count on anything.'

'We are where we are . . .' says John ponderously.

'. . . and that's never a good place to be?' Natasha suggests.

'*Au contraire,*' John says, zeroing in on me. 'Look at Max.' He starts to well with emotion, but composes himself. 'Max has been seriously ill, it was . . . precarious . . .'

'You had a cold, didn't you?' Natasha looks up from her computer.

'It was flu,' I say. 'Quite a serious case. And I have to be careful because of my previous health incident.'

'You are strong,' John interrupts. 'We all are, and that's why this year is going to be a *huge* success for us.'

I feel a self-empowering song brewing. Destiny's Child's 'Survivor', perhaps. John has a habit of launching into song, musical theatre being part of his repertoire.

'Thank you, John. I'm touched. All is well; let's focus on work.'

13

'We did pretty well last year,' Natasha says, before letting loose a considerable yawn. 'Sorry. Lord Edward kept me up.'

'We did well at the end of the year due to two big deals, one of which hasn't landed yet. Before that, we were in trouble,' I say truthfully. 'We can't afford to rest on our laurels. Now: to The Board.'

'The Mighty Board,' seconds John.

We all swing our chairs to face one wall. The Board takes up the entirety of this windowless side of the office. Gigantic for dramatic effect, it's an ever-present aide-memoire of current clients and properties. At the moment, the roster includes:

- The Oscar Winner. My client and future friend. She wants light, high ceilings and a garden or terrace – somewhere to step outside. We're all rather in love with her.

- The sale of the Chisholms' house in Chelsea. A top priority, especially after our almost-buyer did as we expected and chipped at the price on the day of exchange. We told them where to go, so the house is now fully available. It's the second time a buyer has let us down badly. Asking £10 million.

- My old friend Kate, possibly returning to London from LA. An actress and former model, she's made money flipping properties in the Hollywood Hills. She's ready for a new chapter. Budget: unclear.

- The Insta-Kid. Again, budget: unclear. Character: tricky. A contact of Natasha's who's yet to sign terms with us.

- Natasha's Uncle Fortescue and the possible sale of his Kensington house. This has been ongoing for years now, and we hope he will sell.

- Potential new business, follow up leads from the team.

'Do you think things are going to be very bleak this year?' Natasha asks.

'London will always thrive,' John assures her.

'It all feels rather gloomy,' Natasha says, stroking Lord Edward to soothe herself.

'It's going to be our best year yet. We have great things on The Board, and the joy of our job is you never know what's around the corner,' I say, reassuring myself as much as them.

'Exactly,' says Damien. 'We could find a new Billionaire to drive us all crazy.'

'Please.' John shivers. 'I feel we need to carve ourselves a niche more among the artistic community, clients who appreciate what London has to offer: culture, art, theatre, dance, opera, food and restaurants.'

'Let's just find the clients and then worry about their artistic sensibilities,' I say.

7 January 2022

Damien jogs into work and exercises in the cobbled courtyard outside our office. It's not really what I'd call a subtle demonstration of athleticism. Once in the office, there seem to be several urgent calls and emails that need attending to until it's undeniably indecent for him to remain in his body-hugging Lycra a minute longer. He showers and changes before Natasha's arrival, which I sense rather defeats the point of the whole performance.

Natasha is late. Again. Lord Edward trots in reluctantly behind her. John arches an eyebrow at me, but business is always slow at this time of year.

We're chugging into action, touching bases with existing clients and following up potential leads. I've been playing phone-tag with Zara. I found a terrific house in Notting Hill for her and Spencer (husband) before prices hit the stratosphere. Spencer has made a fortune in venture capital, and my optimistic property mind contemplates the notion that they may want to upgrade to a bigger house, which would mean a double deal for us – a sale and purchase. I often find myself cautiously predicting moves, fantasising about what clients may want – which often correlates in some ways to what I'd want. My own particular property porn varies depending on my mood and the season. A finca in Mallorca overlooking the sea on one side, mountains on the other; a modernist new-build with a view of the South Downs; or a first-floor flat overlooking communal gardens in Little Venice. Or all of the above when I'm feeling grandiose.

10 January 2022

Kate calls. She still refers to herself as 'the Mattress', for she was/is a model/actress. The portmanteau doesn't really sit well nowadays, so I reverted some years ago to her real name.

'I'm going to do it. I've booked my flight,' she tells me.

'One way?' I ask.

'Yes.'

'It's a big step; you're so LA. Are you sure?'

'I don't know. It's the pandemic, it's the polarising politics. You know, I even woke up this morning and thought, it's another bloody sunny day. I was actually craving low, grey skies and drizzle.'

'Well, if that's not a sign,' I say.

The pandemic has made many of us rethink life and what's important. And though I hate to contradict Paul Young, home is more than just where you lay your hat; it's partly about who you're with and who is around you. Kate's had a good run in Hollywood, but stardom has eluded her. This is through no fault of her own and is more down to the vagaries of the industry and the luck of the draw of life. She was almost cast in a mega sitcom that would have been game-changing but lost out as the 'star' wanted his friend in the role. A version of that story has played out many times over her career, but she's the type to dust herself off; you have to be in that game.

13 January 2022

Three times in my life, I've gone into therapy. The first time was in my early twenties, when I was coming to terms with being gay (how outdated that sounds, when gay is so positively normal now). I sorted that out (ish) in six sessions and became disconcerted by the amount of positive affirmation that therapist gave me.

The second time I was thirty, in the wake of a heartbreak I didn't know how to get past. Self-medicating with negronis and martinis, I came to realise, was not the way. I always call that break-up my cocktail voyage of discovery.

The third time was after my mother died unexpectedly and I needed to find a way to navigate the enormous grief, look after my dad and stay sane. It was Quentin who helped me steer that path. Since then, I've had top-up sessions on an as-needed basis. It's like seeing an old friend who knows you inside out. I don't need to give him the backdrop and explain who fits where in the jigsaw of my life; I can launch straight in.

And now, after a brisk six-minute walk down Earl's Court Road, I'm examining his bookshelves for new material and assuming my usual seat in the armchair as he faces me, notebook in hand, wearing an earnest expression.

'I'm wondering if it's just all too much, Quentin?'

'Your mean your work?' Quentin has that therapist's habit of tilting his head at a slight angle to indicate how intensely he's listening.

'I suppose it's that. I am fond of my clients. Mostly. But some – well, they do give me stress. And then there's my team, whom I love but feel a responsibility to. I remember you warning me not to be alone in my professional and personal life. And here I am in both. Alone. What I mean about work is that I have workmates, but the buck stops with me, which is another version of alone.'

'Have you thought of sharing this feeling with your colleagues?'

'It's not their problem.'

'Well, your first responsibility is to yourself. Not every heart attack is triggered by something strictly physiological. Do you see any possibility that yours was the result of putting too much pressure on yourself from a sense of duty to others?'

I had a heart attack three years ago, at the age of thirty-nine. I was fit and healthy and my weight was what it should be; I probably drink too much, but that is my only real vice, and my stock response to questions about my consumption is that being a functioning borderline alcoholic is culturally British.

I'd had no indications of a pending heart attack. The doctors were all convinced I'd been on a cocaine binge the night before, as that seemed the most rational explanation. I hadn't been. It feels like old news now, but I am still more heightened to my body's potential frailties.

'Possibly,' I say, doubting it as soon as the word comes out of my mouth.

'Perhaps your subconscious was feeling your isolation?'

'I don't think my subconscious was telling me to have a heart attack because I'm single, Quentin, or indeed because I have a sense of duty to my colleagues,' I say, rather testily.

'Of course not, but you need to be kinder to yourself, you need to minimise the stress in your life and you need to prioritise your needs above the needs of everyone else. You give too much away, Max. The burden can't be yours alone.'

Now, this is the sort of therapy I approve of: the kind where I'm the hero of the narrative.

'Yes, I see that.'

'Good. Now go act on it.' He concludes the session.

On the walk back to the office, I cogitate on how to impress upon the team a shared sense of responsibility. A new incentive system, possibly, reducing salaries in exchange for profit participation.

The fact is, estate agenting is feast or famine. There's little correlation between how hard you work and the fiscal returns. You can toil for two years to sell a property, but if the client belatedly changes their mind and pulls it off the market, you've got naught to show for it. In fact, you're down, as you'll have spent time, money and resources. And on the buying side, you can visit countless properties with a client who then calls you in high spirits to say they've found the perfect flat – through another broker. It happens.

On the flipside, as with the house in Holland Park, you can have a one-hit wonder that requires minimal man-hours and reaps great rewards. Those jackpots are few and far between but I love them landing in our laps.

14 January 2022

The new year brings new challenges, new hope, new possibilities, new adventures – at least, this is the hackneyed line I'm delivering to Zara, the client who morphed into a friend, and now lives with her husband, Spencer, in the house I found them in Notting Hill. They're the couple that I was hoping were looking for an upgrade. The conversation, though, takes a different turn.

'It's happened,' she says with a tone of inevitability that suggests I should know what's happened.

'I'm so sorry,' I reply – then hold my tongue. The lack of context is limiting. And I'm catastrophising; my mind races to the Big C.

'I'm not sure I can stay in the house.' Oh, no. I think it's terminal.

'Of course. Oh, Zara, I don't know what to say.' And I don't – but I realise a speaking role isn't required of me. It's something television's Anne Robinson set me straight on in my early days of agenting: when to talk and when to shut up. While showing her a house in Kensington, I twittered on about the joys of an en-suite bathroom, or something equally banal, and she cut me short with: 'You've got a non-speaking role here.' A lesson learned. I never try and *sell* property now, I simply *show* property – with a certain flair and consideration, I like to think – and answer asked questions.

Zara is still talking. 'He wants to buy me out so I can find another house for me and the children. I told him we're *one* family. She's twenty-eight, his Pilates instructor. Purr-leeese. And, what's worse, *I* found her for him. I mean, as an instructor, obviously. He wanted to go on a health drive . . . for us, supposedly! Can you believe the cliché?'

'It's certainly that.' I feel relief and recalibrate my thoughts.

'We've been together since university; my whole identity is wrapped up in his. And I thought his in mine. Who am I, if I'm not the wife of, the mother of . . .?' She devolves into self-recrimination. 'The choices I've made! The quicksand that I've built my life on!'

Sometimes you need to let people talk. I read somewhere that listening isn't passive, that if you're doing it right, it's active. At times, my head is so filled with information about my clients' lives – the flotsam and jetsam, the mundane detail (usually staffing problems) and the turning of the bigger emotional wheels – that I hardly have space for my own interior emotions. 'Boundaries!' Quentin exhorts, every time I see him. 'Boundaries,' I agree, then fail to draw them up.

The problem with the very rich – and this goes beyond the well-used F. Scott Fitzgerald quote that 'they are different from you and me' – is they are used to everything being about them and everyone being subservient to their emotions, as if their feelings are somehow bigger than anyone else's. Fact check: they're not.

But the situation with Zara is different. This is a truly sad case of a lockdown divorce.

'I hate what you're telling me. What can I do, Zar?'

'Just help with houses. If I have to move, I need to find something that's an equal, not a lesser. Does that make sense? Spencer's got Slick advising him.'

Ugh.

Slick. Our bigger, more successful nemesis. Ruthless. The Goliath to our David. Hustler, poacher and some unprintable words. He's torpedoed two of my most lucrative deals and come close to destroying my relationship with Billionaire.

'And I need a shit-hot lawyer,' Zara says. 'We never did a prenup, we were just kids. We were earning the same amount back then. I gave up my *so-called career*, as Spencer calls it. I have allowed myself to become one of *those* women. I just thought we'd muck along through the rocky patches – I mean, Christ, what a charmed life we've had. Or I thought we did. I am so angry with it all: with myself, with him.'

I go through my list of lawyers: Shackleton, Tooth, the top brass at Farrer's. I tell her she needs to get in to see them immediately, even if there's a chance of reconciliation with Spencer, because once she's seen a given lawyer, Spencer can't use them. And if she sees all the best ones, he'll be reduced to the second tiers.

So yes, I'm not just a property agent, I'm a referral service. It's usually for the things you'd expect: conveyancing solicitors, builders, architects, landscapers and designers. But I've also recommended reflexologists, Pilates instructors, doctors, dentists, masseurs, divorce lawyers, financial advisors, private-jet charters. Then there was the time a client asked me to set him up with Natasha. He was twice her age and comprehensively unattractive. He told me more than once how very rich he was. When I said Natasha had a boyfriend, he asked me to put him in touch with a 'high-class' escort agency. A real Prince Charming. I told him that I thought that's what the internet was for, not his property finder. And just like that, I knew where to draw the line on my referral services.

The moment I saw Zara's number pop up, I'd known something was wrong. They were supposedly in Mustique, where Spencer could work remotely and the children could be home-schooled by a tutor. But no. It all makes sense now. I knew they'd been having slight wobbles, but frankly, who hasn't?

What I love about Zara is this: she looks after herself, but she laughs and has the appropriate fine lines to show it; she's engaged with life and curious about people; she drinks red wine with ice; she's smart and has a throaty chortle that is completely intoxicating. She had a job at Radio 4, but since Spencer's earnings moved into the stratosphere, she left it. They were paying the tutor more than she was earning, and she reasoned she'd return to work when her youngest started school. Inevitably, that didn't happen. Meanwhile, Spencer began manifesting a machismo that was not in his natural character but finally became who he was: a kind of toxic masculine pride demanding that Zara turn herself into the adoring appendage, that she should be the hostess of his parties and streamliner in his life. But she refused to treat him like some pasha to whom she should be in permanent gratitude for all his gluttonous wealth. She was, I'd thought, his touchstone.

18 January 2022

I haven't dared ask John whether there's any acting work on the horizon. His true passion, theatre, is a precarious world at the moment. Perhaps adverts, I'm thinking.

Office-wise, there's not quite enough going on for the four

of us to be full-time, and we all sort of know it. The property game is seasonal; it tends to dip with the school holidays, so things are quiet for big chunks of time that add up to a full three months of the year. With Christmas in the rear-view, the current lull in action should end soon and the phone should start ringing again. Should. Should. Should. The change can't come soon enough for my worrying mind and the business's tight operating margins. Bless John, though, he never fails to deliver, arriving from a socially distanced breakfast meeting to announce he's landed new clients.

'Frenchies. And, surprisingly, utterly charming. You know I feel more *simpatico* with Latins.'

'What are they looking for?' Damien asks.

'A classic three-bed flat, preferably on Onslow Gardens or Square, first floor ideally, but they'd settle for second. Amazingly, given COVID, they're not insistent on outside space. They have three to five million. I'm going to call all the South Ken agents and speak to the porters.'

John has built up a rapport with the porters of London, those holders of the city's residential secrets. 'They're an unsung bunch,' he says now, 'but think of the tales they could tell. And, of course, the world they inhabit is rife with visual interest. I was wondering if we should try to pitch a coffee-table book about them . . . it could even blossom into a series: *The Porters of Paris . . . The Porters of Milan . . . of New York . . . of Mumbai* . . . of the South American capitals. Think of the photography and the architecture and the characterfulness we could capture in their faces. Marvellous.'

I catch Natasha flash an aren't-you-going-to-stop-this look at Damien. Their looks are legion, though who can really tell what these two are thinking about (or at) each other from one minute to the next? To Damien, Natasha is alternately aloof, annoyed, unguarded and obviously interested. To Natasha, Damien is attentive, strutting and, frankly, bristling with sexual energy. When he does press-ups outside after his morning run, one senses that he hopes for rain as an excuse for his sluiced body to come into the office and pump itself up and down on our wooden floor. It's all getting very *Magic Mike*.

Damien takes his cue. 'A book on porters . . . sure . . . So, anyway. I know there's a good flat coming up in a portered block in South Kensington: wonderful views over Onslow, seventh floor, they want a quick cash sale. They could get it for two-point-six million, which is a good price.'

It is a good price; I think of the Oscar Winner.

'I wonder if my Frenchies would go for the block?' muses John.

The block is 1950s and purpose-built, so there's no architectural merit from the outside, but the flats on the upper floors have good open vistas across the surrounding rooftops. And they're relatively good value in terms of pounds per square foot.

Damien stands and stretches out his arms – he's still in his running kit – revealing a midriff that shows the sculpted V-shaped line of his flanks leading to his groin. He turns, angling himself towards Natasha.

'What's their time frame?' he asks, casually.

'They'd act rapidly, for the right property. They have to feel something for the place, though . . . I do understand the sentiment.' John drifts off again, looking around the room as if recalling a flat that had moved him once. 'Artists and creatives need to feel an empathy.'

'Are they artists?' I ask.

'Umm, not ostensibly . . .'

'What do they do?' You can trust Natasha to get to the point.

'For work?'

'Yes . . .'

'He's a banker and she works in tech.'

'I see,' says Natasha, with an all-knowing tone, side-eyeing Damien as he heads to the shower.

19 January 2022

Natasha walks in at 9.40am with Lord Edward by her side. John burlesques checking his wristwatch by raising his arm perpendicularly and studying the face. He thinks, as, I suspect, does Damien, that Natasha gets away with a lot. She does. I should say something to her about it, but I'm biding my time because today is the day. After an eighteen-month purgatory, we're going to see her Uncle Fortescue, the man who's lived in the same magnificent house in the same fashionable part of Kensington for over half a century. He inherited the place from an aunt, who imagined Fortescue would raise a family there. He turns ninety this year. Still single, it seems unlikely he'll produce offspring now.

When we come to 'Fortescue' on The Board, John asks Natasha: 'Is he, to put it the old-fashioned way, a confirmed society bachelor?'

Natasha ignores the question. 'We really need to move him into sheltered housing. Better now, when he's still got his marbles. Poor Great-aunt Lavinia was completely gaga before we got her out.'

'You have longevity in your genes; it's something to be grateful for,' states John.

'My father says it's the curse of the Lane-Darcys; it's drained our resources, having all these old relatives sucking up the family money.'

The British aristocracy can be ruthless. Rather than pointing that out, I look for the positive. 'His house is going to be worth a lot, that should restore the family coffers somewhat.' Now *I* sound like a Lane-Darcy; I don't think I've ever said 'coffers' in my life before.

'Fortescue is so contrary he'll probably leave it to a donkey sanctuary.'

'Family is family,' says John firmly.

'That's sometimes the problem,' replies Natasha crisply. Her grandness permeates from her very being; it's not so much what she says but more how she says it. There's an ingrained hauteur. Here's the thing about her versus me: I'm always accosted by those people with clipboards asking you to make a monthly donation to a charity. The other day, Natasha and I walked along Kensington High Street together, and three such clipboarders literally stepped aside, clearing a path for us.

'How did you do that?' I'd asked.

'What?'

'*What*? These charity touts, they didn't even approach us. I'm always pretending I'm on a phone call or distracted by my own thoughts, but they always step in.'

'Oh, they never come near me.'

And that's Natasha.

'Fortescue needs to be handled with care,' she says.

'But he's committed to us?'

'As John says, he's family.'

'True,' I respond. 'And I hate to be the cynic in the room, but with friends and family, I find it much safer to head off any chance of them behaving badly with a watertight contract. In my experience, there are no guarantees.'

'Fortescue is eighty-nine, and he's my great-uncle. I don't think he's going to be tarting around. But he can be a cantankerous old fart.'

A couple of hours later, Natasha and I walk up Victoria Road, one of Kensington's costlier streets. His house is on the favoured east side, and therefore has a west-facing garden. I sniff the potential in it. From what Natasha has told me, it's clearly a gut-job, and that takes a certain buyer. Someone ready to pour heart, soul, bandwidth and bullion into refurbishing everything from floorboards to mouldings. And the house is listed, meaning building works are strictly regulated, which adds another layer of complication.

Inconveniently for Fortescue, these days there are fewer such buyers ready to take on such a project. It used to be that people yearned for something un-modernised so that they could wipe it clean and make it their own. But the cost of refurbishment (£350–£1,000 per square foot for a super-prime London pad), the time it takes (as long as three years from planning to completion) and the sheer aggro of the process (supply chains in freefall, lack of builders caused by Brexit) has reduced the appeal. Then there's the new reality that the market is no longer on an inexorable upward slope. Your house might lose value before you start living there. All this makes turnkey properties a far easier sell. I get it. I used to be all about 'the potential', but now I encourage clients to let someone else realise that potential and to spend their time enjoying themselves.

At Uncle Fortescue's, Natasha rings the bell.

We wait. Then we wait some more. Then we look at one another, both thinking the unthinkable: is he lying deceased on the kitchen floor, the exertion of opening a tin of sardines having pushed him into the arms of Death?

Finally, after several more rings, we hear a faint shuffling of footsteps from within. Fortescue opens the door, stick in hand. Looking every one of his years, he's attired in a burgundy cardigan, paisley shirt and corduroys worn so thin they're sheer over the kneecaps.

'Hello, sir,' I say with a bow of my head.

'In, in. I can't abide a draught'.

We enter a hall that feels several degrees colder than the air on the street; it's like walking into a queue of ghosts.

'Shall I show Max around, Uncle F?' Natasha asks.

'Certainly not. I'll do the showing around.'

And that sets the tenor of our visit, Fortescue starting as he means to continue.

It's a large house, roughly 4,000 square feet I reckon, though its original rooms have been cut in half, and some of them even quartered, for reasons unknown. The resulting maze is littered with piles, clumps and jumbles of dust-thickened books and yellowed newsprint. The shutters remain closed, *à la* Havisham, while a solitary low-wattage bulb serves to light each room. There's nothing as modern as a light switch by each door, so Fortescue stumbles into each cramped space and feels his way to turn on a lamp, at which point a gloaming hue illuminates yet another depressing and cluttered corner. And in each room, we must pause, admire, and be given a description of what purpose it has served in the past (a nursery kitchen, a butler's pantry, the telephone room) and, more fancifully, how Fortescue pictures it being used in the future. He takes a seat, musing aloud whether the room we're currently in could be dedicated to viewing video cassettes or converted into a spacious extra bathroom. I'm thinking a utility room, fully supplied with the best cleaning agents, as the whole house has a cloyingly claustrophobic odour of must, antique cologne and talcum powder. I long to open the shutters and windows to let in air, light and life.

Oh, and there's no central heating, only plug-in radiators. Two, in fact: one in Fortescue's bedroom and another in the study. The bedroom one has been turned off, he mentions, irrelevantly, but at least the one in the study is on. So that's where we find ourselves, the only warm spot in the house, an hour later.

Left on my own, I could've covered the place in five minutes, scoping the aspect, proportions and possibilities; but then we wouldn't have had the pleasure of getting to know what was important to Fortescue, his own particular brand of prejudice.

'Does journalism hold a special interest for you, sir?' I ask, noticing by the light of a dim bulb that even more newspapers are stacked around the perimeter of this room than the others.

Rather than answer me, he swings around and barks at Natasha, who's just yanked closed the study's heavy door to preserve the warmth. 'Don't knock it off the hinges, girl!'

I'm not sure whether to set aside the newspapers on the chair I've been directed to use or sit on them. Natasha comes to the rescue, picking them up and placing them on what I suppose is her uncle's desk.

'Don't get them out of order,' Fortescue snaps.

'I won't.' Natasha matches his tone and then silence ensues. No tea, coffee or water is offered, and I see that it's for me to lead the conversation.

'Thank you so much for showing us your wonderful house; it really is a treat to see something with such historic interest. You must have been very happy living here.'

'Not really,' he says, and I feel a pang of melancholia for him.

'Oh, Uncle F, don't be silly. You've had a marvellous time here, and we've all got such happy memories of it as our London base.'

'Well, that's something.'

I spot my opening. 'Natasha mentioned that you may be interested in selling? Did you have a tentative time frame in mind? Of course, we'd love to help in any way we can with a potential sale.'

'Steady on, steady on. If I am to . . . sell . . . I want it to go to someone British. And decent. You can't imagine some of the people who have moved into the street. Complete showers.'

If there's one thing I find hard in my job, it's listening as clients spout views unsympathetic to my own. I've had professional dealings with anti-vaxxers, avid Q-Anon supporters, conspiracy theorists: the more extreme their beliefs, the more determined they are to share them.

I try to conjure a diplomatic reply. 'It's the case all over London,' I say. 'The shape of the capital has changed, but then we live in a global world now. And one thing that you can be grateful for is that it has made your house price rocket.'

'I don't give a fig about that. And it's a damn pity we're a global world now. I've nothing against Johnny Foreigner, but they should be as happy being French, Dutch or Turkish as we are being British. And they should stay on their own turf.'

'I understand. I imagine you'll have some of your way with Brexit, though.'

'How can we help?' Natasha interjects, having borrowed that particular turn of phrase from me, I note.

'If I am to sell, I'll want to meet them, see the whites of their eyes. And I've heard these houses go for millions now, tens of millions. Mine must be worth a good twenty.'

I sense disaster looming. 'It's certainly a very fine house, and anyone you may be gracious enough to sell it to will be lucky indeed,' I say. I'm buying time to gather my courage, because I can't avoid what needs to be said; and it needs saying now, to avoid trouble later on. 'But I think that you may be a touch ambitious in terms of pricing. The market is in a rather different place now, and even at its peak in 2014, twenty million – taking into account square footage, comparable sales in your neighbourhood, the need for renovation – would not have been achieved.'

'It's a ridiculous figure.' Natasha backs me up, perhaps a little too staunchly, as Fortescue looks irate.

'What I can promise you is that we will do everything to ensure you achieve the best possible price.'

No reply.

'That is, of course, if you are good enough to give us the instruction, if and when you decide to sell.'

'I'm seeing some chap called Slick, who has been recommended.'

I palpitate, but maintain a smile while turning to Natasha. *Do something, now*, I scream without a word, and she gets the message.

'Really Uncle Fortescue, he's not the right type at all to be selling it. Trust me on that.'

'Your grandfather, I may point out, was a terrible bully to me. I won't be frogmarched into selling just to please you.'

'I'm not my grandfather,' says Natasha sharply. 'Though, rather more importantly, I *am* family. And I want what's best for you. If you don't want to sell, then don't – but if you do, you should use us. Max, tell Uncle F why he should.'

I long to respond by mimicking Meryl Streep in *The Devil Wears Prada:* on being questioned on her role as editor of *Runway*, she replies simply, 'No one can do what I do.' It's on the tip of my tongue, but I suspect that the reference may go over, or at least swerve, Fortescue's head.

'Because we'll work tirelessly and respectfully for you, and we have an excellent track record of finding buyers without resorting to online portals.' That's what I do say.

'What do you mean by that?' he grunts.

'Advertising on the internet.'

'Well, that certainly won't be happening.'

'Quite,' I say, 'but it is common practice now. For most agencies, it's a *sine qua non* of taking on a new client. We, however, are not most agencies. We're specialists in selling properties by placing them discreetly into the view of serious buyers, without fanfare or advertising. We'll treat your house like a work of art, not a commodity. We can also help with lawyers and surveyors. We'll hold your hand through the entire process—'

'I don't need my hand held.'

I feel like I'm going to choke on the dust in the room. I'd give anything for a glass of water. Also, the plug-in radiator has made the place stifling, all the worse after the gelidity of the rest of the house. I'm dying to take off my jacket and loosen my shirt, but even more than that, I want to wrap up this encounter.

'I believe we'd serve you well and get you the best possible price,' I say, keeping it simple.

'All right then, I will let you know. Now, I must get on.'

This is our welcome cue to leave.

'Thank you, Uncle F,' Natasha says.

I second the sentiment, mentioning I'll send along a letter with our terms and a suggested price for the property. The front door is opened and we step on to the street, escaping the Grimms' fairy tale that is Uncle Fortescue's house.

24 January 2022

I've been thinking about how to approach my team chat over the weekend. Walking helped. I strode alternately between Regent's Park and Kensington Gardens. The weather is damp and depressing, and a cloud of January lethargy hangs over us. Spring seems too far in the distance, and the heavy, grey sky has a pessimistic hue to it. This makes me think of Kate: does she really want to return to this from the blue skies of LA? Along the way, I also reflect on Quentin's words and how best to imbue my team with a sense of ownership in the business. I decide they're invincible, very Marvel cinematic universe. And so, at our Monday meeting, I launch in.

'We must deploy our superpowers,' I say, trying not to sound tentative.

'What?' Damien says. He is still in his Lycra. Perhaps his superhero could be some form of decathlete.

'We all have superpowers, and we must harness them.'

'Do we?' asks Natasha archly. 'You haven't been listening to another self-help podcast, have you?'

I've noticed Natasha's been upgrading her look of late. She has flawless skin, naturally alabaster, with a rosy freshness from her morning walks with Lord Edward. Historically make-up free, she is now wearing lip gloss and an ever-so-subtle eyeshadow that makes the green of her eyes pop. She is a handsome woman, and all the more appealing as she lacks vanity. You'd never find her doing the fish gape on Instagram.

I continue with my half-prepared speech. 'Let me start with Damien. You bring us enthusiasm, tenacity, hard work, muscular strength and endurance.'

Silence ensues. Did I choose quite the right words? They feel different said aloud (with Damien standing there in his skimpy shorts and vest top) than they did when I rehearsed them in my mind.

I move on. 'John, you bring us charm, finesse, panache, a turn of phrase, a glide into a foreign tongue that can beguile. You have words that can massage any ego and soothe any ire.'

He smiles graciously, and I picture him winning an award with all the modesty, humility (and clear expectancy) of a Streep or a Hopkins.

'And Natasha. Natasha . . . where we may be blinded, where our weak spots exist, you see them. You are ever vigilant to frailties. You have the gift of vision, of seeing through others, of seeing what they want, and knowing it instinctively before they know it themselves.'

'We do make a formidable team,' John says.

'Have we gone full Oprah?' Natasha asks, unmoved by my encomium.

'As John says, we're a team. We're going to rise to our challenges. And I've been thinking of ways for us to do just that.'

'We're going to smash this year,' Damien declares, and I feel like he's suppressing the desire to do a burpee in support.

'And you, marvellous Max,' asks John, 'what are your superpowers?'

'Ah. My superpower. Hmmm, I hadn't thought of that.' I pause. 'I have you three to enact the superpowers.'

'Come on, mate, don't be so British,' Damien says.

'I like people. I'm interested in how they live and what appeals to them. I want to find that ideal fit for clients, one they haven't even thought of themselves. And I love making a deal, doing that dance and securing the right property at the best possible price.'

'But that makes you sound so mercenary when you have such soul,' says John. 'Your integrity shines through; it positively glares at people.'

I blush. Quentin hasn't got me to a place where I can easily accept a compliment.

'So, we're good at our jobs, both collaboratively and individually,' I say. 'That's not the hard part. What we need are the clients.'

'Networking!' John exclaims in a eureka moment.

'Always,' I respond. 'But we also need to let them know we'll work for as long as it takes,' I add. 'And always with their interests first.'

'Bravo,' John cheers, clapping without a trace of sarcasm. 'Very rousing.'

'And I want us all to be recognised for our efforts, so I am thinking about an incentive structure that could see you potentially earning much more money.'

Damien gives me the thumbs-up.

'Though it would mean a cut in salary.'

Natasha groans expressively.

'I'll put it in writing,' I say, 'and then we can discuss it.'

Our approaches do vary; our good fortune has been in choosing a job that has such a poor public image that it doesn't attract, how shall I put it, the *crème de la crème* of the working world. But we are *la crème* of agents, I reason. Now we just need to show it. It's not too hard. If you turn up on time, if you're polite, if you return calls promptly, if you have good market knowledge, if you're not too pushy, if you have an easy manner, you're already outperforming most of the competition.

Connecting with clients is everything. A wise friend once remarked to me: 'There's always a way in. It may take time, but there is always a way in.' And I work hard to find that way in, to make that connection with people, to ask questions and really listen to the answers. Natasha's demeanour simply commands attention. It's true, too, that behind her upper-class feigned indifference she wants to succeed. Damien's innate enthusiasm is like a bulldozer through any potential opposition or wavering doubts. John channels Wildean wit and charm to entertain clients into submission. There's a sonorous quality to his persuasion, as if he's talking about a rather wonderful production at the National Theatre. I have to work at it. Finding not freedom but my way in.

25 January 2022

John's Frenchies didn't bite on the flat, so I'm showing the Oscar Winner.

I offer to pick her up, as I always do, but she's coming from set so has a driver. After our juice session was cut short, I'm hoping she'll have time for a catch-up after the viewing. The balance between clients and friendship is a tricky one. They're in control of it; they have to set the tempo and parameters. This is heightened with a celebrity client, where the one-wayness of it is like a law of physics.

I have clients who have become friends, good friends. But it's taken time and a certain delicacy on both sides. I ended up dating one former client. He was inscrutable, but I instinctively liked him as a person, though I'm never thinking of romance while in work mode. Also, I'd assumed he was straight. Nevertheless, there must have been something knowing in me, as I remember showing him a house with a charming first-floor master bedroom overlooking the garden and saying, 'What a wonderful room to wake up in and have a lazy Sunday morning, reading the papers and enjoying life.' I did wake up in that bedroom on a Sunday morning, as he ended up buying the house and asked me out on completion. I'd never imagined that happening – and if I had, the scenario I'd have envisaged would have been very different. Mine would have entailed coffee and croissants on a lacquer tray, lolling in the morning light, glances back and forth to say without words how lucky we were to be together. Instead, it was an early alarm clock, then checking emails, followed by a lengthy call to his mother, at which point I discreetly slipped out of bed. There was nothing in his fridge or kitchen cupboards, so I went to find a local patisserie and collected us coffees and *pains au chocolat*. His response to my efforts was a complaint that I'd disturbed his call by ringing the doorbell, and that he didn't like coffee and didn't want crumbs in the bed. The romance, such as it wasn't, didn't last long.

But back to the Oscar Winner. I meet her in the lobby, which has a slight mid-range hotel feel to it. Not quite her. She arrives in a trench coat and a woollen hat, with a scarf wrapped tightly around her neck. I've seen her turn on and off the 'movie star' aspect of herself. She can go almost unnoticed on the street, but she once came to see a flat on the way to a premiere and was in full star-mode, dazzling and camera-ready. When I was sitting opposite her in the café last time, I had to stop myself staring. She is truly beautiful: the symmetry, the grey-green of her eyes, the smile that could launch a fleet of electric cars. She has a timeless quality to her. She is of an age now where she'd normally be playing mothers, but instead has carved out more interesting roles for herself – characters of substance, with real internal emotional range. And her looks can match that part, as she has the ability to morph from drudgery to high glamour, from an embittered housekeeper to an impossibly glamorous femme fatale seducing a younger woman. And that range is driven by an innate intelligence and understanding of the human condition. We're gloved and masked; her film protocol requires such, though social distancing is tricky in the lift. At least we laugh at this. She is one of those actresses who is a real actor: she doesn't play herself.

The flat we see has possibilities, despite having an institutional air to it. The furnishings would not be out of place in a nursing home, complete with an electronic armchair, the type that can heave you out of your seat. The decor is brown-themed (always a mistake) married with chintz. There's even an avocado-coloured bathroom. The light floods in, though, and being above the rooftops means views with a splash of greenery, giving a feeling of space and air, which I know the Oscar Winner enjoys.

'Do you mind if I FaceTime James so he can see it as well?' she asks.

James is the boyfriend. As the phone comes out, the performance begins, and I witness a masterclass. The language, the cadences, the delivery. Even her movement through the flat is ballerina-like as she floats from detail to detail, including ones that I've failed to point out: the cornicing in the drawing room, the craftsmanship of the fireplace, the geometries of light. In short, she has an artist's eye.

'I like it,' I say prosaically, once she's finished her FaceTime call.

'Yes, it's got potential. I think James should see it.'

'I'll organise it. Can I drop you anywhere? Or do you have time for a juice, perhaps?' 'You're kind, but I'm back to filming, so the car is downstairs.'

'Next time,' I offer, as we head back into the lift. She nods a vague assent.

For me, it's off to filming too. We have a bite on the Chisholm house. The potential buyers are in Antigua. They've seen the brochure, they like the Victorian Gothic architecture and want a video to get a firmer sense of the place. I'm ready for my close-up.

On location, I try and emulate the moves and tones of the Oscar Winner. The house lends itself to waxing lyrical, and I sing-song my way through three short videos. 'Look at this room,' I purr, standing on the balls of my feet and swinging my phone around. 'The architrave, the aspect on to the garden, the fireplaces – two, *two*, in one room – and the ceiling heights,' I positively enthuse. As I move into the principal suite, I carry on, gushing, 'Can you imagine waking up here and having everything so easily at hand, the flow of bedroom to bathroom to dressing room? And the potential: look through this window. You could create a first-floor balcony or an orangery of sorts. The house isn't listed. It's rather thrilling to think of all that could be done, though it's also rather perfect as is,' I coo.

I send it to their buying agent immediately, quietly pleased. Six minutes later, he texts back: 'That was quite the breathless performance.'

Sometimes you gotta go big.

26 January 2022

Natasha comes in with a beam on her face and Lord Edward trotting by her side.

'You look happy,' I say.

'And you're early,' says John.

'Would you rather I was unhappy and late?' she enquires.

Fair point.

'Of course not. I like seeing happy people. It's good that you're here; I've been working on my letter to Fortescue and want to run it by you.'

Damien comes in ten minutes later, looking equally cheery, but that's a normal state of affairs.

The measurement of Fortescue's house comes in at 3,850 square feet; I'd hoped we'd tip the scales at over 4,000. I guide the price at £10 million, writing to Fortescue that I believe in round numbers while knowing anything less than eight digits won't satisfy him. I can't risk pricing it any higher for fear of burning it in the market. The equation of pounds per square footage largely dictates value these days – it's the first thing that agents and the more price-sensitive buyers enquire after. There are always new records being set, and figures that seemed inconceivable just years ago have quickly become the norm.

The Candy brothers, the billionaire pair who have been London's most successful developers in the last twenty years, topped sale prices of £6,000 per square foot at their One Hyde Park flats. Some new uber developments coming to the market, and some very unique private houses, are attempting to nudge up to the glass-ceiling figure of £10,000 per square foot, but it's yet to be achieved.

Fortescue is playing his cards close to his withered chest in terms of other opinions he may be seeking – apart from the dastardly Slick.

Launching a new property is a bit like putting up your internet dating profile for the first time. There is a sudden flurry of activity and interest. You're the new kid on the block walking into a bar full of regulars. You're at your optimum, and your chances of having multiple people interested in you will never be so great. A house, flat or individual is inevitably more desirable if you know someone else wants them – human nature being as it is. But, as with the dating profile, you have to be careful how to position yourself: which buzzwords to use, which images to put up. You have to be sure of getting the balance right between selling and overselling yourself. Don't post photos of yourself in a first-class airport lounge. That's an instant swipe left.

I try to explain this fine line to Fortescue in my letter, without using the analogy of the dating website, instead explaining that there's a window when the house is fresh to the market, and that's what we need to capitalise on. I talk of 'decluttering', presenting the house in the best possible light, and say we will of course assist with this under his supervision. 'We always go the extra mile' is the subtext.

I dare to hope that Natasha's parents may put in a word – or, better still, take Fortescue in if we get the green light to sell. The thought of him trailing around after us is not something I want to navigate. I duly run the letter past Natasha; she moderates the language and couches it in slightly more Fortescuean terms. 'There is an optimum moment when I believe we'll achieve the highest price,' is replaced with: 'We'll do everything to accommodate you and get you a rip-roaring price.'

'We won't be able to sell if he insists on being there for viewings,' I tell her.

'What can I do?'

'Take him and Lord Edward for a walk? He may be slow but he is mobile.'

Natasha looks up to the ceiling. 'This house better sell quickly. I'm fond of Fortescue, but there are limits.'

'Gosh, darling, it all sounds *muy complicado*. I'm sure you've got the old boy wrapped around your little finger, haven't you?' John questions.

'He's not that malleable, even by Lane-Darcy standards.'

'This reminds me of a wonderful film I did when practically a child – eighteen, and so full of enthusiasm. I was learning the craft, so I was a stand-in. Johnny G was playing this gruff old codger with such relish. It was just after Hollywood was so wild about him. Can you imagine? One of our finest Shakespearean actors, and Hollywood only perks up after he did that picture with poor Dudley playing a drunk, so true to life it ached.'

'*Arthur*,' I say.

'What?'

'It's the name of the film.'

'Absolutely. Well, Johnny G was marvellous and kept in character for most of the shoot; he hardly spoke to me. Liza was divine – she's never got the notices she's deserved since *Cabaret*. Not fair, really, but then that's the business.'

'And some say life isn't fair either,' I respond.

John sighs.

FEBRUARY

1 February 2022

I go out with Zara, looking at houses. I've been nervous, as I fear anything will be a let-down compared to her stucco-fronted, *House & Garden*-featured Notting Hill pad. She doesn't want to fight Spencer to keep the house but rather has decided that a fresh start would be preferable. I'm not sure what emotional state she's in, so when I see her warm smile and sunny body language, I am heartened and relieved.

'How are you, Zar?' I venture tentatively.

'All things considered, not bad.' She looks good, hints of Mustique still in her tan.

'Well, I'm taking you out of your comfort zone. We're doing two parks and one heath – Queen's, Belsize and Hampstead. We're shaking things up.'

'That's great. I need a new centre of gravity.'

'Zara, you're being amazing. Has something happened?'

'I've been listening to a mindfulness podcast. I know my life is going through a seismic change, but I have much to be grateful for. My kids, my health; I have mobility, I have money.'

'Wow, this feels a bit like that scene in *When Harry Met Sally* when the woman in the diner says, "I'll have what she's having." I want this podcast.'

'I'll share it with you – it's all about seeing the positive. And we've both got a lot of that to be thankful for.'

'A sort of "living well is the best revenge"-type ethos?' I ask.

'I don't even *want* revenge . . . I don't think.' She gives one of her guttural laughs, which always remind me how much I like her. 'Spencer's on his journey, and he's unwittingly set me on mine.'

'Are you sure this podcast doesn't involve some sort of medication?'

'No, silly.'

We proceed to look at the best selection of houses in her budget. London, I always think, is made up of a series of villages. Certain pockets have defining characteristics. Hampstead is full of the moneyed intelligentsia, generally left-leaning. I'm not sure if the term 'champagne socialist' came from the NW3 postcode, but that's the vibe. Notting Hill is now colonised by the hedge-funder; St John's Wood has become an American enclave due to the school for expats there. Meanwhile, South Kensington has a Francophile feel with its Lycée and patisseries.

Queen's Park doesn't yet have a clear identity, but it's leafy and green and tends to be family-orientated. The houses aren't particularly pretty – they're largely Edwardian with a whiff of suburbia – but they're non-basement, built on wide plots and have big gardens. The house Zar and I visit looks like nothing from the outside – bland, pebble-dashed, 1920s – but it has off-street parking and faces a park. Once inside, we see the architect owner has opened up the spaces. There's a huge room at the back that's a kitchen-cum-sitting room-cum-family room with a glass cube opening on to an enormous garden boasting a variety of fruit trees. I particularly like the garden's winding path, which leads to a compost heap and a trampoline. It feels like you've stepped out of London into a rural idyll, even on a February day.

'The children would love this,' says Zara.

The house is full of books and eclectic art; there are tapestries on the walls, and shelves adorned with objects collected from travels across continents. The owners offer us almond cappuccinos, as both are working from home. I watch Zara's reaction and wonder if she's thinking what I am: that this could be a new way of living, not one surrounded by a retinue of staff but one that's more relaxed – in fact, more her.

It's the final house on the tour, and unwittingly, I've saved the best to last. The Hampstead and Belsize Park houses were fine, just nothing special.

'I love this one,' says Zara as I steer her down a parallel road to the high street, Salusbury Road. I just stop myself from saying, 'I love you and your spirit.' Instead, I say, 'This is you, Zara – so much more than playing the rich bitch. I can picture you having kitchen suppers around that table.'

'You know, Max, I'm embracing the Shakespearean edict of the seven ages of man. And I think you're right. My next age is going to be an exciting one. I'm honestly not sure how happy I've been with Spencer in the last few years, and I've just gone along with it because I had this sense that I'd won the jackpot. Or like I'd been told to feel that. But, actually, I don't want a place in the country next door to Soho Farmhouse, I don't want to be friends with Jeremy Clarkson and his gang, I'm not desperate for a house on Mustique. I want a less aspirational life – or, at least, to have different aspirations. I don't want to be constantly comparing myself to others and ticking off what I have or haven't got, or worrying about being part of some Notting Hill cabal that; to be honest, I've never found that appealing. Do you get what I'm saying?'

'I hear you,' I say. 'And I support you.'

2 February 2022

A disappointing viewing at the Chisholms'. The buyers turn up fifty minutes late with their dog, who, reluctantly, I allow to accompany them into the house. I long to ask them for an explanation as to why their time is more valuable than mine. Normally, I would have left after twenty minutes – that's my cut-off point for tardiness with no explanation – but it's the Chisholms.

I care about all my clients but am heavily invested in the sale of the Chisholms' place so much so that I'll put up with a lot for the faintest promise of a sale. We've been let down badly twice. After having laboriously waded through conveyancing, the hoopla of surveyors and architects, the stream of endless questions and the feng-shui experts, one buyer disappeared without a word. I'd been ghosted once before, personally, but I'd never been ghosted professionally – and neither had the Chisholms.

The next buyer we agreed terms with repeatedly assured us of their wealth, their importance, their market knowledge, their ability to perform, that their word was their bond, and so on and so forth. I've learned to be suspicious of people who tell you a) of their vast wealth, and b) of their honour. If they are going to great lengths to point this out, it's usually not the case. I hate it when those who behave badly (and these people did) have the power to suck at your oxygen and invade your head – and, as with Billionaire and his Stasi-style manipulations, I battle against that happening. But sometimes it is hard, especially when you've got emotional skin in the game.

What has been particularly distressing is that the Chisholms are thoroughly decent people, and thus are utterly flummoxed by such deceptive behaviour. They are of their word and expect others to be. And they are great family friends. My father was at school with George Chisholm, I grew up with their children, their grandchildren are friends with my nephew and nieces; it's three generations of history. They have been unflinchingly loyal to me when others would have jumped ship. I wouldn't have blamed them if they had, because you need to have a very clear and rational mind not to blame the agent when a series of buyers behave badly. This year, I am determined, will be the year we sell their house.

In this case, though, it isn't going to happen. These potential buyers, apart from being tardy, are monosyllabic, and the few words they offer are on the vast cost of refurbishment. It puts me in a dark mood, and as I walk back to the office, I feel a tightness in my chest. I pause, take several deep breaths, and stabilise. It's psychosomatic, I'm sure; if the viewing had gone well, I'd be positively skipping down Chelsea Park Gardens.

I haven't heard back after that video I sent off, and I worry that my overacting could have damaged the chances of a sale. I tell myself not to be stupid and ping their buying agent a message. I like him, but he's notoriously unresponsive unless there's something concrete to say. I like an over-communicator, so that I can at least relay information to my clients. I remember the late, great Ed Victor (London's top literary agent) telling me, 'I'm going to give you the second-best answer, a quick no.' These were words he often said, but they were always appreciated, as it's the not knowing that can be so torturous. We all know how to deal with rejection (well, I do, at least) but it's painful to have it dragged out.

4 February 2022

Damien jogs into the office without his usual sprightliness. His step isn't as high, and his general bonhomie seems flatter.

'How are you, Dame?' I ask, using my own abbreviation of his name. Most of his friends know him as Damo; professionally, he's Damien.

'I'm all right,' he responds, the normal glint in his eye missing as he walks heavily across to his desk. There are no burpees or press-ups.

'Not doing your usual set?' John enquires, giving me an on-camera look of significance.

'Not today, I'm not feeling it.'

Natasha looks up when he says this, rather than studiously avoiding his athletic showmanship. The energy that habitually pulsates from Damien has been dialled down several notches.

'Is everything OK?' John asks, giving me another stagey look.

'I'm all right, mate,' Damien says flatly.

I've tried to keep track of my team's emotional well-being over the last tumultuous couple of years, but lately I've got caught up in keeping my own ship steady. I've been less attuned to them than I'd like to be, but it's seemed, surface-wise, they've been doing OK. The job we do demands a certain self-sufficiency – it's low-salaried and commission-based, so you eat what you kill and that necessitates a self-reliance. Due to lockdown restrictions, socialising hasn't been happening as much – and it's inevitably after a glass or two that we tend to share the personal stuff.

Natasha hails from a school that considers it rather bad form to talk about feelings, particularly with work colleagues. There is a robustness to her that I admire, a sense of self that comes from generations of land ownership.

John told me long ago that he'd made the conscious decision that, having chosen the uncertain world of acting, he must always present what the Italians call *bella figura*. It's akin to putting on the show, summed up by Elizabeth Taylor's famous quote that in the face of adversity you should: 'Pour yourself a drink, put on some lipstick, and pull yourself together.' He does it well. It's as if, by force of personality, he chooses to see and celebrate the positive in life. And I think he genuinely does: I've never heard a bitter word leave his mouth, despite his lack of overt success in the acting world. He hates bad manners and unpleasantness, but goes for the high ground when faced with them. 'Surely they must be very unhappy to behave in such a way,' he's oft been heard say, when a client is being belligerent, unreasonable or just plain bloody rude. Who really knows what lurks in the inner sanctums of his psyche – but who knows that for any of us? All I can say for sure is that John leads with kindness.

Damien has an inherent optimism, a natural propensity to see the glass half-full, a straightforward blokeishness that isn't prone to introspection. It's never occurred to me to ask if he's OK, and until now I've never had a whiff of concern over him. But to state the obvious, he hasn't seen his family in two years. His father has health issues, and he's been in a London flat-share without seeing friends, though I choose not to enquire how strictly adherent he's been in following COVID rules. Damien's life before lockdown was one of sociability, of sports, populated by friends, dates and weekends away. Like most Australians, he was taking advantage of London's proximity to Europe. He's great at 'sucking the marrow' (as he describes it), and I imagine, in time, the lure of climate, lifestyle and family will inevitably take him back to his homeland.

'How about we go and look at that new development?' I ask as he's heading to the shower.

'Yeah, sure,' he responds vaguely. 'I could go, or John could . . .' It's not like Damien to pass on the chance to see a property and increase his market knowledge, so I know something is not right. Natasha looks up from her computer.

'I'd like you to come with me,' I say. 'I've got a 10am slot booked.'

John gives me a look of approval and takes a sip of his espresso.

A freshly spruced Damien and I leave the office and start our walk up to Holland Park. There's something about walking or driving that I find makes personal conversations easier – the fact that you're occupied with something else makes them less earnest, and often it's easier to say difficult things when you're not making direct eye contact. Not that I had worked out anything profound or wise to say in the previous twenty minutes.

'Strange times,' I open with, as we cut through the Georgian architecture of Edwardes Square. The square had been built speculatively in prospect for Napoleon's conquering captains, and almost every time I walk through it, I'm struck by this oasis set back just one road from Kensington High Street – only in London can you turn off a shopping metropolis and be in greenery and tranquillity so quickly. We walk past the perfectly symmetrical red-brick terraced houses with wrought-iron gates leading into front gardens. The houses aren't grand or modest, but strike me as being just right, comfortably bourgeois. The square faces a three-and-a-half-acre garden accessed by residents only, containing a grass tennis court. It's almost as if it's been created for a film set, so picture-perfect are the gardens, with wooden benches, arched avenues and even a chocolate-box cottage in the middle, home to the permanent gardener.

'Strange times,' echoes Damien.

'I've always loved this square,' I say. 'It's so quintessentially London, don't you think?'

'Yeah, I guess. There are a lot of Londons, though.'

'I imagine you see a lot more of it than me.'

'I don't know.'

It's not much of an opening, but after we've turned off the High Street and started our walk up Melbury Road, sighting the late Michael Winner's Victorian palace ahead of us (now owned by Robbie Williams and rented to the restaurateur Richard Caring), I take my chance. 'And how are you, Dame? It must be tough. You're missing your family and home, I bet. Well, that's stating the obvious. We haven't really chatted and I'm sorry for that.' The words come stumbling out of me.

'I'm all right, I'm a bit worried about Dad, but he'll be OK. It just got to me a bit yesterday. There was something . . .'

We pass Winner's house. I'd almost sold it to a hedgie before Robbie came along and blew our offer out of the water with his 'Angels' royalties. I'm not sure if he now regrets it, having largely relocated to LA. His neighbour, Led Zeppelin's Jimmy Page, has been in an epic feud with him over Robbie's desire for the ubiquitous basement pool, cinema room and gym. Page had complained it's a listed house of historic interest, and the works would damage the fabric of his own building. I can't begin to imagine the number of unused underground pools that have been built in London over the last decade. Likewise cinema rooms.

'Did something in particular happen yesterday?' I ask, running through the day in my mind.

'You know Good Gym?'

'Yup, the running charity.' We turn into Ilchester Place, which resembles what I imagine the grander streets of Washington DC look like. Wide, low-built, solid and prosperous-looking, with one side of the gardens backing on to Holland Park. They were built in the 1950s, but have a look of American comfort, sort of solidly grand and rather un-London-like. They now sell for around £20 million a pop.

Good Gym partners runners with old people who are largely housebound, the idea being that the runner jogs to the flat or house, has a chat, asks the client if they need anything, runs to the local shops, runs back, delivers and has another chat. Simple but effective in that it combines practicality with fending off the sense of isolation in older people. Not only is Damien an active member but he's encouraged a lot of his friends to join.

'I've been seeing this great old guy, Brian,' Damien explains, as I catch a glimpse of Holland Park through one of its entrances. 'He's alone, doesn't have any family. I get him what he needs and then sit outside and have a yarn with him through an open window. He's very COVID cautious.'

'That's great, Damien. So good of you.' For some reason, I feel tears welling in my eyes. I find this simple act of kindness very moving.

'He's a great bloke – so full of stories.'

'I'm sure,' I say, as we turn into Abbotsbury Road. A peacock from the adjacent Holland Park casually strolls across the road, plumage outspread, stopping cars.

'I go and see him every other day, and last night he wasn't there. He never goes anywhere, so I buzzed the other flats in the building, and he's in hospital. It's not COVID, but an ambulance came to get him, and it's not good being in hospital at his age. I guess it just hit me. And I can't even visit him in hospital. And then I thought, what happens if Mum or Dad get sick and I'm stuck here?'

I really have to hold back the tears now. 'Oh, Damien.' My voice catches. 'It's tough, and we're all still adjusting.'

Damien gives me a slightly quizzical look and asks, 'Are *you* OK, Max?'

'Yes, I'm fine. I was worried about you. You seemed, I don't know, a little out of sorts this morning, but now I understand why. And I just think it's so wonderful that you're looking after this old man. I'm sure your parents will be OK.' We turn into a street of Italianate villas, huge white stucco palazzos that were built to announce the height of empire and the invincibility of the British nation. I feel embarrassed that I've managed to turn my queries into his well-being into him enquiring after my own.

'Yeah, well, I'll be all right.'

We arrive at the development on the northern edge of Holland Park, bringing our chat to a natural close.

The marketing suite resembles the others I've seen over the

years – a slick operation that has a scale model, a showroom and an interactive video presentation. I've become somewhat jaded by the luxury and wizardry of such gizmos, even if someone who sounds like – or possibly is – Stephen Fry narrates the dazzling nature of the new development. The booming voice talks of the twenty-metre ozone pool (*Big whoop*, I think cynically, *I've seen that before*); a private screening room showing all the latest releases (*ring-a-ding-ding, these days I yearn to go to a public cinema with other people*); twenty-four-hour concierge service that promises to source you anything ('Anything?' I want to ask, thinking of that client's request for a high-end escort. 'Do you really mean *anything*?'); restaurant service delivered to your apartment (*so, that's a glorified Deliveroo*). And on it goes.

You see how brattish I am in the face of all these luxuries, and how hard developers try to set an ever-higher sybaritic bar for each new super-prime build. This quest has become farcical, demanding a separation between the super-rich and the merely wealthy, as if entering this world sets them apart somehow. It's all very Tom Wolfe's *The Bonfire of the Vanities*. I remember the passage describing how the Park Avenue elite didn't come into contact with 'normal' people; they went from doormen-secured apartments to chauffeur-driven cars to underground car spaces, never being polluted by contact with the outside world. I think of a client who told me he'd flown back commercially from New York (naturally in first class), rather than in his own plane, and what fun it had been, as he'd bumped into someone in the airport lounge and then another person on the plane itself whom he hadn't seen for years. There is something isolating about being very rich; random encounters are greatly decreased.

The sales agent for the marketing suite is Cassie, a pretty woman in her late twenties with cropped blonde hair. She is wearing a fitted skirt suit and is armed with a well-worn smile. She's got her patter down and hits the high notes in well-practised verse. She takes over where Stephen Fry leaves off. Personally, I don't want to be wowed by 'the extras' – spa treatments, car decks, concierge service. I want to go back to the basics; to ask about the shapes and proportions of the flats, what their outlooks are, whether the bathrooms have windows, what the ceiling heights are – all the things that actually matter in a property. The whizz-bang flashiness of having a Michelin-starred supper delivered to your room at 3am is never really going to be something you want. The point of being in London is to get out and enjoy it. At least, that's what I think. But increasingly, there's a demand from international clientele for these uber-luxury developments to be so homogenised that once you're inside them you could be in Dubai, London, Hong Kong or Singapore. The character and culture of the city is considered secondary to having the right level of gadgetry, service and facilities. Once, I was inside a show apartment being shown a Japanese loo, the kind that offers a sort of wash and blow-dry for the derriere. 'Surely there's someone to do that for you?' I asked jokingly, and the agent looked concerned that they'd failed in some way to provide this essential service. They'd talked, then, of each apartment being assigned a personal concierge. But how far do whims go – and, unless there is a boundary check, when do they become normality?

Cassie continues to run through the marketing spiel, largely ignoring my questions (I don't think she knows the answers). She robotically sticks to her script, trying to sound enthused by the stacking car park that goes down the equivalent of six storeys and can summon up your car within minutes via an app.

'The app is groundbreaking and the first ever to be used in a London development,' Cassie tells us. 'It's been trialled in a Six Senses development in Singapore, and the residents of that building have given it a ninety-eight per cent approval rating.'

'That's great,' says Damien, who is proving more of a captive audience than I am. I suppress a yawn, knowing Cassie is just doing her job, and try to look interested. Damien, being more technologically savvy than me (not hard), appears impressed by the app and its features. I feel sure the novelty of running your bath from your office so it's ready and at a perfect temperature when you arrive home might wear off, but who am I to question the success of the billionaire Candy brothers?

'Sounds clever,' I say, as now even Dame's enthusiasm is waning. We both know that an app like this will inevitably freeze at some point; an operating system will age out, a piece of tech will fail you. Just the other day, John and I went to view a flat that the brothers developed ten years ago, and I couldn't believe how dated it looked – every device seemed laughably antique, and not in a good way. A beautiful brass light switch with a dimmer still radiates chic after twenty years – a Lutron lighting system needs updating after five. That's the reality.

'What's the entry level?' I ask, cutting to the financial nuts and bolts.

'Well.' Cassie wields her mouse and starts clicking on her pad. 'We've got a couple of one-beds coming on.'

'And?'

'They start at' – she clicks ferociously on her mouse as if it may give her a different answer from the one she must know – 'five point five million.'

'Gadgetry doesn't come cheap,' I say, stating the obvious.

Damien and I walk back to the office, discussing the mass of luxury developments being built in London: Grosvenor Square in Mayfair, Chelsea Barracks, Battersea Power Station, the whole regeneration of Nine Elms, where the American Embassy is now located. I wonder where the appetite will come from, and who these buyers will be. I suppose it's a new way of living, but it's so different from Edwardes Square, which we find ourselves walking through again. There is both a housing shortage for key workers and a glut of luxury developments coming on stream – the equation doesn't seem balanced.

'So, how was it?' asks Natasha, in a way that suggests she's really not interested in the answer.

'Oh, the usual,' I say. 'All thrills and spills and not that much substance.'

'And isn't that a sign of the times?' chimes in John.

8 February 2022

I go for my annual tests. There's something reassuring about the pushing, prodding and blood-taking. Then I run on the treadmill as I'm monitored like some sort of bionic man. I'm encouraged to make it to level eight, significantly faster than my usual running pace, and I pant heavily at the end as I'm pushed on to my side and a cold stethoscope is placed on my chest.

'Good, looking good,' says the male nurse.

I'll take it.

On my return to the office, Slick calls me to discuss the value of Zara and Spencer's house. He's been retained by the latter to act on his behalf, which is galling, as I would have happily given an impartial view. Not to mention the fact that it's Slick. The house was bought well, and I'm happy to say I advised them. They purchased it in 2009, just after the crash; the then-owners had bought something else, thinking their place would sell in a flash (which normally it would have done), and overstretched themselves. They needed money quickly, and Spencer and I negotiated a forty-eight-hour attended exchange without a survey.

Zara did a terrific job doing up the house. It doesn't look like the generic variation-of-beige houses that inhabit the area, all of which have an obligatory Damian Hirst butterfly print in the hallway and identikit kitchens and bathrooms. She didn't use a designer (unusual), she used colour (outlandish), and most of the things in the house have a personal story (revelatory) – there's a driftwood bench by the fireplace that came from a holiday in Myanmar, artwork from a safari in Botswana, and an antique bath from her grandmother's cottage in Wales. The place has character and feels like a home rather than a show house.

Lansdowne Road, where the house is, is one of the most desirable streets in the area. And their house ticks the boxes within the boxes: it backs on to communal gardens, via a west-facing garden, and has off-street parking. The best houses in the area have doubled in value in the last ten years, while the rest of the super-prime market (Mayfair, Knightsbridge, Belgravia and Chelsea) has risen by only ten to twenty per cent. The thing about Notting Hill is that if you're a hedgie, in tech, finance or the CEO of a unicorn business, you want to be there. I have been sceptical about the over-inflation of the area in the past, but having bought and sold so much there, I get it. The communal garden aspect is hugely appealing, particularly when you know you're mixing with like-minded types. The architecture is pretty, while the greenery puts oxygen in the air and gives children places to run and adults a place to walk dogs. The garden square hosts firework parties, camping nights, summer parties and the like, creating a sense of community – even if it's a rarefied one. The boutique shops selling artisanal bread and cupcakes (though I'm sure the women of the neighbourhood don't eat carbs) speak of a certain lifestyle. It has become a gentrified version of the film *Notting Hill*, and the writer/director Richard Curtis and his wife, Emma Freud, actually lived here for many years. As do a host of celebs and expensively groomed wealthy people. There's something people find reassuring about that.

Slick, rather than discussing the value, tells me what it is. 'I'd say seven million is a decent price for it. Let's make this easy.' Slick has a condescending *de-haut-en-bas* (literally translated as 'from high to low') manner that doesn't invite any questions. He's tried this technique with me in the past, and succeeded – it's his MO. On a previous deal, I was more generous with commission-sharing than I should have been, but I reasoned I was in the business for the long haul, so could afford to be collegiate now, and then, when the shoe was on the other foot, it would be reciprocated – blah, blah, blah. When such an occasion did present itself, the anticipated reciprocation failed to materialise; what's more, he actively tried to pinch the very client I'd introduced him to. It was utterly ruthless and somewhat insulting; he clearly saw me as someone easily railroaded with no fear of reprisals.

Slick is, unquestionably, a big cheese in the industry: urbane, handsome and surface-level charming. He oozes suavity, and I'm impressed by how easily he's able to take command of a situation. I've tried to observe how he does this, and it seems to be a mixture of self-assurance, a certain gravitas, confidence in the product (whether real or false) and an air of playing in the same orbit as his clients, or even on a level above. This heady combination ensures he's highly per-suasive with buyers and sellers, while he treats his colleagues with a thinly disguised disdain. He's tall, six foot three, with hair that's now receding and greying but swept back, and he's always immaculately turned out in finely tailored suits. If I'm to give a visual, I'd say think of Charles Dance.

'I'm sorry, Slick,' I say. 'That's a ludicrously low valuation.' I do my best to imbue my voice with an authoritative tone.

'I don't think so. You know what they bought it for . . . four-point-five million. This is a generous increase. The super-prime market hasn't gone up sixty per cent in the last thirteen years, as we both know.'

'They spent a million doing it up, they bought it very judiciously, and the Notting Hill market is very different from the broader super-prime market in London. It's gone up way more than sixty per cent.'

'I wouldn't say that. Look at—' and he rolls off some entirely ill-judged comparable sales to support his argument.

'Why don't you put those in writing, and I'll do the same, and then we can discuss this with the lawyers and see what agreement we can come to.'

'My dear boy, the last thing we want to do is get lawyers involved, that will simply hurt both our clients. We must think of them as a family and think continuity. Surely you won't deny the children that? Bigger picture, Max.'

I say nothing. I'm tempted to ask if he even knows the names of Zara and Spencer's children, but I hold back.

'I am thinking of the bigger picture, but I'm also considering a fair valuation. I know two people currently in the market who would pay north of ten for that house.'

'Ten! Ten! I'm not sure what you're smoking, but that figure is way beyond the realm of where we're at.'

'Well, I'm sorry to report that's the figure I am at. And if you and Spencer don't like it, we can always go to the open market and see where the value lands. Your call.'

'You've become very hot-headed, Max. I'm not sure it suits you. And before making ultimatums, maybe you should consult your client. Or would you like me to call Zara?'

'By all means, try. I'll be interested to see if she picks up.'

This is becoming a touch like a scene from *Dynasty*; I'm channelling Alexis Carrington, albeit rather unsuccessfully. Big talk and ultimatums don't really suit me.

'Let's talk when you're feeling more reasonable,' Slick admonishes, and puts down the phone before I'm able to respond.

Round one to him in this particular battle. I'm clearly so determined not to feel I'm being pushed around that I've overplayed my hand.

I immediately call Zara, before Slick can. The critical thing with clients is to communicate, even when there's nothing to say.

'So, how's my property maestro?' she asks. 'Am I moving to Queen's Park?'

'I think so. I hope so. I just wanted to warn you that Slick may call. He's trying to put a ludicrously low valuation on Lansdowne Road, and I'm pushing back. I am determined you should get your due.'

'My due?' Zara asks.

'Yes – half the value of the house?'

'Yes, that's what's been agreed by us both, and our mediator. But I guess when you phrase it like that, I wonder what my "due" is. It's a heavily loaded word that has lots of implications. Let's be honest, Spencer made this money and it's always been more important to him than me. In lots of ways, I'm happy to be freed from the trappings of it all. I want to be secure and have enough to give me work options, but getting exactly half of everything – I don't know, it doesn't feel that important.'

'I know that you get it, Zar. That's why I admire you. But I don't want you going all MacKenzie Bezos just yet and giving everything away. You should get what you're entitled to, and then you can choose what you do with it.'

'But what am I entitled to? I married him because I love him – or loved him, I don't know what tense to use now. We have children, and he happened to make a lot of money. I don't want my children to grow up in a world that is too detached from reality and places too high a value on material goods. I don't want that,' she reflects.

'But you don't want your children to have two different lives. You don't want them to be high-flying with him and—'

'Slumming it with me?'

'That's not what I meant.'

'I know, Max, but I don't want them to equate money with happiness. I want them to be as joyful in a cottage on the Dorset coast with their normal-life cousins as they are in

Dubai with rich kids spending thousands on champagne and thinking that's normal. And that's up to me to teach them. Money won't do that.'

'As always, you are wise.'

'Let's settle this quickly. I really like the Queen's Park house and don't want to lose it; it feels right. I know that I'm not being strategic, but I'm trusting my gut on this one. I met two of the neighbours, and they were great – one works in publishing and the other is retraining as a therapist having left banking. That's who I'm going to feel more comfortable around. People who are trying to make sense of their lives, like me.'

'I understand. Leave it with me. I'll get it sorted out.'

9 February 2022

I meet with Slick at a coffee shop. I've deliberately chosen a high-street chain that won't be his normal habitat, hoping it may disorientate him. He's wearing a perfectly tailored grey lambswool suit, a hand-fitted Savile Row shirt in cream, a fawn cashmere scarf and highly polished shoes. Everything about him is polished, in fact. By contrast, I'm in navy Massimo Dutti brushed cotton trousers, a Charles Tyrwhitt hang-dry non-iron shirt and a dark green Uniqlo sweater – wool, not cashmere. It sets the tone.

'Well, are you feeling a little more reasonable this morning?' he asks, taking in the surroundings somewhat scornfully and then spreading himself across a sofa. He looks rather out of place but is doing his best not to show it.

'I hope we both are,' I say. I'm about to continue but have drummed into myself the power of silence. I've learned that speaking for the sake of it only weakens your negotiating position.

We sit facing each other and I avert my gaze to my Americano coffee as if it holds the answer to world peace.

'So,' Slick says, and then adds nothing else.

I let the silence hang between us.

Finally, he continues. 'Spencer is inclined to be generous, and though I'm not agreeing with your valuation, which is ludicrously high, let's find a meeting point.'

I don't want to overplay my hand, so I take a sip of my coffee and then say, 'I think my valuation is realistic, and I think you know it is.'

'Let's not quibble about pounds per square foot; we can both do that dance. Let's try and make our clients happy, agreed?' There's just a hint of aggression and irritation in the last utterance. He looks at his Patek Philippe watch as if the meeting has already overrun.

'Agreed.' I take another sip of coffee and remain silent. I'm enjoying Slick in these uncomfortable surroundings. He has an air that suggests he thinks his clothes will somehow become polluted by the sofa he'd at first tried to take mastery of.

'Well, what's that figure to be, Max, according to you?' And now there's definitely irritation in his voice.

'I think it's worth north of ten and as my client has a generous nature why don't we settle on ten – and Spencer can get away with giving Zara five.'

'Get away with—' His voice rises, but then he takes a breath and moderates his tone, although he still allows his irritability to come across clearly. 'I think if anyone is getting away with anything, it's you and Zara at that price. It's absurdly overinflated.'

'Should we put it on the market to test the value? We could both be instructed and see what offers we get.'

'Don't be childish. We've been through this. It would be highly disruptive – and somewhat unethical, knowing that Spencer has no intention of selling. How about eight?' he says.

I say nothing, silently amused by his reference to ethics. It's good, though, as it galvanises me to let the air hang between us.

'Well?' he says, dusting away some imaginary tarnish from his trousers.

I wait a few beats and then say, 'There's no point in having this conversation unless there's an element of realism involved.'

'Nine,' he says bluntly.

'I will take nine and a half to her in the interests of harmony.'

Slick seethes as he restrains himself from uttering the barrage of expletives that I imagine are on the tip of his tongue. 'Very well.'

'And you have the authority to make this offer? I don't think either of us want to repeat this chat.'

'I do,' he says getting up. 'I presume you can say the same?'

'I can confirm the price within half an hour.'

'If we are to have any professional dealings again, I will choose the venue.' I let him have the last word as he strides out of the coffee chain.

He'd have probably gone to £10 million, but I suspect Zara would have settled at £7 million. She only needs £3 million for the house in Queen's Park. She's certainly happy with £9.5 million, so I confirm with Slick and the lawyers get to work.

10 February 2022

We visit the Queen's Park house one more time, just to make sure we weren't won over by the day and moment. I always ask clients to visit three times, at different times of day, to be sure of their purchase. And if it's a new area to them, I ask them to walk around the neighbourhood – at night, on a Saturday morning and during a weekday. Just to feel the place and the environs. The architect owners are in, and they tell us how they conceived the space, how they live in it and how happy they've been there. We sit at their kitchen table, with the sliding glass doors on to the garden pulled back and light pouring in. It feels right. The living is all on the ground floor, with the huge open-plan kitchen-cum-sitting room at the rear leading on to the garden, and a TV/children's room at the front of the house. The bedrooms are on the first floor, and Zara's 'suite' will span the back of the house. There's no basement or sub-basement, no cinema room or pool. It's a relief.

'What do you think, Maxi?' she asks after we've left.

'I love it.'

'I do too. What shall we do? How do I get it?'

'It's off-market. There's no competition, currently. I think they're being sensible at three million; I've looked at the comps and it stacks up. You're a cash buyer, we've got my con-veyancing lawyer on standby, we're ready to go. To be honest, I'd offer the asking on an exclusive basis of ten working days from receipt of the full pack of papers, and let's wrap it up.'

'Do it,' she says. 'I feel good about this.' And I see the old Zar back, the one who was confident about life and its possi-bilities.

'I do too.'

'Thank you, Max.'

'I haven't done anything.'

'You've been here for me.'

'Always,' I say and then continue: 'Are you a tiny bit happy that I got you a realistic valuation for Lansdowne Road?'

'Thank you for looking out for me, needy one.'

I get home and call the owners, as I'm dealing directly with them. We close the deal. I love it when things are this easy and all sides are happy. The owners like Zara and are aware of the change in her life circumstances; they like that she hasn't quibbled over price, and they like that she'll give them four months to move out. As with many other Londoners, they are making a move for the countryside. I open a bottle of champagne and toast the first deal of the year – and Zara's future. It doesn't cross my mind often, but as I take the first sip of sparkling nectar, I think how nice it would be to be clinking glasses with someone else.

11 February 2022

Natasha comes in late. Pre-empting any looks or comments, she says, 'I'm pretty sure Uncle F is going to sign with us exclusively. He called my parents last night.'

'Oh, that's terrific Natasha. We're on a roll,' I say. I'm slightly hungover from my drinking party for one last night. It ended with me dancing to Fleetwood Mac's 'Landslide', empty champagne bottle doubling as a mic.

I am feeling it a little today.

And it seems we are indeed on a roll. John announces after lunch that he's landed a new client who, it seems, is rather more than merely a client. She wants a *pied-à-terre* in London. I must look a little despondent at the mention of a *pied-à-terre*, thinking it signifies a studio flat, as John proclaims: 'Now, don't be disheartened, for what Flavia means by that is a flat that can hold a drinks party for forty, has elegance and grace and should be the *piano nobile* in one of London's premier squares. I imagine South Kensington to be close to her son, Keko, who is in Chelsea.'

'We like that sort of *pied-à-terre*. Tell me more about her.'

'She's a woman of the world, a true sophisticate. Think Diane.'

I look blank.

'Von Fürstenberg.'

'Right,' I say, sketchily. I have a vague image of the 1970s, flowing hair and a wrap dress.

'Flavia knows her, of course. She's lent me her biography: *The Woman I Always Wanted to Be*. Can you think of a better title?'

'It's pretty good,' I confess.

'Flavia has led many lives, from fashion – Studio 54, New York, that whole scene in the late seventies and early eighties – to Rome, Porto Ercole and running a textiles business, through to the nineties, the *dolce vita* period I call it. She met Keko's father in Italy then moved to a ranch in Uruguay when they broke up and became a *gaucha* for most of the noughties. Then she went to Geneva briefly – I can only assume for tax – and now she's in Paris, with a bolthole in Tangiers, but she wants to spend more time in London, as Keko has settled here. She dotes on him.'

'And how do you know her?'

'We've known each other for years through the di Robbilants,' he says to me, as if that explains everything. I have no clue who the di Robbilants are. John has an array of Euro-chic friends, and he's the ideal villa-filler and yacht-hopper, spending each August doing just that. He's charming, good company, always has a smile on his face and knows how to sing for his supper – quite literally. 'We became close through lockdown; she got stuck here having come just before Christmas 2020 to be with Keko. We started walking together, then bubbled. I might go so far as to say it's not just Keko that has tempted her to get a place here. I have fallen madly in love, Max.'

'I'm happy for you. Is she your age?'

'What does age mean?' John himself is rather opaque about his age, but piecing together his acting anecdotes would suggest he's somewhere in his fifties. A quick stab at mental arithmetic suggests that this lady of international living has to be at the very least in her sixties. Studio 54 dates her.

'How terrific, John.'

He sighs.

'What is it?'

'The course of true love ne'er did run smooth.'

'Is it because she lives mainly abroad?'

'Oh no, that's easy to overcome. We've both committed to pan-European love affairs before; one craves a bit of space after a certain age.'

'Then what?'

'There's the question of the husband.'

'Ah, I see. Well, that *is* a problem.'

14 February 2022

I'd forgotten it was Valentine's Day until I arrive in the office and find a decoration of simple exquisiteness on Natasha's desk. It's made up of snowdrops and branches, and has clearly been crafted by hand, and with some skill. There's a note attached to it. Damien is at his desk.

'Morning, Dame, you're in early,' I say.

'Yeah, I decided to walk in today.'

I don't mention the flowers.

John calls to say he'll be working from home, purring with satisfaction. And why not? If anyone deserves to be happy, it's him. He'd told me that he left Flavia a voice note reciting Shakespeare's Sonnet 18 after their first date: 'Shall I compare thee to a summer's day? Thou art more lovely and more temperate . . .' I imagine every day is Valentine's Day when you're romantically involved with John. I think of my solitary bottle of champagne the other night and determine that I must do something to change the situation. But then, I've told myself that before.

Natasha arrives and looks genuinely thrilled with her flowers. She blushes when she reads the card, tilting her head *à la* Princess Diana (very unlike Natasha) and looking coyly up at Damien. I knew it, I tell myself. I am sure something is going on there.

15 February 2022

I make the trot down Earl's Court Road to see Quentin, but when I get there, I realise I'm struggling to find anything to say. Quentin and I have covered all life's big emotional wheels and the conversations we have now are usually some variation of ones we've had before.

'I just thought my heart attack would impact me more, if that makes sense?' I say, boring myself as I whine on.

'Oh, it does make sense. But it may take time. And I'm sure it has had an impact, on some level.'

'Yes, it must have. I suppose I'm less likely to sweat the

small things now. A perceived slight, a friend not behaving as I'd like – I let it go now.'

'Well, that is good. And how is your father?'

'He's well. And happy.' My father had dominated my early sessions with Quentin. After my mother died, he was lost. My two brothers were married with young children and I was on my own, so it felt natural that I spent the most time with him. And I think in clinging to each other, we got through it. It was probably becoming just a little too co-dependent, but just in time he met his new partner, a year later. That was some years ago now, and they've remained happily together. We are still very close and he is my greatest champion, but there is little left to discuss about our relationship now.

The conversation descends into repetitive and circular terrain, and I'm tempted to say something shocking, but I imagine that with Quentin, nothing can shock. His head would tilt, his face would maintain its empathetic aura, his hands would remain interlaced, resting on his left thigh in their usual thoughtful manner.

'Shall we pay that visit to Clone Zone today?' The unshockable Quentin succeeds in shocking me.

'Umm, well, perhaps. I'm not sure,' I stumble.

'We can treat it as a field trip.' Before I know it, Quentin is standing up and making for the door, and I'm following him.

It's not like any field trip I recall from my schooldays.

Clone Zone is a sex shop on the Old Brompton Road. An institution, I'm told. Some sessions ago, Quentin had taken something I'd said about the guarding of emotions and equated it to the guarding of my sexual liberation. He'd decided I needed to be more experimental. I'd vaguely assented – who wouldn't wish to be more sexually free? – but I'd never quite imagined it would lead to this. Now I'm walking around a sex shop with my therapist as he earnestly asks an attendant in leather chaps how certain apparatus work and what pleasure they can give individually or as part of paired or group activity.

'And this can bring one to orgasm without a physical touch to the actual phallus?' he asks sincerely as I cringe behind him. 'Fascinating,' he continues. 'We'll take one of those.'

It's a scene of embarrassment, comedy and education.

18 February 2022

A good day. The letter comes in from Fortescue formally accepting our contract. I am delighted to have won this over Slick. In the end, family came first and I suspect the wily old fox was probably threatening the use of another agent to get our fee down. We've given him a great rate of 1–1.5 per cent fee depending on the purchaser. If we sell it directly to a buyer or through a buying agent, we charge the former; if we sell via a sub-agent, we charge the latter, as we'd give them 0.5 per cent. It's competitive, but we have to be. Natasha had insisted we offer Fortescue the *prix de famille* (family discount) rather than the shade less favourable *prix d'ami* (mates' rates).

And now the hard part starts: we need to find a buyer. The usual process is going first to the buying agents and allowing them to present it to their clients as an off-market opportunity before it lands on any of the portals. Of course, Fortescue's place will never have an internet presence, so we just need to stagger who we tell, and when. Who are the strongest agents in the area? Who has the best buyers? Who are the most credible? And who do we like dealing with?

There is an overwhelming array of agents operating in our field – among them, probably ten I'd rate, but the list grows weekly. There are no regulations in our industry, no test you must pass to set up as an estate agent. It's open to all. The lines have become blurred somewhat between the traditional high-street brokers and the plethora of one-man bands who now try to compete, selling properties off-market. I can't complain, as it's how we've always operated, but at least I'd worked in the field first and learned the ropes at a big-name agency.

The various practitioners tend to fall into four broad categories:

1. **The well-connected.** The second son or daughter of a duke, for example, who has a great address book.

2. **The niche player.** The Italian living in London who, understandably, has cornered the market in looking after Italians. The former sports player who looks after athletes. The ex-city banker who 'understands' the Goldman mentality. I'll take any business offered but am always trying to position myself as the dealmaker to 'creatives' – writers, actors and artists. It helps that we've got John as part of our team.

3. **Those who have worked for big-name agencies (Savills, Knight Frank, Strutt and Parker).** They are now fed up with corporate management and reporting to spreadsheet-obsessed managers who fail to understand it's a people business. On top of that, there are the endless meetings they're subjected to that go nowhere apart from serving as a chance to see who can be the most vocal at positioning themselves. Senior management bombard the sales agents with meaningless KPIs (key performance indicators) and targets. It's all pretty thankless.

4. **The runners and chancers.** These are the ones who cling to the very rich and are looking for backhanders. This is the majority, working from cafés or kitchen tables, and looking for their slice of the pie.

We have a list of all of them and it's constantly being updated. It totals just 250 names, so we divide it up and start working the phones.

21 February 2022

Our first day of viewings at Fortescue's. We have just over an hour, as Natasha is taking him and Lord Edward for a meander around Hyde Park. We've checked the forecast and, though cold, it is sunny. We arrive *en masse* to find Fortescue bundled into an overcoat that looks like it's seen better days with a matted woollen scarf wrapped around his neck. He fusses over which walking stick to choose. John, always so well turned out, looks taken aback at Fortescue's dishevelled appearance. All the same, he turns on the full force of his theatrical charm: 'Such an honour to meet our dear Natasha's uncle . . . great-uncle, I can't believe it . . . what a gem this house is . . . how delighted we are to have the opportunity . . .' Oh yes, indeed, he understood the upset of leaving a beloved home, it's more than mere bricks but imbued with memories . . . Did Fortescue ever come across his dear old friend Brian Sewell, who lived down the road?

Fortescue thaws, after his initial look of bemusement. John in full sail is hard to resist. I begin to make circles with my hands, trying to indicate that it's time for him to wrap things up and send Uncle F on his way. He takes the hint and walks Fortescue down the steps of his own house to admire some detail of the façade.

'What a fascinating nugget of history; thank you so much for sharing it with me,' I hear John enunciate clearly, although I can't decipher Fortescue's fainter response.

'Go,' I say to Natasha, and I thrust Fortescue's stick into her hand. She joins him, linking her arm into his, and escorting both him and Lord Edward up to Kensington Gardens.

'Bravo, John,' I say. Then there's a mad flurry of activity, as we have five minutes to de-Havisham the house as best we can. Blinds, shutters and windows are thrown open to the chilled air of February, the musty damp smell gradually receding to a severe chill. John has brought some superior air freshener from Santa Maria Novella and wafts it around. 'Not too liberally,' I shout. 'I don't want Fortescue complaining that it smells like a bordello on his return.' Damien takes photos on his iPhone of everything we move so we know how to put it back correctly. I feel like some undercover agent on a furtive mission.

'Jeez, it's colder in here than it is outside,' Damien announces.

'At least he won't notice that the windows have been wide open, that's one consolation.'

We've lined up back-to-back bookings with finders and developers as our first port of call. As we have a short window, we're going to overlap in the house, which is never a bad thing in terms of creating a sense of competition.

The first time I show a property, I'm anxious that the viewer reacts positively. When you pitch, your aim is to win the instruction and help them see the positive. When you show a property, you want people to see the good you see. In this case, it's the bones, the proportions and the position on the street. The bad, of course, is the work needed and the asking price.

'OK,' Damien says, opening the last window on the attic floor. 'I think we're as ready as we'll ever be. How can people live like this? I don't get it. I mean, the guy isn't poor. He can afford a cleaning service.'

'Never underestimate the eccentricities of the British upper classes,' John proclaims. 'They think it's terribly bourgeois to care about cleanliness.'

James Finch-Stormont is the first through the door – a developer who loves a deal. There are no surprises in liking a deal, it's business. He's scruffy, in his mid-fifties, stubbled and exuding a faint whiff of Old Spice. He wears his ever-familiar faded bomber jacket with leather patches and Green Flash trainers. You'd never guess how successful he is. Unless, of course, you met his wife, who is twenty years younger and a former Miss Estonia. Clichés exist. James's shtick is to automatically start chipping at price – if I say a house is on for £8 million, his immediate response is to comment we'd be lucky to get £6 million. He loves to barter; a smile dominates his face when we get into haggling over price. Of course, when it comes to selling, he's just as convincing, always arguing for a record price.

We're climbing up the stairs to the first-floor study. 'Ten million? You're having a laugh,' he says, a droplet of his phlegm hitting my cheek. 'This is a gut-job. It's four hundred and fifty per square foot and three years' work. You need a developer for this, Maxi, someone who can see the potential. An end-user . . . it's too much for them.' I know what he means. I look at the peeling wallpaper, at the piles of newspapers and the solitary lamp throwing a gloomy light on to the room. I wrap my scarf tightly around my neck as a draught catches me through the open window. I feel rather depressed by the scale of work.

'When have you ever spent four hundred and fifty per square foot on a renovation, James? I may be green, but . . .' The best way to communicate with James is in his own language. 'You've got to look at the bones,' I continue, 'and what it could be. You've got the vision and wherewithal to do this.' I need to inject enthusiasm.

James pats me on the back. 'Don't bullshit a bullshitter, Maximilian.'

We're climbing now to the attic floor on a wooden step ladder. 'Next door went for three thousand, two hundred and fifty per square foot – that's a serious figure. You could open this all up; it would be an amazing studio room. And then there's the basement potential.'

'A fluke, a one-off. When you're ready to talk serious numbers, give me a call.' James leads the way back down the narrow stairs and to the hallway. 'I've got a pad in Mayfair, if you've got anyone – pure class, just off Mount Street. A corker.'

'And how much is that?'

'Twelve. It may go for over, though, I'm expecting competition. It's a top-of-the-line product.'

'And how big is it?'

'It's Mayfair, turnkey.'

'How big, James?'

'Almost two thousand, four hundred square feet.'

We've reached the hallway.

'That's over five thousand pounds per square foot! And how much of that is storage room or vaults?'

James is famous for squeezing every extra inch of square footage and will only use his 'trusted' people to measure a property.

'Don't quibble, Max.'

'Now who's having a laugh?'

'I never laugh about business.'

'This is Victoria Road. You can't beat it. Don't come crying to me when it's sold, like you did with the Holland Park house.'

James leaves without further comment as Simonetta, a chicly dressed Italian and one of the top property-finders in London, comes walking towards us.

'He's a bottom-feeder. I can't stand the type,' John says, a little too loudly. 'No style.'

'He's bloody successful,' is my response.

'Why do the English not wash?' asks Simonetta as she mounts the stairs, her long limbs taking the steps with a swish. She is permanently plugged into her earphones as her calls flit between Italian, French and English. She's known as the quickest viewer in the business.

'*Ciao*,' says John, giving her an air kiss. '*Veni qua.*' And off he goes, in a mixture of Italian gesticulation and accented English.

And so the merry-go-round continues as Damien, John and I pass each other on the stairs. I swerve between positivity and pessimism. It's right for someone, but James isn't wrong: it's a big-ticket number. Whoever buys it will need to have deep pockets. In our business, though, it's rash to underestimate the number of people with deep pockets. It's a tighter circle, for sure, and limited to select career choices, but that doesn't change the fact that there are a lot of rich people about.

Damien shows me a WhatsApp from Natasha, saying she's heading back. Tick, tock. It's time to usher out the remainders. As ever, my optimism is restored by Damien, who enthuses about the couple looking for a project and the buying agent with the perfect client. 'We're going to sell this,' he says. 'It may not be at ten million, but there's interest. It's blue chip. I'm going to create some buzz.'

'Always, Damien. You can always create buzz.'

22 February 2022

The feedback on Fortescue's is that for most buyers, as James predicted, it's too much of a project. Damien continues to bolster my confidence with his potentials. Natasha ruefully comments that we'd better sell it quickly, as she didn't sign up for endless walks with Fortescue. He's now suggesting that he should be there for viewings so he can meet potential buyers. This is to be firmly discouraged.

I cross-reference the list of those who aren't interested in Fortescue's with those who may like the Chisholms' house and line up some viewings there. I don't dare point out that their house has been on the market for two years, and Fortescue's may easily suffer the same fate.

24 February 2022

'I'm not sure if you'll thank me for this, but' – Natasha, who is unaccustomed dramatic pauses, does just that – 'Vigo Portus is now ready to meet you.'

'Should we know who he is?' John jumps in.

'He'd be very upset to hear you ask that,' Natasha replies.

'I'm afraid I'm in the dark too,' I add.

'Well, he'll be doubly upset now.'

'So, Natasha dearest, who is this exotically named creature?' John asks.

'He's the Insta-Kid.'

'Ah, yes! The Insta-Kid. I never knew what his proper name was but, of course, we've been tracking him. A lot of selfies, a lot of self-aggrandising and a lot of letting us know that he's leading his best life.'

'He's ridiculous, but you've been telling us to drum up business, and I've given you Uncle Fortescue and now Vigo.'

'What does he do?' asks John.

'He's an influencer of sorts.'

'What does he influence?'

'I haven't quite worked that out yet. He's occasionally featured in the *Daily Mail* sidebar of shame with someone from *Love Island* or the equivalent. I think he pays them to go to parties with him. It's all rather embarrassing, but he has a rich daddy who is very good at handing out the lolly.'

'I can't remember if you told us his budget?' I ask.

'He didn't.'

'Well, we shall find out soon enough.'

'Be warned,' she says. 'He's one of those types that travels in a cavalcade of cars with bodyguards.'

'Is he in danger of being kidnapped?' John asks earnestly.

'Of course not, but it's a way of attracting media attention and showing he has a *lifestyle*, whatever that is . . .' The withering intonation is glorious, and I want to capture it.

'But his purchasing power is real?' I ask, heading to my nuts and bolts.

'I presume so: he's always flashing the cash. He'll want something desperately naff, of course.' Natasha can be magnificently snobby at times.

'You make him sound so appealing,' John chuckles.

'I just know that he'll put the tricky into tricky customer.'

'Remind me how you know him?' I ask.

'I met him with some mutual friends.'

'You're being a mistress of the opaque,' John observes.

'Let's just say it's some friends that he'd like to be close to, so by association he values my opinion.'

'Ahh,' says John. 'If I throw you some names, will you let on? You don't have to answer, just a yes or no.'

'That *is* an answer,' I point out. 'Any steers on what sort of thing I should show him?'

'It should be a knicker-dropper, you know what I mean . . . a place that wows and blings in equal measure . . . and something utterly tasteless, of course.'

In the forty-five minutes I have, I rustle together a fairly imperfect list, given the need to second-guess what might appeal to a twenty-four-year-old with dubious taste. Natasha shares the latest from Vigo's Instagram with me. It's named 'The Real Vigo', as if the life he's portraying is more real than any other Vigo out there. It's certainly not. Every photo shown is of him, occasionally with an (unknown to me) reality-TV star, in various stages of spending money or showing how much money he has. Even the pandemic hasn't slowed him down; there are shots of him on a private jet, shots of him in a pimped-up Range Rover, shots of him opening designer packages with little pleasure – and, in one case, disdain, where he's evidently unhappy with the cashmere.

After three minutes of scrolling through these photos, I'm convinced I won't like him and that we'll need a flat that screams money and luxury: something like the development that I went to with Damien, but they're not going to be ready for six months, and I have a feeling that the wannabe-influencer will demand instant gratification.

I arrive at his serviced apartment just before our 11.30am appointment. I'm greeted by a man who introduces himself as Zee, dressed in a black tracksuit. He is, apparently, Vigo's head of private office, manager, communications director and general dogsbody. Zee leaves me in the hallway on a rather uncomfortable chair and tells me that Vigo will be out shortly. I hear some indecipherable bickering, one voice more shrill than the others. 'That bitch, I'm going to block her from my Insta . . . there's no way she's got that many followers, she's bought them in China . . . they're such dumbass shots . . . I want that reality-TV show, Zee . . . I could do *Celebrity Big Brother*, that would be a great . . . what's my agent's word? . . . platform . . . for me.'

I deduce that this could be my man.

I turn my mind to Fortescue's house as I wait, mentally running through the list of potential buyers and wondering if I've called everyone I need to – it's always better to pick up the phone rather than send a group email. My mind switches to the meditation podcast that Zara put me on to. I mean, it worked wonders for her, but I haven't quite found my rhythm with it. And on a practical level, I hadn't thought to bring my headphones with me. It's at times like this that I need to rise to a different state of consciousness. I try.

This higher state lasts all of about five minutes. After over forty minutes (wishing I'd remembered my mother's advice to take a book everywhere), I've exhausted my note-making as to whom else I need to contact regarding Fortescue's and the Chisholms'. As my irritation rises to the point of leaving the suite (it's well past my twenty-minute rule), the door to the bedroom opens.

'This is Vigo,' says Zee. Vigo wears red Adidas tracksuit bottoms and a white V-necked top. His arms are adorned with tattoos, which are written in a version of Sanskrit as far as I can make out. I wonder if he even knows what they mean. Some trite philosophical bunkum that he no doubt fails to live by. His tardiness has put me in a bad mood, as do his reflective dark glasses, which he keeps on. There are two flunkies waving iPhones in my face, and I soon realise they're filming me and the conversation. They're not introduced and nor am I asked if I mind being filmed.

'Hello,' I say, getting up to shake his hand and then remembering not to, I offer him a quasi-bow. He's about five-five, with peroxide-blond hair and skin pitted with acne. He looks like an unattractive version of Justin Bieber, and I presume that's who he's modelling himself on.

'You know Natasha?'

'Yes,' I say. 'We work together.'

'Is she here?'

Does it look like it? I want to say. 'No, she has another meeting. Do you know Lord Edward?' I venture.

'No, I don't think so,' he says. 'Should I follow him?'

'Oh, definitely,' I say. 'Now, down to the business of property. How can we help?'

He turns to his tracksuited cohort.

'We're hoping to start filming a show,' says Zee. Vigo turns his head so Zee is now reflected in his glasses. 'Correction. We *will* be filming a show, and it will follow all aspects of Vigo's life: his friendship circle, his leisure pursuits and his quest for a suitable base in London.'

Riveting, I want to say, but instead I simply respond with, 'I see.'

'This suite is fine for the odd night, but we need something more substantial.'

'It all sounds very exciting,' I say, forcing an up-tempo note.

'It is. So, you could potentially be our property guy, showing us stuff. Top end. Big budget. Have you done camera before?' Zee asks.

'Very little,' I demur.

'That could be problematic.'

'Obviously, I've done some.' I'm not going to be fobbed off so quickly. 'I lived in Los Angeles after university and worked in the industry. I was lucky enough to collaborate with some great talent – big names.' That'll shut them up, I reason.

'Really?'

'Yes.'

'Who?' Vigo asks.

'Discretion is essential in my business, but several Oscar winners. We're still in touch,' I add juicily.

Negotiation features in every aspect of my work.

'Sure,' says Zee.

'I must warn you that I've been approached by TV companies before, and the problem that we come up against is simple – this isn't the US. If you're looking at the upper echelons of the London property market, people do not want cameras in their homes. We're not going to be making *Selling Sunset*.'

The conversation is awkward, as we're still standing in the hallway of the suite – no one has suggested that we go and sit down in the living room. Maybe there isn't one and it's just a bedroom, but I'm beginning to feel claustrophobic.

'Can we work around that?' Zee asks.

'Well, it rather depends on whether you're looking for something to buy or if you're just looking for TV footage.' My bullshit detector has gone into hyper-sensitive mode, and I can see the scales of time-wasted versus deal-making tipping unfavourably against me.

'Both,' Zee says. 'It must be good publicity for them, if someone like Vigo is coming to look at their place.'

They're deluded, I think. I step back, trying to create some space around me. 'The thing is, Zee, lots of people value their privacy and don't want to be on TV.' I was losing them. 'I'm sure we could find some of the bigger developments to film in.'

'Yeah, that could work.' Zee turns towards Vigo, who is still wearing his glasses.

'Yeah,' Vigo says. 'But properly pukka ones, with pools, spas – the works.'

'Right. Could I ask for some guidance?' I say.

'You've just got it,' Vigo says, testily. The two chaps holding iPhones exchange a look. Can they believe this is interesting content?

'Of course, but what I'd love to know, and what would help with the search, is what areas you prefer, what your budget is, what you're looking for in terms of accommodation . . . that sort of thing.'

Vigo remains mute. After a silence that careens towards awkward, Zee speaks. 'I think a penthouse, with concierge and parking. We're building a car collection. Central areas.' He looks to Vigo. 'We can be flexible. Vigo likes the restaurants in Mayfair. Somewhere to entertain, where we can party. A master suite with a dressing room, maybe a guest suite or two for visiting friends.'

'OK,' I prompt after some silence. 'I'm beginning to form a picture. It's often a process that we go on together. And budget?'

'Whatever,' says Vigo.

'Well, I have one client looking to spend seven hundred thousand and another a hundred million, so it would be great to have some sort of parameter that I should be working within.'

'Yeah, well. Somewhere in between those two,' says Zee.

That plan backfired.

'How about we take a two-tier approach?' I say, determining that the time has come for lateral thinking. 'There are limited properties that we can get into with cameras, so why don't we keep the spectrum on the price range wide open and focus on the super-luxury end of the market – the ones with media suites, indoor pools, games rooms and all the trimmings. And then we'll simultaneously conduct another search, one where the cameras are not allowed in, and that can be for your actual purchase. That way, your privacy will be protected.'

'Sweet. I don't really do privacy, though,' Vigo says. It's the most direct thing that's come out of his mouth. He's scratching at his crotch as he speaks. The dark glasses have remained on, and the two iPhone bearers are still recording this banal conversation. To what end, I'm not sure.

'That sounds good. Well, this has been helpful. I'll get Natasha to come around with the contract.' I make towards the door, which I've now been next to for over an hour.

'And what's in the contract?' Zee asks.

'Well, it simply outlines how we work and confirms the percentage fee we will get if we successfully find, negotiate and secure a property on your behalf. And then as soon as the deposit is paid, we get going.'

'Deposit? What sort of level are we looking at? Remember, this could be great press for you. Free PR.'

'The deposit is two thousand, five hundred pounds.' I'm at the point of suggesting it could be bad publicity too, but I leave it. 'We ask all clients to put down a small deposit that's offset

97

against the final fee. It's a way of showing good faith and goes a very small way to accounting for the hours that we will put in on your behalf.'

Silence.

'OK, mate. We'll have our people look it over. And we'll look forward to working with you.'

'Me too,' I say disingenuously, determining this is a client for Damien.

MARCH

2 March 2022

John comes in singing: 'Fly me to the moon and let me play among the stars, tralalalala, deedee, la dee-da, dee-da, Jupiter and Mars.'

'You're in a good mood,' I note, rather obviously. He has his espresso cup in hand and bends down to stroke Lord Edward – who, true to Natasha's word, has been very little trouble and sits peacefully in his basket.

'I am indeed. It's spring, it's all about renewal and starting afresh. I feel bolstered and nurtured by it.'

Natasha gives a withering look.

'And all is well with Flavia?' I ask.

'It is, we are *simpatico* together.'

'And dare I ask about the husband?'

'Happily stuck in Paris and not wanting to fly or take a train for fear of COVID. Fortunately, despite being preposterously rich, he's too cheap to go private.'

'Ugh,' I say as a name flashes up on my phone that fills me with both a lunge of panic and a pulse of opportunity. 'Here we go.'

It's Billionaire. I remind myself that throughout our long history he's always been broadly loyal to me. I take a deep breath, wave my hand in the air to silence Natasha and John and put on my best up-tempo voice: 'Hello, how are you, my friend?'

'My house in Regent's Park . . .'

'I remember when you bought it.'

'I may sell it. For the right price.'

'Oh no, I love that house. Surely you should keep it?' Reverse psychology in its most basic form.

'I hate London. Dubai is a much better place to live.'

'Well, if you've really decided. It's a shame, I think—'

I'm cut off mid-muse.

'What agent would you recommend I use?' he asks.

A pause.

'There are lots of good ones who operate in that area. Knight Frank, Savills, Russell Simpson.' We do this particular shuffle every time, as if I'm not in the business of selling houses myself.

'Who do you think?'

'They're all good, and I can happily make an introduction. Of course, we'd love to have a chance to sell it too.'

'Be honest: should I have got more money for the flat?' He's referring to the £22-million sale that saved our work-bacon at the end of last year.

'You know I have always been honest with you. It's a fabulous flat and you got a record price for it. I was very happy with it.'

'You were very happy with the commission.'

'I was happy with both.'

'I don't need to sell; get me a good offer and I will consider it.'

Truthfully, his reason for being anti-London is he doesn't like paying British taxes, and his non-dom status can no longer be claimed. Billionaire resents paying any tax. All the rest of us happily, or should I say willingly, hand over our income tax, funding a National Health Service, a welfare state, education; all the things that makes us a civilised country. But some of the very rich seem to find it an affront to pay. And so Dubai, Monaco, the Bahamas and Switzerland become their places of domicile. I often wonder – but have never had the guts to ask – where their huge wealth will go when they're gone? Because you can be sure that those who are tax-avoiders are not likely to be great philanthropists.

I've made some of my biggest transactions on Billionaire's behalf – he's helped give me a place among my peers. We met via his personal trainer, who worked in a basement gym in Vauxhall. That sounds seedier than it really was. We got on: I matched his straight-talking with that of my own, and I think I made him laugh. And for some reason, I wasn't scared of him; I was more entertained by his effing, blinding brand of straight-talking. My father was born and brought up in Argentina, and thus has the requisite Latin temperament. My Texan godmother christened him 'Big Wind' to my mother's 'Heavenly Breeze'. And that nickname in turn got adapted to 'Big Daddy' from the Tennessee Williams play *Cat on a Hot Tin Roof*. And so 'a character' doesn't faze me. Through my years of working with Billionaire, we've done nine deals together. We've met for walks when he's in London, occasionally an espresso in his office, but our communication is mostly via phone. Frustratingly, he doesn't really 'do' email or text. I'm fond of him (in my own way), and we've even spent a day hiking together in the Lake District, as I happened to be nearby (it took a train and a taxi for me to be nearby, but hey-ho). A visit to his principal residence in Dubai has been a journey too far for me.

Billionaire is short and slim, with cropped hair cut in a monkish-type pudding bowl and angular features that reflect his hawkish nature. Nothing gets by him; no phrase or use of language can be lazily deployed. He, himself, is economical with language and has a stillness to him that always makes the other party blink first. He's in his seventies, though has a sprightliness that belies this. He's hard to figure out; beyond doing deals, there's not much that seems to give him pleasure.

As I've said before, though, I believe there's always a way 'in'. I ask myself what my clients' drivers are: what gives them pleasure, what are they interested in? With Billionaire, the only driver I've ever got to grips with is his desire to get one over on the other side.

He has the attitude, not uncommon to those at his level of wealth, that everyone else is out to get him, and as a result he determines to get them first. He creates an aura of paranoia around him: pitting those who work for him against each other, encouraging them not to speak but rather to report on one another. It's like being sucked into the world of the Stasi.

Through my sessions with Quentin, I have come to accept

that Billionaire is who he is, and I am who I am. I can't change his behaviour, but I can change my own. I can adjust my expectations. I can be careful about what I say, how I say it and to whom. And whatever integrity I have can be maintained. I can take agency for my own actions and how I treat people. My mantra with Billionaire is: 'You do you and I'll do me.' It was also with Quentin that I came to the epiphany that Billionaire can only win if everyone else loses.

My instincts are torn with Billionaire, as there is a part of me that cares about him and wants him to be happy, which I don't believe he is. He's estranged from his two sons and two ex-wives ('money-grabbing whores') and just about speaks to his daughter. I once suggested he set up a charitable foundation. The look I received was one of complete incredulity. His mentality is about preservation, not giving.

And so, another journey begins with him as I book in to see the Regent's Park house.

8 March 2022

Dare I hope? We have a second viewing at Fortescue's. It's Damien's people, and they've been tempted in from the country for a second time. Promising, particularly as they live in Yorkshire. They like it 'a lot', apparently, and I'm in a state of cautious optimism. Damien has always said they'd be right for it, and they have the appetite, vision and means to do work. Natasha is doing her best to manage Fortescue, though he appears to be in a perpetual state of irritation that we haven't had an offer yet.

I daren't point out to him that the Chisholms' house is still lingering too – like a debutante, seated bashfully in a darkened corner, waiting for that elusive request to dance.

It's crushing.

14 March 2022

It's our Monday meeting. The furtive looks between Natasha and Damien have turned to ones of avoidance. The lightness in the air has become an atmosphere. I do my best to ignore it and press on.

'I've got to do a valuation on Billionaire's house. Damien, will you come with me for that one?'

'Sure, that's a great instruction.' Bless Damien, he's trying to sound upbeat too.

It will come with its own set of trouble – managing Billionaire is not easy – but we know the terrain. 'What's happening on Fortescue's?' I ask.

'I'm pretty sure my people will offer,' he says. 'They've had their architect, designer and builder around, so they're doing their due diligence. I've given them the whole song and dance, but I'm just not sure the comps stack up. Is it worth fifteen million when done – when you look at stamp and the other costs involved?'

'It could be,' I observe. 'There's an argument to be made.'

'You know I'll make it.'

Natasha remains silent, which is odd considering it is her uncle's house.

'That sounds positive,' I conclude. 'Anything else?'

'I think I've found a flat for Flavia,' announces John. 'It's not quite what she expected – it's a penthouse rather than a *piano nobile*, but it has wonderful light and a terrace. She hates the lift – it's tiny – but I've told her that at least there is one, and once in the flat it's rather charmingly Mary Poppins.'

'Terrific. And in other good news, we exchanged on Zara's house in Queen's Park,' I add. There are general whoops of pleasure. 'And the Oscar Winner has a break in shooting soon, so I need to find her something. She passed on the South Ken flat.'

'Oh, she's marvellous. I adored her in that period drama, you know the one. If I wasn't so enraptured with Flavia . . .' John is one of the campest straight men I know. He's so debonair, he uses language so lavishly, and every sentence is almost inevitably accented with a foreign word. He's genuinely interested in women, which is rare in a straight British man. He asks questions and listens to the answers, and I think that's why he's often mistaken for being gay. He doesn't set out to be a lothario, which he accidentally is; he's simply like Sebastian in *Twelfth Night* – in love with the idea of being in love.

Later that day, I catch John alone. 'Do you know if something has gone on between Damien and Natasha? I sense an atmosphere.'

'Absolutely. He's mad about her.'

'I've got that, but there seems to have been a shift – and not in a good way.'

'So,' he half-whispers, leaning in conspiratorially, 'it's been romantic, but then her ex-boyfriend Piers came back and made *une grande declaration*.'

'And?' I ask, feeling anxious on Damien's behalf. Piers has been around forever, but he and Natasha broke up six months ago.

'She's gone back to him. I feel for Damien, but he's young and handsome and has that Antipodean spirit; he'll bounce back.'

'Is he OK? I thought Piers was a terrible stuffed shirt?'

'Australians are very resilient,' John declares knowingly. 'And, yes, Piers *is* a stuffed shirt, but he owns almost half of Northamptonshire. And you know what they say about love, *c'est la guerre.*'

Do they? I ask myself. 'We're not in a Jane Austen novel,' I say.

'You may not be, but are you sure Natasha's family isn't?'

'I'm not,' I respond truthfully.

15 March 2022

Damien and I go to look at Billionaire's house overlooking Regent's Park on Chester Terrace. It's white stuccoed and set back from the outer circle of the park. It meets the demands of your average oligarch: lift, cinema room, gym, basement swimming pool, garage for four cars. Unfortunately, it was done up for one of Billionaire's son's, whose colour palette ranges from dark grey to black. There are chain-metal chandeliers everywhere that give one the sense of having entered Dracula's lair or some sort of sex room. It should be a house filled with natural light, yet it's depressingly dark, the lighting is set to a brothel red and all the blinds, secondary blinds and curtains are closed, blocking out daylight.

'Well, this is grim,' I say to Damien.

'You're telling me, mate.' His shirts seem to get ever more fitted – or else he's working out manically. He's practically bursting out of this one, Hulk-style.

We start to open the layers of blinds and get some natural sunlight into the place. It does make a difference.

'I'm not getting into the lift,' I say to Damien. 'I fear we could get stuck in there and waste away until someone eventually finds us in six months' time. Let's take the stairs.' The house has clearly not been occupied for at least a couple of years.

'It's creepy, man, like they're going to have some weird séance here,' Damien says, getting out his iPhone and turning on the torch.

We descend to the sub-basement. From the gym area, I open the glass door to the pool under the vaults, Damien shining his phone at the ceiling.

'Steady,' I hear him say as I step forward, and I realise I'm descending straight into the pool – it's a literal drop from the door. I let out a whoop (well, it's probably more like a scream) as I lose balance, my arms flailing for something to grab so as not to fall face-first into the fetid water. But there's nothing, and in that split second I brace myself for the inevitable and close my eyes. Suddenly I feel two arms around my chest and my whole body, bent forward in an Ealing-comedy-like pose, is lifted into the air, as if I were a fluttering silk handkerchief, and pulled backwards. I'm pulled into Damien's body; he holds me tightly against him, and I realise what I'm now feeling are the contours of his torso against my back – it all happens in an instant.

'Thank you,' I say, feeling embarrassed. 'That's incredibly dangerous,' I add, nodding towards the pool and mustering irritation into my voice, while internally reflecting on what an idiot Natasha is for having opted for Piers.

'You're all right,' he responds.

I do my best to recover my equilibrium as we look around the gym area. Like the pool, it has a slight sense of decay and feels like a winter sports retreat for Communist block leaders in the 1980s – a *fin de régime* feel. As if it should be nice, but they don't quite know how to make it so.

I make my way up to the first-floor drawing room and plonk myself down on the hideous black leatherette sofa, avoiding looking at the kitsch, semi-paedophilic art on the walls. I'm feeling strangely out of breath, and charge Damien with closing the blinds and shutters and turning off the lights in the house. By the time he returns, my cold sweat has dissipated and I feel back to normal – ish. It's amazing the power the mind has over the body. Prior to my heart attack, I'd taken my body for granted. I'd blithely ignored an ache here, a shortness of breath there, something not feeling quite aligned somewhere. Now, I am super-sensitive to anything out of the ordinary.

'So, what do you think?' I ask Damien as we emerge on to the street, relieved to be in the daylight.

'It's got good bones. That's what you always say, right?'

'I do when it's true – and it's true in this case.'

'Is Billionaire going to want to get his usual overinflated price?'

'Of course. And the problem is, I found this for him, but everything was brand-spanking-new when he bought it. And now, apart from the hideous decorative changes his son has made, it's all fraying at the seams.'

'Yeah,' he responds distractedly.

'How are you doing, Dame? We haven't really checked in since last month. How's Brian, the man you see from Good Gym?'

'Thanks for asking. He's out of hospital and he's doing good.'

'And you?' I ask.

'Yeah, things are all right.'

'Great,' I say, deciding not to enquire any further. Whatever is going on between Natasha and him is their business.

16 March 2022

Kate calls and gives me her return date to London.

We met what seems like a lifetime ago, at the Coffee Bean on Sunset Boulevard. I was straight out of university and she drama school. Her youthful confidence was something I aspired to – and still do now. Back in the early nineties, Kate had a clear path drawn – she was aiming for movie-star success. My own path in those Californian days was more vague; I had notions of being a screenwriter or working in production. My first job was on a studio film, where I was tasked with getting Susan Sarandon her non-fat decaf latte. The young woman playing Susan and Paul Newman's daughter was a then-unknown talent, just a few years older than me, called Reese Witherspoon. On that film set, she was, as I imagine she still is now, filled with Southern charm: a pleasure to work with. As were Susan Sarandon and Paul Newman, so my first gig was a lucky break and gave me an idealised version of the film world. The director, a terrific man and three-time Oscar winner called Robert Benton, set the tone. He'd made one of my top-five tearjerkers, *Kramer vs. Kramer*, which I believe stands the test of time as one of the greatest – if not *the* greatest – divorce films.

I spent three years in Los Angeles, learned a lot, realised that I wasn't tough enough to cut it as a producer or talented enough to be a screenwriter, and came home. It was a happy experience though. Kate stuck it out. She got roles, came close to the big time, did some modelling, dated some big-name actors and began a sideline and profitable career in flipping houses. After her first big pay cheque, she bought a cute little apartment in Los Feliz and sold it almost by accident when someone made an unsolicited offer. And that's how it started. Two decades later, she's accepted stardom has passed her by, and the optimism of youth has turned into a well-adjusted acceptance that she's an actress in her forties who's never had a big hit and is unlikely to now. She's coming home.

'I will be very happy to have you in London,' I tell her.

'It's funny, I do still think of it as home. I'll need a house or a flat – and you're going to help me find it. And maybe I can get into the flipping game in our beloved capital.'

'You're the queen of the flippers. If anyone can make it work, you can. And what about Dave?' I ask. He's the man she's been seeing, though it's always seemed rather half-hearted. When I was last out there visiting, she said to me, 'He's good on paper.'

'Lockdown put paid to that,' she says. 'I woke up one morning, had breakfast by the pool, and looked out across the city below. It was one of those rare clear days in LA and I could see all the way to the Pacific, twinkling in the morning sun. And it struck me then. Am I here for the view or the man?'

'It's a great view,' I say.

'I shall miss it. But on that note, guess who I ran into the other day?'

'Who?'

'Andrew.'

'Andrew?'

'Your Andrew.'

'Oh, goodness. I'd hardly call him *my* Andrew. Where did you see him? When did you last see him?'

'Questions. Questions. I don't think I've seen him for a decade. I was in Gelson's in the Palisades and this guy called out my name. I recognised him immediately.'

'And?'

'He looks good. The same really. Older, there's an inevitability to that, but in a kind of Clooney way. He asked after you.'

'That was good of him. I'm surprised he remembers me.'

'Don't be stupid, Max. You lived together, you broke his heart – he remembers you. Don't do that British self-deprecating thing. Anyway, he's coming to London, and I gave him your email. You don't mind?'

'Of course not.' I digest what Kate is telling me. Andrew had been my first male love. I'd been naive and it had almost felt like I was playing at being an adult when I was with him. I'd had an unhealthy and not particularly happy-making 'thing' (it couldn't stretch to the label of 'relationship' though it lasted for almost two years) at my boarding school with a fellow pupil. It was furtive and we'd both officially been 'straight' – he quite actively. Then, at university, I'd fallen in love with a woman who meant – and still means – the world to me. She was the first person I came out to, which was ironic as we were dating. She encouraged me to go to LA and live my life. It seems absurd now, but back then I was ashamed of myself, and it took me time – too much time – to accept my sexuality.

Andrew was a big part of that. He was a few years older

than me but so much wiser; he'd got his act together at a much younger age and knew who he was, unapologetically. I admired him very much. He had exacting principles and worked for an NGO as their in-house lawyer. He was filled with passion about the injustices of the world and wanted to correct them all, which at times felt overwhelming. But he taught me to be happy in myself, and within months of our meeting I was living with him in his wooden cabin in Laurel Canyon and was co-parent to his rescue mutt, Sid. We spent the weekends hiking and talking about the world: what was important and how we could make changes for the better. (My contribution – fetching Susan Sarandon her coffee – admittedly wasn't great and didn't entail huge social impact, but she's a campaigner herself, so I reasoned that I was one degree of separation away.)

Andrew was a serious person. For him, being gay was an incidental fact; it didn't determine the kind of life he was going to live. He broke down my erroneous perception of what it was to be gay. The politics now are so different, but the representations of gay life and gay people were so much more limited then. And my ingrained homophobia from hearing the word 'gay' only as an insult and a sign of derision during my childhood needed heavy reprogramming – and accepting. In the end, I chose to come home after three years. I didn't see the right fit for me in the film world, and the pull towards my family and friendships was too great. Much as I loved Andrew, I found the bar he set so high that I'd always be failing it some-how, as if I'd be censured for dancing to a Britney Spears song, for being frivolous and having fun. And I wanted a bit of that; I wanted to feel happy. It was about the first time in my adult life I'd got there, and ironically, that was in large part due to him. I know that I hurt him when I left, and he'd found it hard to forgive me.

'So, I'll see you next month, kiddo,' says Kate, wrapping up our call.

'I'm excited,' I tell her – and I am. It will be good to have her back in my life and feel reconnected with that bygone time of our twenties.

21 March 2022

It's finally come in. We've brainstormed, we've lured every agent, developer and buyer we can think of to see it, we've practically built a shrine to it in the office, and finally it's here . . . the offer for Fortescue's.

It's from Damien's buyers, who have stepped up after receiving reports from their builder and architect. Dame begins by telling us it's the good news, bad news sandwich.

I don't care for the sandwich analogy; I just want to cut to the chase. 'OK, how much? Don't kill me here, Dame. I'm counting on you.'

'The architect said it's a three-year project and could cost close to four million.'

'That's ridiculous,' Natasha insists.

I'm not quite sure what she knows about it, and the figure doesn't seem out-of-kilter to me.

'It's what they've been advised,' Damien says flatly.

'Well, this is too tantalising for words. Can you just spit it out?' John, like me, is raring for the grand reveal.

'Eight and a half.'

Natasha lets out a guffaw.

'It's not as bad as I thought it could be,' I admit. 'Is there wriggle room?'

'I think so, but we'll be lucky to squeeze them to nine.'

'I can live with nine.'

'But it's not really about you, Max. It's what Uncle F can live with,' Natasha states.

True. But it's not a half-bad price – that much is also true. Once we have a concrete offer, we're in a position to start nudging other potentials. Buyers can be sheep-like; if a property is in demand, it gives others reassurance as to the value and validates their own opinion. We have several potential purchasers who have expressed interest, and now is the moment to strike and let them know that they could possibly lose the property. Another old psychological trick – as is not overplaying your hand.

We all have our different approaches to this: John goes into poetic descriptions of what their life could be like in a property; he conjures up images of the parties, the anniversaries, the Sunday lunches. Damien takes a more direct and amicable approach, talking of value and working along the lines of *I don't want you to regret this.* Natasha is a study in nonchalance, and has a demeanour that says, *If you're going to be such a fool as to miss out on this, then that's your loss.*

I am factual; I sit down with them and discuss the pros and cons, and what the realistic alternatives are, and come to a consensus decision.

We agree that now it's time to start hitting the phones and actioning our various styles so we can leverage the eight and a half we have on the table and hopefully push up Damien's people. Or attract another party.

22 March 2022

It's just me and Natasha in the office, as Damien and John's phone calls have resulted in second and third viewings at Fortescue's. The great man himself has decided today is not one for walking as it's raining, so he'll stay in his study and have a good 'butcher's' at the 'punters' who are coming around again. My phone call with him was a template of brevity. After, admittedly, a long-winded build-up, I put forward the offer and got a simple 'No,' then heard the click of the landline going cold. Why couldn't I match Fortescue's brevity? I followed up by putting the offer in writing, as is the correct procedure, and dropped it round to his house. Damien has told his buyers that it will have to begin with a nine to stand a chance, and they're going away to do 'their sums.'

Zara calls, as she's having a wobble about her move. I reassure her that all will be well; that's what she needs to hear. Sometimes, and I hope it's true in this case, a trusted voice telling you that you're doing the right thing is what's needed.

I remember when I was living in Los Angeles and having a tough time on a film set. The so-called producer had got the gig as she'd secured her famous sister to come on board as the 'star'. I'd brokered the deal, offering her a producer's credit and hefty salary (she'd never come near a film set prior). In turn, she got her sister to sign on for a four-week shoot (it was an indie) and, hey presto, the film was greenlit. In the snakes and ladders of Hollywood, the sister's star was riding high, as she'd just been nominated for an Oscar in a critically and commercially successful film. I'd thought the 'producer' would be grateful to me for facilitating the deal; instead, she tried to diminish me whenever possible – and did a pretty good job of it. Like the privileged person I am, I felt the unfairness of it. I remember calling my mother.

'Darling, you can always come home, you know. I'll book you a ticket.'

'But I can't.'

'You can, darling,' she said gently, and I knew in that moment of unconditional love that I could. Hearing those words strengthened me because I had the luxury and privilege of choice, and I had the reassurance of my mother's words.

I hope that I've been able to do something similar for Zara today.

'Is everything OK?' Natasha asks as I put the phone down.

'It's Zara. She's having second thoughts about the move.'

'Oh, well, that's a bit late.'

I look sharply at Natasha.

'Isn't it?' she adds more tentatively.

'She could fight Spencer to keep the house,' I mused, 'but I feel she'll be better in a new place, having a new start and being shot of the memories.'

'Is she regretting the divorce?'

'It's hard to regret what you've got no control over; it's all being driven by Spencer.'

'People can be so stupid.' Natasha sighs and strokes Lord Edward.

'Yes, I agree.'

'My grandmother always said to me, you'll find the same problems whoever you end up marrying, so you might as well find someone who's from the same lane and just rub along with their good and bad.'

'Well,' I say, taking this in, 'I'm not sure that I entirely agree with that.'

'Oh, I do. Relationships are hard enough, so why not stay in your lane, as Granny used to say?'

'For a thousand different reasons. The lane you end up in could be with an alcoholic, an unkind person, a serial adulterer, a fraud – and just because they're in your lane, it won't make it OK.'

'You know what I mean, Max,' she says, somewhat defiantly.

'I don't, really.' I deliberately moderate the irritation in my voice. It's such a moronic notion that old Lady Lane-Darcy has instilled in Natasha that I want to root it out. 'I know what your grandmother means by "your lane", but haven't we evolved from that view? I think of all the people that I've met in my life who are out of my lane and what enormous joy and pleasure they've given me.'

'But you're not married to any of them.' Natasha punches back.

'I'm not married to anyone, Natasha.'

She gives me a look that says: *EXACTLY*.

25 March 2022

As I'd thought, Zara is just fine. I go round to the new house and talk about where her furniture should go, and what pieces she'll take from Lansdowne Road. It turns out she did just need a trusted voice to tell her the move was the right thing for her and the children. I truly believe it is. I have a quote, attributed to George Elliot, stuck to my desktop computer: 'It is never too late to be who you might have been.' I frequently repeat it to myself.

There's a huge part of the job – if you're doing it well – that is part-therapist. It's one of the most satisfying aspects for me, helping people get to the right decision without being overly directional. My instinct is to steer; in fact, an ex used to say, 'No unsolicited advice, Max, thank you.' But I manage to rein in that impulse with clients and wait to be asked, only offering the faintest of signposts if I think they're making the wrong decision. I've talked clients out of buying more properties than I have the opposite. I remember being slightly put out when a client brought her actual therapist to view a property she was about to buy, rather than simply relying on her property-therapy expert: me. Fortunately, both the therapist and I agreed it was the right place for her.

28 March 2022

I pass the Insta-Kid on to Damien, who will 'get' the whole thing more than I do. Who am I kidding? I just don't want to deal with him, whereas Damien is younger and more tolerant. I feel that I've done my time looking after young brats. And there's something I find a bit demeaning about running around for someone almost two decades younger than me who may simply be using us for 'content'. Increasingly, I only want to work with people I like – or at least respect. I've been incredibly fortunate to have had among my client roster a Booker Prize-winning novelist, several Oscar nominees and one winner, a stadium-filling musician, an HRH, two national treasures, countless FTSE board members, some serious entrepreneurs, titans of business, editors, a duke, a duchess, a marquis, two countesses, untold barons and baronesses and two supermodels.

Damien gets into the office at noon and recounts his time with the Insta-Kid. Everything, as predicted, was being filmed by a paid-for crew, along with the Insta-Kid's own team and their ever-present iPhones. No channel has commissioned the series, despite Zee's efforts, and it seems Vigo's followers are a pitiably low 22,000 (which actually sounds like a lot to me) and there's very little actual engagement from them. The crew, reading between the lines, were more drawn to Damien's easy-going manner than the farcical demands of the Insta-Kid, who screeched the indoor pool wasn't an ozone one and boo-hooed that the massage suites weren't up to Dubai standards.

Vigo's USP seems to be complaining about everything, which is a bit tone-deaf to the times we're living in. Does anyone really want to see a spoiled child whose accomplishments amount to zero berate Damien on camera over the quality of the spa?

It all got heated when Zee overheard the hired crew suggesting Damien get in touch with a producer they knew who was wanting to make a UK-style version of *Selling Sunset*, the glossy Netflix series following the lives of impossibly glamorous real-estate brokers in LA. Their work attire looks like they're attending the Oscars, and the cat-fighting is worthy of the best daytime soap. Zee desperately tried to persuade the crew that they had the perfect material in Vigo, pleading: 'People love looking into the world of the rich and famous, and you've got it in Vigo – he's great TV.'

'Do you think he'll actually buy anything?' I ask.

'Who knows? I'll give him another try, but I've said it needs to be without the cameras next time.'

'I suspect he'll be delighted, darling,' says John. 'He won't want the competition.'

APRIL

1 April 2022

I visit the Schulenburgers in their South Kensington house. As we emerge into the new-normal of living with COVID, they've decided to dip their toes into the selling market . . . again. I love both their house and them. We first met seven years ago; it must have been in late May, as their wisteria was in full bloom. Florence has exquisite taste; as one of my oldest friends, an antique dealer and aesthete, said to me of their house, 'This sort of style takes years to create, it doesn't happen by accident.' I get it. The little flourishes, like Italian tomato soup cans cut in half and used as vases for flowers on the kitchen table, are what make the place.

The house itself has grand Victorian proportions: the kitchen leads on to the garden via French windows; a drawing room that comes off the first-floor landing is elegant and comfortable with perfect symmetry; and the aforementioned lilac wisteria clambers through the windows and competes for space on the drinks table.

Florence is American but has lived here for forty years raising their four children with Aleco, who is German-Greek. He'd been a banker but gave that up at fifty, left behind his Wharton degree and took one in philosophy and theology, then proceeded to set up an educational charity. On our first meeting, we sat in their garden after a quick tour of the house, which was diametrically opposed to the tour I'd endured during my first meeting with Fortescue. We shared a bottle of Gavi and talked about life in general, with the sale of their house coming almost as an afterthought.

That was the start of our journey and it's been a long one, but I've never minded a moment of it as they're such good company, and I've seen some terrific properties along the way. I still get a buzz from a beautiful house.

We've gone from Georgian terraces in Hampstead to riverside flats in Battersea, and from artist's studios in Belsize Park to modernist houses in Richmond. One of my personal favourites was a Queen Anne beauty on Chiswick Mall, with a wonderful bay window looking out to Barnes Bridge and a garden that ran down to the Thames.

Throughout all the merry-go-round of looking through various parts of London, they've never quite been tempted to move. And I don't blame them. Besides, we've had fun.

'Are you sure you want to do this again?' I say, as I'm parting. 'You know how I love this house.' Which I do.

'We are,' says Florence. 'But only as long as you promise to still be our friend once we've found something.'

'Oh, you're stuck with me for life,' I state matter-of-factly.

I walk back to the office happy, as I always am after having seen them. As Virginia Woolf noted, some people are radiators and others drains. The Schulenburgers fall most firmly into the radiator category. I'm reminded of our tenth work anniversary party. I invited most of my clients and it was, I modestly declare, a fairly impressive turnout. We hosted a drinks party, and halfway through I coughed for attention to say a few words, which ran along the lines of thanking my team and thanking the clients who'd entrusted us to assist them with such hugely important decisions. I expressed my gratitude that they put their faith in us. There were vague murmurs of assent and then everyone got back to their respective conversations. At that moment, an adored international TV personality (who transcends that tightly framed bracket, as she also publishes, and is beautiful, considered, eloquent and much more) spoke up. We had become close during the purchase of her house and I liked her enormously. Our friendship has since faded, but not in a bad way, just in a life-moves-on-way.

'I'd just like to say,' she said, 'that not only will Max find you the perfect place to live but, in him, you've also found a friend . . . for LIFE.'

It was very touching, but as I looked around the room, there was a rather awkward silence, as I imagined my stellar guests thinking to themselves: *He's sort of lucky that we've turned up to this drinks party for half an hour, but the idea that we're going to be his friend for life and he's put X up to saying that . . . well, that's a bit much. Let's get our coats and get out of here.*

I chuckle to myself in recollection.

5 April 2022

Good news. Damien's buyers have increased their offer to £9 million for Fortescue's house. Natasha and I go round to present the offer to him in person. Normally in the sale of a property, there's a pivotal moment when things have got as good as they're going to get. And we may have reached that point. The lay of the land is as follows: Damien's buyers have stretched to £9 million, we have a developer at £8 million (not James, he wouldn't go above £7 million) and we have a third party, brought in by me, who is making promising sounds but frustratingly hasn't committed.

It feels like, with all these spinning plates, we need to lock it down. There's no perfect alchemy in knowing when to get out, and people only regret not having taken an earlier offer in the belief they could get more. If they do take the early one, then they can't know what might have been, so it's all down to the temperament of the seller. I'm hoping that Fortescue will have tired of his walks with Natasha and Lord Edward (though perhaps they're an incentive for him not to sell, as I imagine he's seeing more of his great-niece than he ever has before).

As Natasha and I retrace the steps we first took almost three months prior, I share my views with her.

'It's time to conclude this, as there's a risk that the house will grow stale. Everyone knows about it, the marketplace is active, and we have three parties in the mix. We need to parlay them into the best offer.'

'I have no desire to prolong this,' she responds, pointedly.

'Well, you must guide me; you know your great-uncle. This is in his interests, but what's the best strategy to try and persuade him into moving this towards a closing point?'

'Hmmm,' she reflects. 'I'm going to suggest something controversial.'

'Oh, yes?' I ask, as we turn into his street from Eldon Road.

'The truth.'

I laugh. I sometimes get so caught up in the psychology of it all that I forget the best advocate is often simply just that: the truth.

Fortescue ushers us into his study with what is almost a shove and his usual charmless greeting of, 'Oh, it's you,' delivered with a slight note of annoyance. I can't imagine he has many other visitors. I do note that he's taken to leaving the shutters open, and occasionally a window, so our influence is having some beneficial effects.

'Very good to see you, sir,' I begin.

'Yes,' he replies. This family is a tough audience. He's got the same patchy cardigan on as always, though the musty smell has been somewhat alleviated since we've started visiting. I catch a faint whiff of faded Santa Maria Novella incense that John left in the upstairs landing, to which Fortescue never goes.

'I thought it would be good to catch up in person and go through the various interested parties, so we can decide together on a strategy that you're happy with.'

'Very well.' He pulls down the sleeve of his cardigan. His eyes are deep-set and there's a mournful look to them. I wonder what his life has been, what memories there are in this house, what loves may have passed in and out of it.

I go through the three possible buyers, two of whom are solid, the third less so.

'I think we have a window of interest and now would be a good time to draw it to a conclusion,' I tell him. 'I suspect you're bored of having people traipse through your house.'

He gives a vague nod of assent – or it could just be an involuntary tick.

'So, who is offering ten million?'

'I'm afraid none of them. We always knew it was a strong price, perhaps unrealistically so, and we've given it a good test in the market. I believe the offer we have is a decent one.'

'You do?' He peers over his glasses, giving me an inscrutable gaze.

'I do'. I look to Natasha, who has remained mute through my discourse.

'And how much do you have, then?' He looks towards a portrait over the fireplace, which is so in need of restoration that it's hard to make out. I suspect it's an ancestor, judging from the dour expression on the Victorian man's face.

'Nine million . . . we can try and push them up, though they've already come up by five hundred thousand pounds.'

'And who are they?'

'They're a terribly nice family from Yorkshire. He's made his money in retirement homes.'

'Made his money?' Fortescue spouts.

'Yes, he made his money. Given that we've got him and the two other parties, are you happy for me to go to a best-bids scenario?' I push on. This is the strategy employed when there are several interested parties. They're invited to put in their full and final offer, along with lawyers' details, proof of funds and anything that might be favourable to their cause.

'Do what you think is best. I can't promise to accept any offer.'

'I understand,' I say. I do understand: he's a cantankerous old so-and-so.

As we're walking back to the office, I say to Natasha, 'You weren't an awful lot of help.'

'There wasn't much to say. You told him what the situation was, now we'll get the best bid and it will be up to him.'

'But he does need to move. I mean, he does. It's not safe for him to be in that house.' I hear the shrill tone in my voice, and I don't like it.

'He should move.' Natasha tosses her hair. 'Whether he will or won't is rather up to what price we get. And him.'

As we walk into the mews, I see a Porsche parked bang in the middle of the cobbles outside our office. Normally, some-one would tuck their car in to allow another to pass, but this is what I call 'territorial parking'. I tut to myself. Natasha quickens her pace and we walk in to find Piers languishing on the sofa, chatting with John and Damien.

'I said to him, "Jeremy Clarkson is a god, you oik – what do you know about it anyway?"' Piers has that particular braying voice that I associate with the worst type of character from my boarding-school days. It usually indicates a fairly toxic combi-nation of stupidity and arrogance – two qualities that don't gel well together. He doesn't get up when he sees Natasha come into the office, and it's only now he's finished talking that he turns to me, almost as an afterthought.

'Yeah, hello,' he says.

'Hi, Piers,' I respond, as coolly as I can manage.

'Selling masses, are you?' He says it in a tone laced with *Schadenfreude*, as he knows we're not.

'We're getting by,' I say, and turn on my computer screen, quickly becoming engrossed by my inbox.

'All right, woman, shall we get going?' I presume he's trying to be funny in addressing Natasha as such, though she has the good grace to colour. She collects her things as quickly as I've ever seen her do it, and picks up Lord Edward before saying, 'Bye, everyone.' We mutter our responses.

While John and I are lost for words, Damien has a rather colourful four-letter name in mind for Piers. I can't disagree.

'What is she thinking?' asks John.

'That he's rich, her parents like him and he's not some Aussie bogan,' replies Damien.

7 April 2022

'It has a certain charm, don't you think? *Piccolo*, of course, but one doesn't need more, really.' Flavia is chicly dressed in a burgundy poncho, jeans and suede boots. Her hair is dirty blonde and expensively tousled. She wears simple gold jewellery and a large sapphire ring that complements her eyes. There's something magnetic about her.

'Oh, yes, and I'm sure you can really make something of it,' I add. The flat is on the top floor of a Kensington side street. It would have been a grand Victorian house originally, but was converted in the 1960s, at which point a small lift was also put in. One of the previous owners cleverly got permission to go into the eaves of the building, so the flat has vaulted ceilings with skylights, giving it a sense of airiness – a Parisian loft vibe. There's a huge living room with a kitchen behind sliding doors, a study leading on to a terrace, a generous master bedroom and bathroom suite, and another bedroom and bathroom. The common parts of the building are shabby, and I suggest Flavia pays to have them redone, as it would put her in good stead with the residents of the building.

'And what of the neighbours?' she asks. 'I had a horror story in Rome. I can't even talk of this deranged woman.'

'No, you mustn't,' John says soothingly.

'I could put lemon trees here' – she waves towards the terrace – 'perhaps an olive too, and have my own slice of Italia on the terrazzo. Surely the sun must come out sometimes in London?'

'Sometimes,' I promise. 'John tells me you have wonderful taste.' I follow her on to the terrace, and though there's no greenery to see, it has rooftop views including a glimpse of the Victoria and Albert Museum. I can see how she'd make a charming suntrap up here, with a table for drinks and a canvas umbrella for shade.

'Oh, she does,' John says admiringly. 'Everything Flavia does, she does impeccably.'

131

'*Basta*, Johnnie, I never knew an Englishman to be such a flatterer. I have always found the Anglo-Saxon temperament rather, *come si dice*, different, to that of the Italians.'

'John is not your average Brit,' I say fondly.

There is a warmth between them, and they keep finding excuses to touch one another: a palm on the small of the back, a squeeze of the hand, a brush of the cheek.

'And a little table here' – she throws a hand to the corner of the drawing room – 'just for six, maybe eight, a simple pasta supper. I won't entertain properly here, of course.'

'No, of course,' I concur. I think the sophistication level of my hosting is probably rather different to Flavia's. A simple pasta supper is about as far as I go.

'And the price, what can we do about it?' She ruffles her poncho.

I feel it's sensible at £2.95 million, and I tell Flavia this.

'*Ma certo*, we can have a discussion. Who are the owners?' She wraps her arms around herself, shivering. 'I suppose the heating is "on the blink"?' I'm charmed by the way she pronounces the colloquialism with an Italian accent.

'They're a British couple; they've lived here for twenty-five years. I'm sure the heating is working, they've probably just got it turned off.'

'This is evident.' She looks around discerningly.

'They rarely come up to London, and I think they want to give their children some money and increase their pension pot.' I'd spoken to the agent and got a full debrief.

'And are they amenable to an arrangement?' Flavia eyes a stuffed pheasant in a glass box suspiciously.

'What were you thinking?'

'Perhaps we pay a little offshore to make things more agreeable for everyone. You British are so ferocious with your taxes, just like the Americans.' Flavia allows a light chortle to accompany this observation.

'I'm afraid everything will have to be onshore. That's just the way it is done here.'

'So formal.' Flavia sighs. 'Let Johnnie and I discuss.'

'Of course.' I head home as the pair walk down the street, hand in hand. I get why he's fallen for her. She has an allure, an unidentifiable quality that makes one want to be in her presence. I know several people who have it, and it's a magical stardust that is hard to define. A glow, an ease, a natural and immediate intimacy, an open smile indicating a generosity of spirit, a curiosity suggesting a sense of adventure. Everything with Flavia seems fun. She came on the bus from an art exhibition and was delighted by seeing London from the upper deck: 'Such a new perspective, so wonderful to be among the trees, and I met such interesting people,' she proclaimed. She's another one of life's radiators – as is John.

8 April 2022

As the week draws to a close, I decide to take the gamble and send out the best-bids letter to the three parties interested in

Fortescue's. They have until next Wednesday to put their full and final offers in. It's a way of drawing the deal to a close, but it can scare people off; some don't like feeling pressured and walk away. But as no one is budging, I have few cards left to play, bar the ultimatum. I press 'send' and determine to forget about it until the following week.

11 April 2022

First thing, I go to preview a flat for the Oscar Winner. The duplex makes up the ground and first floor of an impressive white stucco-fronted house. Critically, it has the garden, which is unusual as that's usually assigned to the lower-ground-floor flat. It doesn't have a lot of rooms, but the rooms it does have are large, with the original features in place – cornicing, fireplaces and shutters on the windows. The Oscar Winner is a fan of period features. The property has been restored with charm by the owner, who is a designer and has expensively bohemian taste. The floors have been stripped back and painted white, the conservatory is filled with greenery and has a lush orangery vibe. I think this could be the one.

I call the Oscar Winner, trying to temper my enthusiasm, as I walk through Hyde Park to the office. We arrange to go first thing tomorrow, as she's filming from 10am. The agent had been tricky about timings, but as soon as I mention who my client is, the viewing schedule opens up. Funny that. It must be nice having the level of fame that facilitates such matters.

As I turn into our cobbled mews, I see that the office door is open and Natasha is standing outside, smoking. She doesn't see me. She is shouting into the office: 'Well, that's just typical, you would say that. You're just so bloody predictable.'

'*I'm* predictable? Well, that's horse shit. Look at who you're dating. If that's not predictable . . .'

'This has got nothing to do with Piers,' Natasha seethes as I come to a halt, wishing to turn invisible.

'Forget it, Tash, just forget it.' Damien walks out into the mews and sees me frozen in place. I resume walking. 'Hey,' Damien says. 'I'm just getting some air.' He walks past me. 'I'll meet you at Billionaire's.'

Natasha inhales hard on her cigarette. I smile weakly and ask, 'Is everything OK?' as Damien disappears round the corner.

'Fine,' she says hotly. 'It's just, well – it's just—'

For one awful moment I think she's going to cry, and I move clumsily to put an arm around her. 'I didn't know you smoked,' I say, for want of anything else.

'I don't,' she says, tossing the cigarette to the ground and grinding it into the cobbles.

'Can I get you anything?' I offer. 'A coffee? A martini? A world free of COVID?'

She chuckles indulgently. 'A martini sounds good, but ten in the morning is a little early for it.' She rests her head on my shoulder for a split second, and then steps back into the office.

I go to join Damien and Billionaire's team. The plan is to declutter the house and make it as saleable as possible. It's hard to know where to begin as everything is so hideous: the gadgetry, the artwork, the black velvet walls.

Frankly, I'd paint the whole place shades of white, get rid of the furniture and present it as a blank canvas. The problem with that, though, is that rooms read more easily with furniture in them; even if it's the wrong furniture, it gives a sense of what the space could be. And rooms look bigger when furnished.

Damien and I go around with Trisha, Billionaire's designer, working out the most effective and least expensive way to get the best result. You have to be confident in your opinions to inspire others. It's the *September Issue* school of thought. The documentary shows Anna Wintour putting together the eponymous issue of *Vogue*, and what's clear about her leadership is it's totally decisive. When she's going through the photo board, it's an instant 'Yes, no, yes, yes, no, no, no.' It's done without explanation or consultation, as several months' worth of work is left on the cutting-room floor. This is the style I try to adopt with Trisha.

'This has to go,' I say, of a particularly ugly leopard-print pouffe in the dining room. 'And this semi-pornographic art – all of it has to go. It's offensive to most people.' I don't know who the artist is, but it's a kitsch version of Humbert Humbert's darkest fantasies.

'But Billionaire's son paid a lot for the art collection,' Trisha protests.

'Well, he can keep it in his house. We're trying to sell this place and this artwork doesn't cut it.'

I'm rather enjoying my morph into 'Nuclear Wintour'.

'All this' – I sweep my hand, indicating everything in the media room – 'has to go.'

'But—' Trisha begins to protest

'No.' I'm in full swing. 'I want a clean palette here. And move some of the sofas in the bedroom down here. Let's buy some throws to go over them.' I'm surprising myself with my decisiveness.

It takes about an hour to power through, but I have to be ruthless if we're going to stand a chance with the house.

'Wow, mate. That was a whole new you back there. I was almost scared.' Damien chuckles as we walk to get a coffee on Marylebone High Street.

'How are things?' I ask, once we're sitting outside in the spring sunshine.

'So-so . . . It's Natasha.'

'Yes, I gathered that. Do you want to talk about it? I don't want to pry.'

'She's got under my skin. I thought we had something but I guess I was wrong. I'll be fine.' He averts his eyes.

'You will,' I say, trying to sound reassuring.

'I don't tend to get hung up on girls.'

What about boys? I have a sudden desire to ask mischievously, but I know now isn't the time for humour. 'Yes, I imagine it's normally the other way round,' I say.

137

'No,' he says, unconvincingly.

'Well, Natasha is special,' I say.

'She is.' And he raises a smile.

'Who knows what goes on in anyone's head? And things may change.' I want to strike a note of optimism.

'If she wants to be with that jerk, then good luck to her.'

'Well, you won't have any problems moving on, if that's what you want. But some things in life are worth fighting for – you just have to work out which ones,' I say wistfully, having made my own mistakes in the past.

12 April 2022

I meet the Oscar Winner – she's always five minutes early, so I've learned to be as well. We stand outside, chatting about our favourite aspects of the neighbourhood: the Persian restaurant I like; the sushi one she does; a secret bicycle path up to Regent's Park; a coffee shop in the direction of St John's Wood; the institution that is the deli Panzer's. We're bonding. She's in civilian mode, wearing jeans and a navy jumper, with her lightly blonde hair tied back and the grey-green of her eyes slightly dimmed by glasses. The impeccable raised cheekbones can't be hidden, though, and there's no visible sign of make-up. A natural beauty.

When the agent arrives a couple of minutes later, she asks him if we can look around on our own. He is in a fluster; he'd brought the wrong keys with him, so had to run back to the office, and is panting heavily as sweat pours off his slightly pasty face, running on to the collar of his shirt. Poor chap. I feel embarrassed for him. It would seem to be the first rule of estate agency to bring the right keys.

I love that I'm part of Team Oscar Winner as we examine the flat together, leaving Huffy-puffy in the hallway to recoup. She looks approvingly at me as we go from room to room, and when we get to the garden, I look at her expectantly.

'You've found it. It needs some work, but it's rather perfect.'

'I'm so pleased. I did think so when I saw it yesterday.'

We leave after having shown muted interest to the agent.

The Oscar Winner and I head to Clifton Nurseries and discuss tactics for the purchase. I can't resist a bit of fandom at the same time, and run through various films she's starred in, skirting around the subject of co-stars. She throws me some crumbs of information that I readily hoard, and gives me a flash of movie-star wattage by re-enacting a scene she did with someone who was, at the time, one of the most famous people in the world.

And then we're back to business, as she sips her herbal tea and I my Americano. The owners of the flat are reputed to be tricky, but I confidently say that we'll pass over any obstacles. I practically skip out of the Nurseries, intoxicated by having found the right place and elated by the idea that the Oscar Winner might soon be living streets away from me. I run away with myself, picturing casual Sunday-night suppers, easy intimacy and a lasting friendship – although I come back to earth as I think back to the speech at my work anniversary party and remember the awkward looks on the other guests' faces.

13 April 2022

The offers are in for Fortescue's. The deadline is midday, and Damien pings me our most eagerly awaited one at 11.55am. It's been hair-pulling up until now: the developer has stuck to his guns at £8,400,000, and my buyers have continued to do what they've done to date – a lot of talking and no delivering.

As Quentin has oft repeated, people tell you who they are through their actions, not their words. I've had promise after promise that an offer will be forthcoming, and then instead come the excuses: I'm working on a £400-million deal . . . I'm flying to Switzerland . . . one of my PAs has COVID . . . we haven't yet decided which lawyer to use . . . You believe the first excuse, you believe the second even, and then you begin to doubt. We tend to believe what we want to believe, but the property world has taught me to have a healthy cynicism.

'It's come in,' I say to Natasha and John.

'And?' Natasha says eagerly.

'Yes, yes, yes.' I punch the air. 'Nine-point-three-five.'

'Hallelujah,' says John and jumps up to hug me. 'This is why I always advocate a champagne fridge, for moments just like this.'

'But will Fortescue take it?' Natasha asks.

'He has to,' I say. 'It's a terrific offer.'

'But it's not ten.'

'I know, but ten was never going to happen. Come on,' I say. 'We're going round there. I want to share the news with him.'

'Let me bring Lord Edward, he'll be our lucky mascot.'

Ten minutes later we're walking through the back streets of Kensington – with frequent interruptions. It seems Lord Edward wants to sniff every tree and cock his leg at every turn. I'm impatient and call Damien to tell him we're in transit. He's going to join us there, as I want him to emphasise the credibility of the buyers and for us to operate in a unified pincer movement.

'Do you have good news for me?' Fortescue asks upon opening the door. I realise he could be enjoying our regular visits. The poor man must have been dreadfully isolated through the pandemic, probably nervous about catching COVID (though he's far too stiff upper lip to admit it), and finally he's got some action around him. Action that he's at the centre of. He'll be making a huge sum of money, tax-free – there's no capital gains on the sale of a principal residence. But then it will be over; his life will be back to normal. And I'm not sure normal is much fun for him. He'll also have the reality of the next step, which he's been obfuscating. There's been talk of him moving into a new development that is exclusively for the over sixty-fives. It's a terrific idea, in that everything is five-star standard – there's a cinema, swimming pool, restaurant and bar, along with a degree of nursing assistance. It's not very Fortescue, as everything is so swanky, but he may enjoy the company. Or, rather, he may enjoy not enjoying it. But wherever he ends up, it will be a huge change and that must be scary. As I walk into his study, the prism of how I've looked at this sale shifts. I don't want him to feel pressured into moving; I want him to feel supported.

'We've got the offers back,' I start, matter-of-factly. 'The developer is still there at eight million, while Damien's buyers have gone up to nine million, three hundred and fifty thousand.' I inject my voice with a soaring enthusiasm.

'We think it's a terrific price,' Natasha adds.

'Hmmm,' says Fortescue.

'May I speak candidly, sir?' I ask.

Fortescue looks a little taken aback. 'Must you?' he says, finally.

'I'd like to,' I say, smiling.

'Go on.'

'For over nearly twenty years in the business,' I begin, trying to find the right words even as I speak, 'we've helped many people who have lived in their beloved family homes for decades. It's always a wrench – more than a wrench, in fact – and without meaning to sound too . . . too American . . . it's traumatic. If, and I realise it is an if, you decide to move, we will help you every step of the way. We will ensure there's a delayed completion so you have time to pack up and move things. We have the marvellous Tina, who can help you with all that too. We will also make sure that the next place you move to is the right place and that you are happy with it. We are here to support you through the whole thing. And if you decide you can't face the idea of moving and want to stay, we would quite understand.'

I stop. I don't dare look at Natasha. I'm not sure whether

this is the right or wrong thing to say in terms of getting the deal across the line, but it feels like the right thing to say for Fortescue.

Natasha stands up and gives me just the briefest of looks. 'We'll let you mull it over, Uncle F,' she says. 'Do you want to come for a walk with me and Lord Edward in the park, if I promise we won't say a word about the house sale?'

'I'd like that,' he says. 'Let me get my scarf.'

As I walk down the steps, leaving great-uncle and great-niece together, Damien comes bounding up.

'So?' he says.

'Let's leave them to it. You've done an amazing job in getting the offer. Now it's up to Fortescue.'

15 April 2022

Hallelujah. Fortescue calls and tells me he'll accept the offer; he even seems satisfied with it. There's no thanks, but the growling tone has been replaced by one of inevitable acceptance. We structure that he'll have a six-month delayed completion after exchange, during which time he'll grant reasonable access to the new owners and their architect. I put Fortescue in touch with the marvel that is Tina, who will help him move.

Tina's in her sixties. She's comfortingly reassuring, and she walks with a purposeful swish that suggests she's heading in a linear direction. She's firm but fair, and trucks with no nonsense. I've heard her on the phone saying, 'No, I'm not having that' – and when Tina speaks, you listen. Over the twelve years she's been helping me and my clients, I've learned of her past careers – a rock 'n' roll singer on a cruise line, the manager of gay bar in the eighties ('I *saw* some things, Max'), running a division of a moving company. She's someone who is the same with everyone – polite, somewhat foreboding, always taking pride in her work. Whether you're a duke or a dustbin man, you get the same Tina.

With the news in from Uncle F, I dash up Campden Hill Road and buy a case of champagne, balancing the bottles in my backpack, then I cycle precariously back through Holland Park, knocking on a neighbour's door in the mews and putting all six in their freezer. Damien is out with the Insta-Kid, John is seeing a new Italian client referred by Flavia, and Natasha is accompanying her father to the hospital for a routine test. I wait until they're all back in the office and then share the news, producing the now-chilled champagne with a John-like flourish and filling four glasses.

'We did it. Congratulations, everyone. This has been a major team effort and I'm thrilled for us all. Fortescue has accepted.' I give a particular nod to Damien as I raise my glass.

'And Fortescue's happy?' Natasha asks somewhat tentatively, taking a sip of champagne.

'Yes, I do believe he is,' I say. 'But this is the start of the journey. We need to see this through until he's safely settled in his new place. I've introduced him to Tina so she can help. Now come on, we deserve this.' I clink glasses with each of them in turn.

And so the fizz flows, and I realise we haven't had a moment like this since pre-pandemic. I've never been a great believer in weekend off-sites, reasoning we see enough of each other during the week, but there is something to be said for taking your work hat off and putting a friendship one on. We chat away happily from our desks, and then end up in a closer huddle: John and me on the sofa, with Lord Edward sitting between us, and Natasha and Damien opposite on chairs. John is in full raconteur mode. By the time the third bottle is open, we're all quite light-headed.

I suggest that we should check in with one another more often.

'You are a sentimental old sausage, Max. I've always known it. But on that note, having had this charming *coup* with you all, it's time to say goodbye.' And then John breaks into the Andrea Bocelli/Sarah Brightman song of the same name: '*Quando sono solo, Sogno all'orizgonte.*'

He reaches the crescendo of the first verse, belting out in a deep baritone: 'Time to say goodbye, *Paesi che non ho mai.*'

When he finishes, we, the captive audience, give a round of applause, as much to cut him off from launching into the second verse as for the merits of his vocals.

'Where are you off to, John?' asks Natasha.

'Flavia beckons. We're walking through the apartment one more time with the prodigal son, Keko, and then she'll decide. He is the sun and the moon to her. I've never been jealous of a mother's love for a child, but I'm coming close.'

'Ironic when you could be more jealous of the fact that

she's got a husband,' Natasha says under her breath as John swans out of the door.

The three of us are left, and there's a slight shift in atmosphere. Without John's bonhomie filling the room, it feels just a tad deflated. Thus I make the executive decision to open one more bottle.

'We are celebrating, I suppose,' says Natasha.

'Did everything go OK with your father at the hospital?' I ask her.

In her usual reserved style, she simply tells us that he is fine.

'Tash, you never told me that your dad was going in again,' says Damien. 'Is he OK?'

There's a concern in his voice that takes me by surprise, and he leans over instinctively and touches her hand. Natasha lets it rest there for a moment and then gets up.

'It's fine, really. Thank you. I've just got to blow my nose.'

I'm pretty sure I see a tear in her eye. I look to Damien with a what's-going-on? face but he doesn't pick up on it. She comes back, and there's another shift in atmosphere. Damien is trying hard to connect with her, and she's glugging back the champagne; suddenly, I feel rather redundant. Always leave while you're still wanted, I tell myself, knowing that I could quite happily remain settled on the sofa.

'I've gotta head, guys,' I say adopting one of Damien's phrases. 'I'm meeting someone.'

'Good on you,' chimes Damien.

He's got the wrong end of the stick, but I don't disillusion them.

'Don't let me break up the party.' I gather my things and start making for the door before they can protest, and as I'm about to leave, I hear Natasha say she can stay for one more drink.

The beam on Damien's face is undeniable. I leave the office with a 'Byeeee,' but, to them, I'm already superfluous.

The champagne has given me a buzz and I decide to walk home through the park to sober myself up. I'm confronted by couples holding hands, couples laughing, couples with other couples. It's a warm spring evening and people are making the most of it.

I get home and respond to the email Andrew sent me yesterday. I say how happy I'd be to meet up when he comes to London next month. His message was brief, giving me simply his dates and availability.

16 April 2022

I send a message to the office WhatsApp group letting them know I'm working from home. I need to poke around some local agents and get some comps before we offer on behalf of the Oscar Winner. There's jovial banter from the group, with references to sore heads and hangover cures. John lets me know that he's put in an offer on behalf of Flavia as Keko gave his approval.

I wonder how the evening ended for Natasha and Damien. For me, it ended with several pints of water, some cheese toasties and an episode or two of *Selling Sunset*.

20 April 2022

Kate is back. She landed yesterday and is borrowing a friend's Chelsea flat. She's full of her usual energy and keen to get on. I'm summoned.

'Maxi, it's so good to see you,' she says, embracing me.

'And you too.'

She puts her hands on my shoulders, pushes me back and takes me in. 'OK, you're maintaining . . . you haven't attacked the bread basket . . . hair's looking good . . . skin's OK, though I'd like you to see my dermatologist – I think a deep-pore cleanse could help give an extra glow . . . keep an eye on the waistline – it's looking fine, but it's often the first area to slip . . . with men, particularly.'

'What is this?' I ask.

'I'm just doing the LA thing, measuring you up.' She laughs.

'Well, you look bloody fantastic,' I say. 'It must be that combination of yoga, carb-avoidance and ever-so-expensive non-invasive surgery.'

She has that polished LA veneer: glossy hair, glossy skin, lightly made up. Kate has always known how to make the best of herself. She has that Elizabeth Hurley quality. An old-school approach means she's permanently 'on', as if the paparazzi could appear from round a corner at any moment. She's five foot eight with thick brown hair that has myriad light brown, blonde and darker tones, along with hazel eyes.

'Can you believe how long we've known each other? Twenty frigging years, Maxi,' she enthuses. 'We're grown-ups now!' Her tone changes to one of mock seriousness. 'Don't tell anyone how long we've known each other . . . ever.'

'I shan't, but it's hardly as if *I* know anyone,' I protest.

'Don't be silly. You know everyone.' Kate has an endearing quality of over-promotion. I've heard her tell people I am without question *the* real-estate broker in London; her screenwriter friend deserves an Oscar; her massage therapist is out of this world; her yoga teacher she got from Brad Pitt.

'So,' I say, after the niceties, 'what's the plan?'

'The plan is there is no plan.'

'That's unlike you.'

'I know, it's fun. I want to buy somewhere and then I've got lots of ideas on the boil.'

'Well, I can help with the home front.'

She picks an errant croissant flake from my stomach area, giving my belly a gentle prod. 'That does need some work. I've got a great vibrator strap-on thing. Not *that* kind, but one you attach to your stomach. It gives you a mini electric shock as you're watching TV. I sort of like it in a vaguely masochistic way. I'll get you one.'

'Thanks, but honestly, just send me a link.'

'Sure. Now, there's a fund that's approached me about buying blue-chip properties here, doing them up and holding them for ten years, taking the rental yield and capital growth.

There's so much money in LA, and a few of them are betting on London as a long-term solid. I told them I'd scout.'

'Wow, that could be great,' I say enthusiastically. I am reminded of how much I love Kate's energy. It's rather a hackneyed cliché, but she has that twinkle in her eyes.

'I'd love us to be a team, but hold your horses for now – I'm looking at some other options. I'm talking about partnering with a lifestyle app – and before you say anything, I know. Gwyneth is doing a great job with Goop but I think there's space for something a bit different. And I've told my British agent I'm here and available. I want him to put me forward for *The Crown*. I'm exploring, but one thing is for certain: I need a home.'

'I'm on it,' I say, and then take her brief.

It's great to see Kate and be infused by her positivity. If I didn't work as an estate agent, I'd be completely unemployable. It's this or nothing. I used to muse that I could be a butler in Hollywood, though I'm not sure the accent cuts it any longer. But here's Kate, moving to somewhere she hasn't lived for twenty years, and already she has so many options in front of her. After the property chat is done, she moves on.

'So, any eligibles to set me up with?'

'Hmmm, it's a tough market,' I say. 'We're probably looking at a divorcee.'

'I could go younger,' she says, considering the idea. 'I'd like a bit of fun, nothing heavy. It's a sort of relief that the child question is out of the way.'

'Kate, you're forty-two,' I protest.

'Oh sure, it's possible. But in my head, it's out of the way.'

'OK.' I note her Californian candour. Everything is on the table for discussion.

'And you, Maxi? Who are you seeing?'

'Oh, no one.'

'Well, that's just ridiculous. You're a catch. And while we're on that subject, did Andrew get in touch?'

'He did. I'm seeing him in a few weeks.'

'Interesting.' She infuses the word with heavy meaning.

'It will be good to see him.'

'It's very on trend of you. Could be very Bennifer.'

'Oh no, it's nothing like that. For goodness' sake.'

'We'll see,' Kate says.

We rattle on, recollecting old times, our respective first houses on stilts in Studio City and Laurel Canyon. Drinks at the Sky Bar, parties and gauche tales of us playing it uncool with various celebrities. My contented coupled life versus her bionic dating back in the day. I catch a glimpse of my watch and realise I need to leave, as I have a viewing at the Chisholms'.

'Are you OK, Maxi?' she asks as I leave.

'All is well,' I say.

'Come here.' She pulls me in and gives me a big hug. 'Hmmmm, I've missed you.'

'Me too.' I blow her a kiss and turn away.

I can't say the words out loud but it's my mother's birthday today. And I can't believe that it's ten years since she died. It's always a tough day for me, but it's one that I guard privately.

I haven't even booked in to see Quentin, who I'd normally share my interior thoughts with. It feels like there's something sacrosanct about keeping this to myself.

22 April 2022

Amazingly, the sellers have accepted Flavia's offer. She put in the low-ball via John and it worked. I'd thought they'd be offended by an almost fifteen per cent reduction on the asking price. It makes a little more sense when I learn that there is, in fact, a troublesome neighbour who is in constant litigation with the rest of the building. Flavia has been warned, but I suspect she's convinced she'll charm the grumpy old man into submission and has already invited him for drinks. I have the sense she's got faith in her own powers of persuasion.

As John reports the news, he seems a little despondent. It transpires that Flavia is having a pang of spousal obligation and is going to see her husband in Paris.

'It's been this blissful spring honeymoon, and I haven't wanted to think about the future,' he tells me. 'But now, well . . .'

'Reality bites,' I suggest.

'I'm not sure how keen I am on reality.'

'It can be tiresome.' That's all I can offer by way of comfort. It seems prosaic to point out this was the inevitable. 'Let's think positively,' I say banally.

'Absolutely,' he says, rallying.

28 April 2022

I meet Tina at Fortescue's. I've briefed her in advance, letting her know that he's a gentleman of a certain age who's a little stuck in his ways. Nothing tips Tina's steady equilibrium, though, and she's standing on the steps when I arrive.

'Nice house,' she says.

'It is. Slightly like taking a step back into the Dark Ages, though.'

'Not a problem,' says Tina, and immediately I'm reassured. I try not to be a control freak, but when Damien, John or Natasha are doing a deal, it's hard for me not to offer advice – thankfully, it's usually asked for. My way isn't necessarily the right way, but I have learned over the years how to reassure clients and find pathways forward. But with Tina in charge, I can always relax.

I remember a client of mine once telling me how fond he was of his chauffeur.

'Why, particularly?' I'd asked.

'He says my two favourite words in sequence: "No prob-lem."'

That's what I try to make our clients feel: the no-problem-feeling. Sometimes it's best just to keep things simple, and if that mantra is running through your mind, it helps inform how you present to clients. It's like the story of Bill Clinton having a block of wood on his desk at the Oval Office bearing the legend: 'It's the economy, stupid.' It got him two terms.

Fortescue greets us in his usual attire and ushers us into the study.

'Tina is a genius at helping people move,' I offer by way of an introduction. 'She can help take the stress out of it.'

'There are some very valuable items here,' he barks. 'Are you familiar with Meissen porcelain?'

'Not as such, but I know how to deal with valuable possessions.' This Tina delivers in her no-nonsense manner.

'Hmmm,' grunts Fortescue and looks skyward.

'Now,' Tina says, 'what are we going to do with all these newspapers?'

'They have important information,' Fortescue retorts, meeting Tina's gaze directly.

'Oh really, what?' Tina plays the question with a straight bat.

'Stuff.' Fortescue is stalling.

'I'm sure we can sort through them.' Tina starts making notes. 'Would you be good enough to show me around?'

Faced with Tina's notepad and efficient manner, Fortescue begins to adopt old-world manners and takes on a courtly form as he shuffles her around the house. As I wait in the study, I think I hear faint chortles coming from the distance.

I flick through my phone and find a message from Andrew confirming supper next week. The message after that makes me seethe. It's a mail-out about a Belgravia flat that looks familiar. I realise why as I study the floorplan: I acquired it for Vera, a client and friend, only three years ago. It seems she's selling, and Slick has the listing. Vera and I are proper friends –

I've been to stay with her at her family house in the Caribbean. What's gone wrong? Did I undertip? And how has Slick engineered his way in there? It's very distressing, but I'm brought back to the moment by the disorientating sound of Fortescue's laughter – something I've never heard before.

'Well, I think that's all sorted then,' Tina says, upon re-entering the room. 'We've got a plan of action. I'll be round next week to start making an inventory.' And with that, she picks up her handbag, swings it onto her shoulder and exits stage left.

'What a terrific gal she is,' Fortescue says as I remain sunk in the decrepit springs of the armchair. 'She rather reminds me of Nanny.'

'Oh, yes, she's wonderful,' I say distractedly, pulling myself out of the chair and trying to clear my head of the mail-out I've just seen. 'I'm so pleased you like her.'

'Rather,' says Fortescue. He steps towards me and I wonder if he's about to lose his balance. I move towards him and then understand that he wants to touch me. His liver-spotted hand gently rests itself on top of my left one. 'Thank you, Max,' he says simply.

I'm so touched by this unexpected gesture that it's all I can do not to cry. I look to the ceiling and respond: 'You are very welcome.'

MAY

3 May 2022

Damien jogs in, and along with his burpee press-ups he performs the highest star jumps I've ever witnessed. It's as if he's auditioning for a back-up role on one of those exercise videos that stars released with such regularity in the nineties. I picture him wearing a sweatband around his head and gyrating up and down on plastic steps behind Cher, both of them in body-defining Lycra.

'I'm positively exhausted just watching him. What energy he has to burn,' John exclaims. He adds, 'What it is to be young,' with a pointed look at me.

I slightly bristle at this, considering myself closer in age to Damien and Natasha than John, though that may not be the reality.

'He's a frightful show-off,' remarks Natasha. 'Prancing in front of us like we've got some ghastly musical theatre performer in our office; I'm surprised he doesn't have speakers and a soundtrack.'

'Don't give him ideas,' I warn.

'If music be the food of love, play on; Give me excess of it, that, surfeiting, The appetite may sicken, and so die. That strain again! It had a dying fall,' recites John.

'What?' asks Natasha.

'Shakespeare. *Twelfth Night*,' John explains.

At this point, Damien emerges from the shower room, hair still wet, shirt wide open as he fiddles with his cuffs, taking an inordinately long time in doing so, leaving us all to see his glistening chest and core.

I do wonder whether this is entirely appropriate office etiquette.

Time to bring the focus of the room back to the job at hand. 'John, how's Flavia's purchase coming along?'

He explains that the lawyers are in touch and that we're using Jayne, our safest pair of hands, so all should be well. The relationship between an estate agent and a conveyancing lawyer should be a happy one, with both working on the same side. I do see that lawyers can get frustrated with agents trying to push things through, sometimes too speedily. It can seem they're just focused on their commissions, particularly when the fees they make can be significantly larger than the lawyers' fees. The lawyers are paid either way; agents aren't. I try and stay on the right side of them. I don't push, and as soon as a deal is agreed, I phone, introduce myself and let them know I'm there to help. I also do my best to persuade clients to use lawyers we know, like and have a direct line to. It can be the difference between a deal going through or falling apart. A good lawyer is worth every penny they're paid, in my mind.

'Any news on the Insta-Kid, or have we given up on him and his cameras?' I say to the now fully-shirted Damien.

'I'm not sure. Zee says he's still furious that the TV people got on with me. In fact, I'm having a drink with one of the producers of that show next week.'

Natasha raises an eyebrow. 'What's this person called?'

'Tanya, as it happens.'

4 May 2022

I'm not sure what the etiquette is with an ex, particularly one you haven't seen in over a decade. It feels very much as if our relationship was part of another time. It's like the famous opening line of L. P. Hartley's *The Go-Between*: 'The past is a foreign country; they do things differently there.'

As I walk to the Fitzrovia restaurant I've chosen near Andrew's hotel, I reflect on those Los Angeles days. Kate is back in London, and now Andrew is visiting – the past is upon me. I remember the intimacy between us, the ease, what Andrew taught me – what he gave me, really, in terms of feeling utterly secure with someone. I'm not one for looking in the rear-view mirror, as we can't change what's gone, but as Quentin is at pains to point out to me, we can learn from it. And I'd discussed it recently with him, when I knew I would be seeing Andrew.

'Tell me about your relationship with Andrew.'

'It was good. I was naive, but he never made me feel that. In fact, I don't think anyone has made me feel as loved. I always knew with him that we were a team, that we had each other's back.'

'And that's what a healthy relationship should feel like.'

'Yes, I see that now. I didn't realise it back then. I expected it – the folly of youth.'

'Hmmm.' Quentin tilts his head knowingly and makes a note in his pad.

'It's later that I realised people can be optimisers. Could they do better, be with someone more attractive, someone richer? Are they settling? And that feeling is *un*settling. I don't know if that's the malaise of being a metropolitan gay.'

'It shouldn't be,' Quentin states very matter-of-factly. 'And it's a crude and unattractive way to look at a relationship.'

'I know. Maybe I'm just mixing with the wrong people. I never felt like a compromise with Andrew; I always felt wanted. And needed. That's probably a huge indictment on my own neediness, but I liked it.'

'I don't think there's anything wrong with having those emotions, Max. They are yours and they're honest. We all want to feel needed on some level.'

'So, I don't know how to be with him. What to say?'

'Be yourself, Max. I think we can safely say Andrew rather likes that person.'

Entering the restaurant, I have butterflies in a way that I haven't for many years. I'd googled Andrew earlier, as I needed to calibrate my visual recall to the man of today rather than the one of my memory. He looks reassuringly the same, just older. His hair is flecked with grey, but he's in good shape. He always did have a naturally athletic frame that I envied: broad shoulders, slender waist. A swimmer's physique. He'd been on his college swim team. His strong jawline remains and only shows the faintest signs of softening; his pale eyes, which had first drawn me to him, are still the same, the light behind them still strong. He holds himself well and stands to greet me. I give a broad smile and stretch out my arms to hug him. He draws me close.

'Wow,' I say. 'It's you.'

'It is.'

'Ahhh, Andrew, it's good to see you. It's crazy, but I feel a bit nervous, and yet also like this is so familiar, almost a *déjà vu*. I must have dreamed this scene.'

Quentin would be happy with me. Honest and open. I'm mentally preparing my report to him.

'So tell me, what are you doing here?' I remind myself not to fill those silences unnecessarily. They don't have to be awkward if both parties decide they're not.

'I'm here to see you,' Andrew says.

The silence that follows *is* awkward.

'Oh wow, gosh. Really?'

Again a silence. Again, awkward.

And then Andrew laughs. 'Oh, Max. Still so gullible. I'm here for work. We're doing a collaboration with Client Earth and there's a meeting.' My face must betray something, as he continues: 'And it's good to see you too.'

'Tell me about Client Earth.' I regain my balance, not sure if I remember this joker side of him.

'It's an organisation that holds corporations and governments to account and tries to get laws changed to protect the environment.'

'That sounds like it's right up your *strasse*.'

'It is.'

I make a move for the wine bottle that Andrew has ordered (a Pinot Noir, which was always our preferred red). He reaches for it too. Our hands touch. And there it is, that charge. I feel a jolt, just as I had when we'd first touched, years ago. It's funny, that purely chemical reaction. I've had it with people at one time, and then met them again and wondered how I'd ever felt that way. It can seem alien, like a remote memory of another person. But with Andrew, the force of it takes me back.

The wine helps the conversation flow. It's odd having both that deep knowledge of one another and yet also a huge vacuum of what's gone on in the last almost two decades. I know about his childhood, his inner hopes and fears, his vulnerabilities. I'd held his head in my hands and comforted him as he wept over his alcoholic father. I'd been there when one of his best friends died in a car crash. I'd encouraged him to heal the wounds of his childhood with his sister, and I was there to smooth things over when she came to stay. I remember every contour of his body, and where and how he liked to be touched. Yet this is also a person I haven't had a substantive conversation with for fifteen years. We talk in broad strokes and then catch up on our families, friendships and work. He asks me about the impact of COVID, what it's brought to me in terms of clarifying what I want from the next chapters of life.

(I can't very well answer 'Nothing much,' so I try to work up something more profound).

As we get to the end of our main courses and the second bottle of wine – that's typical of me but unlike the Andrew of old – I ask: 'And is there anyone in your life?'

'I'm seeing someone, yes.'

'Oh, that's good,' I offer.

'Why?' he asks.

'Well, it's nicer to be seeing someone than not. And I know you well enough to know that you wouldn't be seeing someone just because. You'd be seeing them because you like them.'

'I'm pleased you know me so well,' he says, holding my gaze and taking a sip of wine.

'I'm not saying that, Andrew. I mean, I am, but you know what I mean. It's a compliment. You wouldn't muck anyone around is the point. You've got integrity and you're a good guy.'

'And you would muck someone around?'

'I would hope not,' I say. We're on dangerous ground. 'Andrew,' I go on.

'Yes, Max.'

'I know it's a long time ago, and you probably don't even consider it, and I'm sure that I'm saying this more for me than for you.'

'What are you saying?'

'It's just something that Kate said to me.' I haven't thought how to express this. It seems rather arrogant to just tell him that Kate thinks I broke his heart.

'Which was?'

'Well, I don't think, when we ended, that I handled it well.'

'You didn't. And *we* didn't end it. You did,' he jumps in before I can continue.

'I was young.'

'And so was I,' he says, fairly.

'And inexperienced, and it seemed that this whole life was mapped out and I had so much of my life here, at home. But I did it badly, just leaving so quickly and definitively. And I'm sorry.' I take a sip of wine and tell myself to be quiet and let him speak.

'OK,' he says neutrally.

'OK,' I parrot, and then stay silent.

'So, you've said your piece,' he finally says. And I remember the lawyer in him, the careful use of words, the noncommittal language, as if waiting for me to slip up.

'And do you have anything to say? Or should I not be asking that question?' I feel something rising in me.

'You can ask any question you want, Max. I just don't know if you'll want to hear the answer.'

Now it feels like we're in a game of poker, and I'm not sure if I want to call his bluff or quit. I catch the waiter's eye and signal for the bill. We're the last but one table there, so it comes promptly and with a flourish, just to remind our neighbouring table that they are now the last diners.

'Let me get this,' I say, putting my card down.

'Are you sure?' Andrew asks.

'Of course. You can get the next one,' I add reflexively.

*

As I walk home, my foggy head tries to understand the evening. We parted with a hug, and I found I didn't want to let go. We'd been happy and laughing and reminiscing through most of the evening, but the conversational turn at the end has left a sour note. And I don't know if that's it, if I'll see him again in a decade or never, or if he'll call tomorrow and suggest supper.

I get home, brush my teeth and get into bed. I'm too tired to deconstruct and second-guess what Andrew may be thinking. I feel unsettled by having seen him, but part of that is because it was a reminder that I miss sharing my life with somebody.

5 May 2022

I wake up to the following email:

> Max, I've been thinking about our dinner. I realise I must
> still be angry about how we ended. It's a long time ago, but
> I guess you only care if you cared. I'm back again in London
> next month. Can we meet for supper and talk?

I respond immediately:

> Dear Andrew,
> Thank you for your email and for being honest with me.
> I know I handled things badly all those years ago, and I
> think you know the reasons why, though I'm not seeking
> justification. And, of course, I care very much. You mean
> a lot to me and always will. So, yes, please, let's meet for
> supper when you're here. xx

9 May 2022

A good day. I have a call from a National Treasure (NT). One I've known for most of my life as she's friends with my father and lives close to where I grew up in Gloucestershire. She wasn't an NT when I first knew her, but like those other Dames, Judi and Maggie, she's earned it. My Dame has served on many government committees and done lots of good works, but her NT status has been secured by being a judge on the most successful cooking show on UK TV. She has that ability that the discerning viewing public appreciate – she's entirely the same person on camera as she is off. And that's a thoroughly nice one who has a *joie de vivre*, an interest in others and a sparkling turn of phrase, all of which is undiminished despite her being in her ninth decade.

She wants to sell her house. She bought it almost fifty years ago with her then-husband to raise her family, but now it's too big and she's undertaken her own architectural project (with her second husband), building her dream home. It's a more manageable size, with three bedrooms, and, crucially, it has the kitchen she's always wanted. We don't often work outside of London, but as this is a patch of the countryside I know well and it is for NT, it's hard to say no.

I tell NT that I'll be entirely honest with her; if I think that I can do a good job, I'll take it on, but if I think she'd be better served by a local agent, I'll find the right one and make the connection. Either way, I'll support her through the process.

She says the words that every agent dreams of, and rarely hears: 'I'm entirely in your hands.'

12 May 2022

Chester Terrace. Damien and I are meeting the removal men to ensure that our directives are being followed to de-blingify the house and lighten the palette so we can hit the market at the beginning of June and have a six-week run before the summer exodus.

At the house, we find Billionaire's sometime-estranged daughter, who is laying claim to things that she wants. It seems that Billionaire's relationship with her has been reset to neutral, as she's ditched the gold-digging boyfriend and is off the following day to see her father in Dubai. The machinations of Billionaire's family dynamics are hard to keep up with, and any time he or one of his retinue try to draw me in I move myself into 'no comment' mode. Like the couple who break up continually and then ask for your opinion: never give it, as inevitably they'll get back together. The see-saw of who's in and out is constantly changing. And to be honest, his brood are a fairly unattractive bunch (not in looks but character) who are driven by their desire for a share of his fortune; the internecine politics of which wife or mistress is in favour, and therefore which children, is impossible and undignified to follow. I can't pretend that Billionaire doesn't encourage such politicking.

This daughter, Florentina, is a pretty woman who's corrupted her looks with so much surgery and so many artificial additions that it's hard to remember the fresh-faced nineteen-year-old I first met. The last few times I've seen her, she was so addled on Xanax that it was like talking to a cyborg version of her former self.

'Florentina, how lovely to see you,' I say.

She's eyeing a painting of a young girl in a transparent dress. She looks at me blankly, despite the fact that I found her starter flat, then her second home a few years later, before she got involved with a fraudster who successfully distanced her from her family but not her trust fund.

'It's Max,' I continue. 'Remember your first flat on Redcliffe Square, and then the mews in South Ken?'

'Oh, yeah,' she says vaguely, showing no actual recognition.

'This is my colleague, Damien.' On cue, he steps forwards. Though her face is frozen into inertia, I swear there's a flicker of interest in her eyes.

'Hey.' Damien leans in to kiss her on the cheek, placing his hand gently on the small of her back as he does so. 'Have you taken all the best gear?' he asks and holds eye contact.

She giggles in response.

'I'll just go and have a chat with Trisha,' I say, upon hearing her voice upstairs. Trisha and I are now bonded, after that slightly wobbly start. I suspect her first reaction to me was that my accent lumped me in the posh, patronising and useless category. I'd once heard an agent say, when she was in the next-door room: 'But they CAN'T use that woman as their designer. Look at her.' I'd wanted to apologise on behalf of the pompous ass, but thought it kinder if Trisha and I pretended we'd never heard the comment. She doesn't have the sort of *World of Interiors/Architectural Digest* coverage as an Axel Vervoordt, Veere Grenney or Rose Uniacke, but Billionaire and the family like her, and she knows how to deliver their look. She also passes on all her trade discounts, while only taking a flat fee. They hate anyone making commissions.

'How's it all going?' I ask, as I walk into the first-floor drawing room and find her bubble wrapping a life-sized pink-painted porcelain tiger, thankfully with a sticker that reads 'TO BE REMOVED'. I may disagree aesthetically with Trisha, but she gets things done. I'd earned some brownie points when one of her delivery team didn't turn up on the day of completion at Billionaire's flat and I spent six hours loading a van with her son, my back aching after a mere two hours and Trisha commenting, 'This is what I'd call a day's work.'

'We'll get this place sorted for you, Max,' she says, heaving the bubble-wrapped tiger into a wooden crate.

'Has Billionaire approved?' I ask.

'I told him it needs a slap of paint and I'd get the lads down, have them sleep here on blow-up mattresses and have it done in a week for five thousand. I can't say fairer.'

'You certainly can't. And it will probably add a couple of hundred thousand to the value of the property, just by making it look clean and fresh.'

'And I suppose you aren't going to let me have any fun with the colours, are you? Florentina always has done, she likes her baby pinks and mauves, but I know you, it'll all be blancmanges and taupes. I wish there was a bit more Dolly Parton in you.'

'What do you mean? I love Dolly Parton,' I protest, 'I went to see her at the O2.'

'Well, you know what she said: "More is more, not less is more."'

I am tempted to riposte that what I think she actually said was: 'It takes a lot of money to look this cheap,' but I decide to let it go.

'We've got to neutralise, let people believe they can put their own mark on it. You know what I always say . . .'

'Yes, I do: a blank canvas. You can start showing in few weeks.'

If only all decorators had as little visual sensitivity as Trisha. I remember my Texan godmother explaining to a Dallas client that they had to make sure they got exactly the right shade of white for the skirting board. 'What can it matter?' he'd queried. 'The wrong shade of white can ruin your life,' she'd responded.

I don't think it would ruin Trisha's.

I go downstairs, pleased that we can get going soon. Historically, May and June are the optimum months for selling in the super-prime London market. The city is at its best, and there are a host of events tempting people to the capital: the Chelsea Flower Show, Wimbledon, the Masterpiece Art Fair,

Ascot, Henley and endless garden parties. There's sunshine and the sense of optimism that spring turning to summer brings. The light glows with a golden hue, the parks look ravishing, people sit outside, pubs overspill on to streets – and the property market reflects this.

I don't see Damien on the ground floor, so I descend to the depressing gym, avoiding the treacherous swimming pool, and pass through the cinema room, finally arriving at the garage of the mews. I find Florentina sitting on the bonnet of a vintage Ferrari and Damien leaning over her, his arms on either side of her as he whispers something into her ear, his mouth almost kissing it, and they both laugh.

Florentina notices me first. 'Oh, hi,' she says, barely trying to disguise her irritation.

'Hi,' I respond. 'Damien.' I nod a greeting.

'I was just telling Florie about the time I raced something like this at Brands Hatch.' He's still leaning over as he says this, his body casual and toned, almost encircling her.

'Mmm-hmm,' I say. 'We need to go and check out that flat for Fortescue.'

'Sure.' He reluctantly straightens up and offers his hand as Florentina slides off the bonnet. 'Great to meet you, Florie.' And he flashes one of his white-toothed smiles.

'You too,' she says coquettishly, pulling down her skirt, which has ridden up to a provocatively high point. 'You can get my number from . . .' And she tilts her head in my direction.

I can't believe she's forgotten my name, again – and already.

16 May 2022

It's my birthday. It's not a big one, so I decide to go low-key. I do my Hyde Park exercise class at 7am, have lunch with the team and then supper with Kate in the Japanese restaurant round the corner from my flat. Kate's news is that she's started looking at houses in the country.

'I fancy a change,' she says. 'And who knows? A combination of country and London life may suit me.'

'Don't be fooled by this unseasonably hot spring,' I say. 'Remember the countryside has winters too. You're living back in the land of seasons.'

'I know, I know, but I'm thinking of reading by log fires, long walks, pubs – a dog, even.'

'Are you sure you haven't just rewatched *The Holiday* and you're imagining meeting your Jude Law?' Kate was up for the lead role in that film; it went, in the end, to the 'Other-Kate' as we like to call her. The hugely talented Winslet. I'm not sure how far my Kate got in the casting process, or if it was just mentioned to her by her agent, but she has never let hard facts get in the way of a good story.

'I love that you know me so well. It is one of my go-to films.'

'I know,' I say.

'And you have your ones.'

Kate and I drift into our favourite quotes over sake and recollect our Los Angeles days.

'OK, enough,' she says eventually, picking parts of her seaweed salad out of her mouth. 'Let's make some new memories.'

I agree, taking some tuna sashimi in my chopsticks.

'You know, Max, I'm so happy to be with you on your birthday.'

'Thanks, Kate,' I say. 'Me too'.

'I missed you in LA; you were a big part of why I came back. Our friendship means the world to me, and I love that we can hang out together now.'

'Awww, Kate. Don't.' I have a tear in my eye.

'Why not? It's the truth, and if I can't say it on your birthday, when am I supposed to say it. On your deathbed?'

'No, don't do that. It almost happened once, and I don't want to repeat that experience. And I feel just the same way, Kate.'

'Let's drink to that,' she says.

And we do.

18 May 2022

The couple from Antigua are delayed and aren't coming back until the autumn. I dread telling the Chisholms, as I've billed the Antigua couple as the perfect buyers. I've protested to their buying agent, Charles, explaining that we'd made a sale via WhatsApp last year.

'Well, my friend,' he responds. 'Not that you didn't do a marvellous job with your video and your – hmmm, what shall I call it? – performance, but believe it or not, they're not going to spend eleven million pounds based on it.'

'But can't they fly over? They may lose it.'

'I've told them that,' he says.

After doing this for twenty years, I've learned that you can't will people into making the decisions you want them to make. You can only put the right decision in front of them and then hope they make it.

22 May 2002

On the subject of the right decisions, the Oscar Winner's offer for the Little Venice flat is hundreds of thousands of pounds from the price the sellers want. They're asking far too much, and I'm telling the Oscar Winner not to pay it. The sellers are counting on the fact that they have a garden that leads directly on to a communal garden, and we're in prime garden season.

24 May 2022

More stalemate news. The managing agents of the flat Flavia is planning to buy have still not delivered any information on how the building is run, what the future expenses may be, and what may or may not be in the sinking fund. John has called them, emailed them, even popped down to their office, but it seems that they have a Soviet attitude towards admin and are not to be rushed. Flavia doesn't understand why we simply don't charm someone into expediating the situation. If only we could.

27 May 2022

Damien comes in with a swagger, a grin and a whiff of expectation.

'You know the crew that were working with the Insta-Kid? I told you I had drink with Tanya, the producer, a few weeks back. Well . . .'. He lets the pause hang in the air. I think John's theatrical training has taught us all the importance of the dramatic pause, and we've now learned to let each other have that moment. 'They want to do a show on us,' he finishes at last.

'You are joking,' Natasha says bluntly.

He's not.

'I did a great job of selling you guys,' he breezes on.

'I'm not quite sure how much *selling* we need. I think we could have stood respectfully on our own.' John bristles.

'I'm kidding, guys. Of course, you're all amazing. All I had to do was tell T about you, and that was enough.'

'Well, that's good to know. And you think we really want to be on camera and open to ridicule and discussion?' Natasha's voice is clipped.

'There is only one thing in life worse than being talked about, and that is not being talked about,' John remarks.

'I'm not sure I agree,' Natasha fires back. 'Granny always said you should appear in the papers three times: birth, marriage and death.'

'I'm only quoting Oscar,' says John defensively.

'What?' Damien asks.

Sensing tension, I step in. 'He's quoting Oscar Wilde. But that's a sidebar. Before we go any further, what are they wanting from us – and what have you offered them?'

'So, they want to film a teaser. If we don't like it, they won't send it out. If we do, then they'll send it out with a proposal to the channels. And pitch a three-part series, following us.'

'Max, please,' Natasha implores. 'We'll lose our clients. How would Fortescue react if we turn up with a film crew? Or the Oscar Winner, for goodness' sake? Our whole USP is discretion. It would be career suicide.'

She has a point, but John, devoid of camera work for so long, adds his voice in support of Damien. 'If we have the guarantee that we'll see the *teaser* and we have to authorise it, what's the harm? Nothing ventured, nothing gained, *mes braves*. And we have to consider what it will mean for each of us individually. I don't want people just to associate me with property. No offence, Max, but you know my first love is acting. Always has been.'

I try to put an end to this, suggesting we think about it, circle back later and take a vote, but Damien persists. 'This is an amazing opportunity for us, the best kind of free publicity. And, as John says, if we don't like it, we don't do it. What's there to lose?'

'Our integrity,' scoffs Natasha. 'I don't want to be a part of it. And neither does Lord Edward,' she adds, petulantly.

30 May 2022

I have a call from Trisha. There's been some delays with materials coming from Europe, and Billionaire isn't happy that her team of painters have put their prices up by a paltry ten per cent, so it looks like Chester Terrace will be behind rather than ahead of schedule. Building costs have increased so much due to supply chains, Brexit and the knock-on effect of COVID. The opportunity cost of the delay is going to be much greater.

Damien offers to chat with Florentina to see if he can smooth things along. I don't enquire as to why he may have any influence, and I don't take him up on his offer.

JUNE

1 June 2022

It's an office day trip. A time for bonding. I take the team along with me to NT's house. I know the house but the others don't, and it's important they get a feel for it.

Damien has persuaded me the film crew should meet us there. Natasha is duly incensed. During the drive, our resident actor asks if the directors have provided us with any notes, and wonders aloud if we should be getting into character.

Furrowing his brow, Damien responds, 'It's reality TV, John. We *are* the characters.'

'But are there any angles they're looking for?'

'You know what they want – intrigue and in-fighting,' Damien says.

'That's exactly what I feared.' Natasha sighs.

I sense a need to redirect the conversation. 'Now, let's remember what our focus is here. The TV crew is incidental. We're here for NT. It's a terrific house, you'll see that soon enough, and I want us to get her a record-breaking price. And so we're all on the same page, it's completely off-market: no print, no internet, discretion all the way. We need to keep the tabloids at bay. It will all be done through a stealth sales strategy.'

Natasha points out that it's not very 'stealth' having a camera crew tailing us around. Hard to disagree with.

'If, and it's a big *if*, anything comes of it, it won't air until long after the house is sold, and nothing will be broadcast without NT's permission.'

'I've told you,' bursts in Damien, 'this is just the teaser. *If* we approve it, they'll pitch it to various channels, and then they'll construct a show around it. Tash, you might as well be in it, we need some female content. T said it would help. And she'd like a will-they-won't-they? element.'

I look in my rear-view mirror to try and catch Damien's eye. If I didn't know him better, I'd swear he was being deliberately provocative.

'I'm not *content*. And I really don't care what *T* wants.' Natasha splutters the letter 'T' with as much disdain as she can muster.

'I think it's rather fabulous that people will see us as we are: honest brokers. It could change the image of estate agents in this country, rehabilitate them. And, dare I say, it may help a little that I have some experience on camera.' Always the optimist, our John.

We turn off the motorway in under an hour, and wind our way through the B-roads as the landscape takes on a pastoral hue: mellow-stoned grey walls, sheep idling in fields, pretty villages of the same famous stone. We reach a hornbeam-flanked driveway and arrive at NT's house. It's Arts and Crafts in style, with a Lutyens influence. There are well-proportioned principal rooms at the rear of the house opening on to a lawned garden. The position is exceptional, with the grander rooms facing south across a valley with a lake at the bottom of it, and no other property in sight. NT greets us warmly, me with a hug and a 'Hello darling,' followed by my family nickname, surprising my colleagues.

'Help yourself to the house and the gardens,' she says. 'I'm just writing an article and need to get it polished off before lunch.'

NT bought the house in the 1970s when, she tells us, her part of the Cotswolds was rather unfashionable. Everyone wanted to be along the M4 corridor heading towards Bath. I chuckle at the irony; she is now in the most desirable (or, at least, the most expensive) corner of the British countryside. Her house sits plum in the middle of the 'golden triangle', being almost equidistant from Stow-on-the-Wold, Daylesford and Soho Farmhouse. You can't get more prime than that. It's become what the Hamptons are to New York. And the prices reflect that.

I've found there are two types of famous people – those who are generous with it, see that fate and good fortune have played a small part in their journeys, and share. And those who guard it closely, somehow concerned that their own wattage may dim. NT falls in the former category and has a spirit of giving. She's happy to support others, not just with her time but with her advice, input and endorsement. I'd called ahead to ask her if she'd mind a film crew (she must be sick of them, what with her day job) capturing us for an hour. 'Of course,' she responded immediately. 'And let me give you all lunch.'

I walk the team around the house, outbuildings, gardens and fields.

'This is a gem,' says John, as we cross the formal lawn and pass beneath an ancient yew tree, admiring the view.

I can't help thinking, *Wouldn't you rather all this than a three-bedroom flat in the new Grosvenor Square development or a nice house in Chelsea?* The lake, the vista, the proportions, the space. It just makes one happy. It helps that it's a perfect day: the sun's out, the fields look resplendently green and the garden is in full bloom. A part of me is pleased the film crew is coming to capture it all, whatever happens with them down the line.

We continue our tour, walking through the formal rose garden, and hear a car on the gravel driveway. Damien has been busily looking at his phone during our tour, and he now announces excitedly that the filming team has arrived.

A Ford Fiesta pulls up and two affable, Hoxton-bearded men in their late twenties get out, introducing themselves as Paul and Joe. They wear jeans and T-shirts; Paul holds the camera, Joe the mic.

'How lovely to meet you. Are the rest of the crew following on? We do have some time constraints.' It seems John is going to take the lead.

Paul chuckles and says, 'It's just us.'

'Ah. No director, no cinematographer, no grips?'

'Just us, mate. We're only doing a teaser, and budgets are tight. You haven't been commissioned yet, have you?'

'No, we haven't,' I say. 'We've got an hour. It's just the three of us being filmed, Natasha won't be a part of it.'

'That's a pity,' Paul says, eyeing Natasha. Then he asks, 'Will NT be on camera?'

'Definitely not.'

'And what is it you're after from us? How shall we play it?' John queries, more accommodatingly.

'You know what sells: celebrity and money. So give us names and figures, and that should get you commissioned. This place is mega.'

I eye Paul. 'But don't you think we're underestimating the British public? Don't you think that seeing a beautiful house and understanding how people inhabit their homes, what they use them for, what gives them particular pleasure in them makes a more interesting show? I don't just mean expensive places; it could be a bothy in Scotland, an artist's flat in a converted warehouse in Liverpool or a stately home. How about that for a concept?'

'I don't know what a bothy is but I do know what commissioning editors are looking for. Right or wrong, that's the way it is.'

And so our directional chat concludes. As Natasha walks down to the lake, John, Damien and I walk across lawns and practise looking intense, earnest, amused and awed as we're filmed. John interrupts almost continually with questions that 'the crew' seem to have little interest in: 'Where's my marker?' 'What angle do you want me from?' 'Should I look more quizzical or impressed when Max says that?' And so it goes on.

Damien is a complete natural, while I'm an embarrassment. I stride across NT's lawn uttering such ridiculous statements as, 'Well, if Harry and Meghan had stayed here, they would have snapped this up; they were apparently looking in the Cotswolds before Montecito beckoned. And as for the Beckhams, they must be devastated they've already bought by Soho Farmhouse, as this would have had their name all over it.'

For good measure, I toss some ludicrous numbers around. 'You couldn't put a price on this . . . twenty million . . . it's a work of art, a *Les Demoiselles d'Avignon*, a *Mona Lisa*.'

Even John looks surprised as I continue, but it's almost as if I can't stop myself. My inner desire to hog camera time must be coming from a buried place.

Paul turns to me just after my *Mona Lisa* monologue and says, 'Thanks for all the names and data. I'm not sure how to say this but maybe you could be a bit more . . . I don't know . . . Actually, a bit less . . . hammy.'

John turns to me, concerned, and then snaps at Paul: 'It's the first time he's done camera, I think he's doing fantastically well. I told you to give us notes. Now, maybe you need to pull the focus to me a little, stop putting all this pressure on Max.' He turns back to me. 'You really are doing marvellously, but it's about pausing for those beats, taking those moments. I think you're a natural, Max, but it does take time.'

I feel suitably chastened, and let John and Damien film the next segment. John does know how to 'pull focus', but it's clear the camera loves Damien.

I walk down to the lake and find Natasha, sitting and looking out across it.

'Penny for them,' I say.

'Aren't you busy becoming the next Phil and Kirsty?'

'I think the crew have found them.' I gesture towards Damien and John, who are engaged in animated conversation. 'I've been told I'm for the cutting-room floor.'

'Best place to be.'

'Are you OK?' I ask.

'I'm fine.'

'And your dad?'

'He'll be OK.'

'I'm sure he will be.' I sit beside her on the grass. 'If you ever need any time off, or for me to look after Lord Edward. Or if you just want to talk. You only have to ask.'

She turns to look at me and I face her. 'Thanks.'

The British aren't very good with death or illness. I know. I remember a family friend's father dying when I was nine. I knew it had happened, but it took him saying to me, 'Max, you know that Dad's dead,' as we were playing *Monopoly*. I simply said, 'Yes,' and that was it. And then the same thing happened when my closest friend from school's father died grimly of alcoholism. He came to stay, and though the death was acknowledged, I thought that I could best serve him by not talking about it. How crazy is that? But since my own mother died, I feel better equipped to face it, to visit friends in hospital when they are close to the end, to hold their hands and cry and say I'll miss them and ask what I can do. Death is part of life, it's the finite nature of it that is so brutal.

'That's a wrap,' shouts Damien from the house. 'Lunch.'

NT gives us a lunch of cheese, soup, salads and bread – all

homemade. She chats happily with Paul and Joe, and even signs a copy of her latest book for them. She's a true pro, and I can tell the lunch and meeting her have meant the world to them. As we part, Paul tells me, 'With so many of them, it's an act but she's really as nice as she seems.'

'She is,' I confirm.

4 June 2022

I've made up my mind. It's not a hard decision, but I just needed to be sure we could do as good a job as anyone else, if not better. It makes things so much easier when you love a place and can speak with genuine superlatives about it. And here I can. I know the terrain, I know the players and I know how to make a deal work. I tell this to NT, who says how happy she is. It's us that are the lucky ones, I tell her, to have this opportunity.

I share the news with the team: 'I've told NT we're in.'

John is all smiles. 'I am thrilled – and what a marvellous woman NT is. I adore her.'

'Now, I'm going to hit the phones. John, how are you fixed? I'd like you to come with me for the preview day. NT is filming there for the next month, but as soon as there's a gap, we're getting people in.'

'I'd be honoured,' he says with a beam.

He needs something; although Flavia is back for the signing of the flat, I sense that having seen her husband has reminded her that she is, in fact, married. Funny that. I can tell John is doing his best *bella figura* but, poor chap, it seems there's an inevitability about where their relationship is heading.

A general rumble purrs through the office as we bat around figures, wondering what to ask for NT's house. It's hard getting the price right. Normally, you'll be in competition with other agents and therefore you have to be competitive, but you want to be realistically so. If you become the agent known for over-valuing and never achieving, that's not good. And it can burn a property.

When it comes to pricing, there are two schools of thought. One, in contrast to the Michelle Obama edict, is you go low. The hope is to create increased footfall, which will translate into competitive bids. This stratagem, when it works, results in people offering over the asking price. It's a higher-risk approach, because you are dependent on competition; if there's only one party interested, well, then, they're not going to bid against themselves. It works when there are multiple parties, particularly when you successfully access their desire to 'win' so they end up paying more than they should have done to fulfil that very desire. And with the price point at which we operate, most of our buyers are used to winning and wired to do so. The second, more conventional route, is to go high and wait for an offer.

NT's house is unique, having no direct comps, and is therefore much harder to value. I play with the figures, look at recent sales, and calculate that despite the fact we're creaking towards a recession, prices in this part of the countryside are still at an all-time high. But how do I value, for example, a disused stable yard? It could be turned into office space, a gym, spa and indoor pool, or extra accommodation decorated *à la* Soho Farmhouse. The possibilities are endless – as are the costings. We have to figure this out, and quickly. We settle on optimism. Why not? I call NT and give her the figure, and she says she's happy. Have I mentioned that she's the dream client?

8 June 2022

Trisha has had sign-off from Billionaire to go ahead: that's the good news. The bad being her team has taken another job for a month, as it took him so long to confirm, so we're now looking at a July launch, which is suboptimal.

'Did you speak to Florentina?' I ask Damien.

'Maybe,' he responds.

'Don't be coy.' I tut. 'And Damien, please be careful.'

'It's just a bit of fun, you should try it.'

And he's right. I'm in a relationship rut. I don't know if it's because I got out of the habit during COVID but my romantic life has wound down to very little. I was never a New York dater, but still.

10 June 2022

The evening arrives for my follow-up supper with Andrew, and I'm half expectant and half not wanting it to happen, for fear that it won't work out as I want – although I'm not sure what that is. Kate has now been informed, consulted and suggests a haircut: 'Shorter makes you look younger, though I know you're still stuck in that Hugh Grant foppish *Four Weddings* look.' She's also insisted I have my eyelashes and brows dyed dark brown, and we go together to her 'place' in Notting Hill to have it done. 'It will take years off you,' she promises. In fact, I look weird, as if someone has burned a cork and rubbed it on my eyebrows. Kate did also lobby for some Botox but I drew the line there, despite her saying, 'Maxi, it will just look like you've had a good night's sleep.'

With my preened hair held tightly in place, neat curves around the sides and neckline, my panda eyes and brows meet Andrew at a Persian restaurant near my flat. I'd thought about the Japanese place, but delicious as it is, it has rather an in-and-out vibe, as if they'd like three table sittings per evening. I know the gang at the Persian restaurant, and though the seating is tightly packed, it has an intimate feel that makes one happy to hunker down there. I arrive and put myself in the corner seat. I order a negroni, and as it arrives, I catch the eye of a client, who nods at me.

This client has proved a valuable lesson to me. She'd entrusted the sale of her house to me and, much as I love it, I've failed to sell it. I'd done my calculations and valued it based on what I thought were the right comps, factoring in that it has a carriage driveway with parking and a huge garden backing directly on to arguably the best London communal gardens I'd seen, which are several acres in size and have a tennis court. It truly has the feel of a country house in London. It needs work, but then almost everything in London, unless entirely brand new, is deemed to need work. My suggested price is strong but I think within the realm of possibility. If the property were in Notting Hill, it would be double what I'm quoting. But it hasn't sold. I've done everything right . . . I think. I've been in touch with all the right players and connected the property dots. But we just haven't found the buyer. So often at this higher end, luck plays a part. I feel the disappointment of my client, who rightly points out that it was me who named the price. In retrospect, I'd been swayed by my own love of the house, as I'd rather have it than the equivalent in Notting Hill. We have a brief and pleasant chat, avoiding the topic of her house, which she's handed to another agent – inevitably, Slick.

I'm in the midst of this chat when Andrew arrives, looking preppy in khaki chinos and a bluey-grey button-down shirt that matches his eyes. I introduce him to my client, who gives me a look of approval, and we sit. As I pick up my drink, my hand does a swerve. The negroni splashes to the side and a trickle runs over the rim of the glass.

'Sorry,' I say reflexively.

'Don't be sorry. It's clearly telling you that you need to drink it.'

I take a gulp. 'So,' I begin. 'I've got this whole speech prepared, and I'd really like to get it out of the way so I can then enjoy supper with you and not have it fermenting in the back of my head.'

'Sure, but shall we order first? You know you can get hangry.'

'Don't worry, I've already got that covered. I've ordered a selection of mezes. But you're wise to consider my blood-sugar levels.'

As if on cue, some flat bread, baba ghanoush and hummus arrive. I tear off a strip of bread, add a dollop of the aubergine dip and put it into my mouth.

'So, here it is: workshopped with my therapist but entirely my own thoughts and feelings. When I moved to LA, I was sure but unsure of my sexuality, as you know. I knew I was gay, but I wasn't comfortable with it. *At all.* I've done lots of work on myself since then, read all the books, seen the aforementioned therapist, and it has taken me time to feel comfortable in my own skin. I think I'm there. So, first off, I owe you a huge debt of gratitude for everything you did for me. As a role model, for showing me you could live the life you want and that being gay is an incidental part of that, not a defining one. And for being the first person to make me feel it was really all right to be me. Thank you, Andrew. Really, I can never thank you enough for that.'

'Max . . .' he says.

'Don't!' I laugh. This had been a catchphrase between us, because a crazy friend of my dad's says it the whole time. 'If you start, then that's it, I will be gone.'

'OK.' He wipes his eye with his napkin. 'It's just a fleck of dust, actually.'

'You had this life, you were fully formed, and I was just this little thing incubating, working out who I was, who I wanted to be. And everything was so good with you. It really was; I was so happy. But it felt somehow that I was playing at life, that it wasn't quite real. And I know you were mad that I hadn't told my parents about you, about us. And that's all on me, on my shame, because I was so proud of you, of being with you. I wanted to shout it from the rooftops but I didn't have the voice. And I don't think I could have found it if I'd stayed in LA then.'

'I think I understand.' It's his turn to take a piece of flat bread and attack the dips.

'I panicked and I missed home and my family, and I couldn't see myself having a life in the film world. You know how crazy it is. What was I going to do, bombard Reese with scripts because we'd build up a small friendship on a film set? Ingratiate myself with Susan Sarandon because she'd been kind enough to ask me to Thanksgiving once? It was just too transactional for me. And I'm not good at that.'

'You could have written. That's what you really wanted to do.'

'I didn't believe in myself. I didn't think I could, and I wasn't brought up to fake it until you make it. I've got over that; I do it constantly now.' I laugh. Then: 'I'm sorry. I'm sorry that I left so abruptly and without letting you talk about it with me. I knew that if I didn't go, I never would. And that would have been bad for us in the long run . . . I think . . . I don't know for sure, and never will. I know you'll think this is chasing after forgiveness but the thing is, I loved you too much, and I knew you'd talk me round, because there was such a huge part of me that wanted to be talked around.'

Andrew is silent now, but he can't pretend the tears in his eyes are due to a fleck of dust any more.

'OK, I'm done now. What shall we have for our main course?'

He stretches his hand across the table, and I put my hand out to meet him halfway. He squeezes it and simply says, 'Max.'

We spend the night together. I feel a huge release after saying what I've said – what should have been said long ago. I take the morning off work and we walk along the canal up to Regent's Park, passing Billionaire's house, letting our hands brush against each other's and drinking coffee on a park bench. *This is what life could have been*, I think to myself. And I'm sad for a moment. But life is a series of sliding doors and I could easily be someone far less fortunate. My door hasn't turned out so badly.

14 June 2022

We finish half a day's filming. We get a couple of developers and fellow agents to show us several properties, with Kate playing our 'client'. I get a few straight-to-camera moments, explaining why I set up the agency, what we offer and how we're different (read: better).

'You didn't tell me about him, Maxi,' Kate says, tilting her head towards Damien as we view the first flat together.

'You knew I had an Australian chap working with me.'

'I did but I didn't know he walked straight out of a surfing catalogue and made the Hemsworths look like his ugly cousins.'

'Well, he's a little young for you.'

'I'm desperate to be a cougar,' she protests. 'And I've had some practice.'

And, inevitably, she charms both John and Damien with her warmth and infectious nature. Kate has that skill of making whoever she's speaking to feel like the most important person not just in the room but the world. Her focus is like a laser, to the exclusion of anyone else. And with Kate, it comes from a genuine interest in people; she loves to understand who they are and what motivates them. I imagine it's part of her craft of acting – getting inside 'the character'.

16 June 2022

Andrew emails:

That was a special time, Max. Thank you for being honest with me. It's amazing how easily we fit back together – it says something.

It's suitably cryptic, but I do my usual thing of responding within minutes rather than waiting hours, or preferably days:

I loved seeing you, Andrew. And thank you for hearing me. There's so much to say, but you know my instinct leans towards verbosity so I'll keep it simple. It was a special time for me too. Love, Max

20 June 2022

We go to an open house in Chelsea. They're not like the ones you see on *Selling Sunset*, which offer Burgers and Botox; the best you can hope for here is a free glass of champagne. These events used to be weekly pre-COVID, but now they're a rarity, so more widely attended. It's the penthouse of a new development with wide-reaching views across the Royal Hospital and towards the river in the much-fought-over development that was Chelsea Barracks. Prince Charles famously used his influence with the Qatari royal family to block a modern scheme by (Lord) Richard Rogers and have it replaced with something more traditional. That was back in 2010, and led to a Candy brothers lawsuit and the judge declaring that PC's interference was 'unwanted and unexpected'. The £3.5-billion development is now complete, and the price tag for this particular flat is £35 million. All the thrills and spills are included: porterage, parking, swimming pool and gym, and access to a private cinema and conference room (which you pay extra for, naturally). The service charge is £80,000 per annum, over three times the median national wage. It's an outrage, of course.

The selling agent works for one of two big international firms, and he's of the newer breed: slicked-back hair, sales figures at hand, sharply tailored suit, oozing estate-agent chat. Not the Tim-Nice-But-Dim public school type with a speckling of dandruff on the shoulders of his pinstripe who'd dominated the scene when I first started working in property. This agent tells us that, unsurprisingly, there's a lot of interest from Hong Kong at the moment. We admire the marble bathrooms, the walk-in wardrobe with cedar cupboards that effortlessly glide shut, the electric blinds and the oddly cut rooms. The furniture is slick and modern, and framed photos of models from a Ralph Lauren catalogue litter the apartment. John chats with everyone, Natasha puts on her best neutral face and stays close to me, while Damien has the two prettiest girls beside him, offering him drinks and canapes. We're heading out of the gilded tower when the lift opens and out comes Slick. He sees me and raises himself to his full six foot three, tilting his head back.

'Max,' he offers condescendingly. 'Good to see you.'

'Hello, Slick.'

'How's Zara getting on? Where is she again? Kensal Rise? Willesden?'

'She's very well. And she's in Queen's Park.'

'Oh really? I'm so unfamiliar with that part of town. Aren't you clever to have found her something so off-beat?' He makes it sounds like an insult, fingering his signet ring as he speaks.

'Yes, it's a great area, full of life and terrific people.' Natasha steps closer beside me, as does John, forming a centurion guard of sorts.

'How . . . sweet. You must come and see our penthouse flat in Belgravia.' And then he leans in confidentially. 'So much more tasteful than this one, done with real flair.'

I feel a lurch at his words. 'Do you mean Vera's flat?'

He smiles that smugly Slick smile. 'Of course, she mentioned she knew you.'

I swallow. 'I know her and the flat well.' I try and keep my voice even.

'Well,' he says gleefully, 'I don't have to sell you on it then. But do hurry, we've got some serious interest, so if you have anyone, act quickly.' A waiter walks past and Slick lifts a glass of champagne from the tray. '*Salut.*' He raises the glass in our general direction.

John puts his hand gently on my back and says: 'Max, we must get down to Dame NT. There's a lot of activity there.'

Slick blinks, recognising the name, then walks across the room to acknowledge an agent who greets him with: 'The King of London property! How good to see you.'

24 June 2022

I arrive in the office to find Natasha with Lord Edward in his basket beneath her desk.

'You're in early,' I say.

'I couldn't sleep, so I took a long walk through the park.'

'Things on your mind?' I ask.

'One or two.'

'Do you want to talk about them?'

'Not yet.'

Later that day, I make my way to Quentin's, treading the familiar steps. I vent about Vera and the fact she's given her flat to Slick for sale; I express my concerns about doing a good enough job for NT; I share my horror that it's almost the end of June and we're not closing deals.

'Have you been experimenting with the toys we bought in Clone Zone?' Quentin asks, throwing me with the change of topic.

I look to the floor and say, rather guiltily, 'No, I haven't.'

'Might that be symptomatic?'

'In what way?'

'You've got Kate back from Los Angeles now. She's single and you're spending a lot of time with her.'

'I am, yes, and I love having her here.'

'So, are you two filling a void for one another? Since she's been back, how many dates have you been on?'

'Umm, there was that guy who worked in the complaints department of the BBC.'

'So – one?'

'She hasn't been back that long.'

'I'm not criticising. But I am observing. And if there are things that you want in life, you have to go about seeking ways to achieve them. So, you have to ask yourself, do you actually want to have a romantic relationship with someone?'

'Yes, of course.'

'You say that, but you have lots of relationships, and they're all fulfilling. You have your family, your work colleagues, your friends – and you have Kate, who is, in many ways, forming the role of partner. Perhaps that's easier and simpler than risking your heart to someone?'

'I do want a relationship. But I'm not someone who wants a relationship at any cost. I don't need anything from anyone. I am self-fulfilled, but I would like to share my life with the right person. And why do we have to define relationships in such a way? I love Kate. The fact that we're spending so much time together is great.'

'There's a lot to unpack in that last sentence.'

I am so tempted, in that moment, to say, 'Well, I don't think experimenting with a butt plug is going to help.' But I don't. Instead, I nod profoundly, wrap up the session and walk back to the office.

I have supper with Kate that night, although I don't repeat to her Quentin's theory that we are each other's substitute partners.

But it does make me think of Andrew. And I wonder why I didn't tell Quentin about the night we'd spent together. I reasoned it would almost make it too real.

28 June 2002

John has blagged tickets for the opening of the Masterpiece Art Fair. It's become a staple part of the London season. It's held in a huge tent in Ranelagh Gardens in the shadow of Christopher Wren's masterpiece The Royal Hospital, happily sandwiched between the King's Road and the Embankment. The Royal Hospital houses army veterans in the majesty of Wren's building and surrounding sixty-four acres. It's one of the things I love about London: that you can stumble upon such gems. If you come in via the Embankment entrance, you have a terrific view across the Thames to Battersea Park and the ornate Albert Bridge, which looks particularly spectacular when illuminated at night.

The fair lasts nine days and houses mainly art dealers, but also jewellers and Savills (one of the big two estate agents). The VIP opening day will be tomorrow and the grand opening the day after, but, for the elite, they have what they call 'the collectors' opening', which is today. It's skilful marketing that makes everyone feel special to varying degrees. The collectors' evening is for those with very deep pockets, and John has got us tickets through a fabulously wealthy New York friend who has decided not to fly over to London this year. It's the perfect place for picking up clients, hence Savills taking a stand. The problem is that if I walk into a room and someone points out a person who is looking to buy or sell a house in London, I'll then do almost everything I can to avoid them. Quentin tells me that ninety-five per cent of our actions are controlled by our subconscious, but I can't think that my subconscious is telling me to fail.

'Perhaps,' Quentin has suggested when I question him on this, 'it's telling you that you don't deserve to succeed.'

I've been to the so-called VIP night in the past, at which there was rather an undignified scramble for the free drinks, with people waiting by the catering exits to grab a glass. The collectors' evening has a rather different feel of hushed money – people turn down the offer of a chilled glass of Ruinart rather than trying to grab two at a time.

'How do we let people know what we do?' I ask John.

'Shall we loiter by the Savills stand and grab people as they're leaving?' he suggests, taking a sip. Then it was, *'Ciao Edmondo, como stai?'* And we're off. John seemingly has a passing acquaintance with half the guests here, and even I know one or two. We're drawn into stands admiring Joseph Albers, Duncan Grants, a particularly fine Henry Moore. These are the works I recognise. I pass David Linley, now the Earl of Snowdon, the Queen's nephew and chairman of Christie's. One side of the tent hosts several pop-up restaurants, including Le Caprice, a stalwart of Arlington Street and a favourite of Princess Diana's and many other celebrities of the old school. Elizabeth Taylor always ate there when in London, and it was a haunt of Mick Jagger's and Princess Margaret's; many a famous face would pop in unannounced for a seat at the bar, a refreshing glass and some grilled squid (or, for those with a sweet tooth, their celebrated iced berries with white chocolate sauce).

John and I walk the aisles and are greeted by an American couple from Houston, both of whom have confusingly double-barrelled first names, Daisy-Irene and Bluewater-John. It seems John once met them at an opening in Fort Worth, at the Kimble Museum. I can't follow quite how he got to Forth Worth or why he had been there; he is too busy extolling the talent of the architect Louis Kahn. I work out Kahn designed the Kimble, but by then John is on the Salk Institute in La Jolla, another one of Kahn's buildings (which Daisy-Irene and Bluewater-John have visited). They haven't been to the National Assembly

Building in Dhaka, Bangladesh, though, and John implores them to visit, stating it's Kahn's most ambitious project. John always has the capacity to surprise me; I don't know many people who have visited Bangladesh, let alone ones who are architectural connoisseurs. The Texans seem pleased to have one of their museums so admired; despite their sneakers, anoraks and fold-up umbrellas, they apparently possess one of the finest Impressionist collections in Dallas. I'm just relieved that we stay away from politics, as from the signalling they gave and a general haranguing about 'wokeness', I feel our opinions may diverge. The situation has apparently got so bad in the US that they want to spend more time in London, although they're also here to avoid the Texan summer. John goes straight into his good ol'boy routine, and morphs into J. R. Ewing. He's practically wearing a Stetson by the end of it and promises to follow up with lunch next week. They are wavering over buying, as they're so fond of their suite in Claridge's and love the concierge there.

I'm up next, as I see a friend, Anne, for whom I'd found a flat in Bayswater. She's an art aficionado and is walking round the exhibit with a seemingly distracted pal, Henry, who is wearing an expression of slight puzzlement. He looks professorial, with thinning grey hair and second-hand-looking clothes. Anne introduces me to him, telling him I'm the best agent in London and he has to use me. I say I'd love to help. He examines a Brâncuşi sculpture and fails to respond. Anne nudges me, so I try again.

'Where are you looking to buy?' I query.

'London,' Henry says, vaguely.

'Anywhere in particular?'

'I don't think I want to live in Clapham,' he responds.

Well, that narrows it down. I suggest I email him and arrange a meeting so we can follow up when art isn't distracting us.

But at least the night has ended with two potential new clients who haven't been swallowed up by the Savills desk. And I came out floating on too many glasses of Ruinart.

JULY

1 July 2022

Kate and I walk across Hampstead Heath. She wants to explore all parts of London before committing to a particular area. She's used to the borough of Kensington and Chelsea but tells me she doesn't want to be staid. I love Hampstead and the surrounding areas, and it's one of those pockets of London where I like to picture an alternative life.

I know a successful film director who lives close to the Heath in Highgate. He invited me to his housewarming party, and our close mutual friend had said to me, 'Do get there punctually, as I'm not sure if many people will turn up.' I'd arrived shortly after the party started and been met by wall-to-wall celebrities with a splattering of politicians. I pretty much hid in the corner as the likes of Helena Bonham-Carter, Sacha Baron-Cohen and Ed Miliband chatted easily. The host said to me, 'Do take a look around, you know about property,' and so I found myself climbing the stairs of his Highgate house. A pretty young woman asked if she could join me and I graciously agreed, so up we walked together to the roof terrace, where we admired the incredible view across London. And then I got it: this is why it's called Highgate. I offered this explanation to my companion.

'Yes, I figured that,' she said politely, in an American accent.

I breathed in the purer air and looked across the Heath. 'I'm so sorry,' I said, 'I haven't introduced myself. I'm Max.'

'I'm Anne,' she said, and as she did it dawned on me that it was Anne Hathaway. Our host had directed her in the role that was a one-take scene and won her an Oscar as she emoted to 'I Dreamed a Dream'. I was desperate to start reciting lines from *The Devil Wears Prada* but was rendered mute instead. We both admired the view in silence.

I'm recounting the tale to Kate as we walk close to the Highgate perimeter of the Heath.

'I'm over actors,' she says, 'but what's happened to your director friend?'

'He's with someone, and has children.'

'Pity,' says Kate, as we swing around to see Kenwood House, the imposing Georgian mansion that commands another great view of the Heath.

'Do you keep up with him?'

'I haven't seen him since that party, rather embarrassingly. That COVID break seems to have created a distance from people who are on the periphery of your friendship circle.'

'Get back in touch. I haven't given up on all my acting aspirations. And if I move up here, it would be good to know people.' Kate is able to make the wonderful assumption that people will be happy to know her; she is so unlike me.

Later, over lunch, she books me in for an August weekend to go cottage-hunting in the Cotswolds. Her talks with the

LA fund regarding investing in prime-residential London are ongoing. Sterling is weak against the dollar, so it's a good moment. Kate suggests we work on our pitch over that weekend. They're not going to decide anything until the fall, she tells me, so we have time.

4 July 2022

We're into July, and deals should be done by now. I request an update from the team, including any potential new leads. Natasha kicks us off.

'I've looked at some flats for Uncle F. He's reluctant to have a live-in carer, which he really needs if he's going to have his own place, and he won't entertain a serviced flat.'

'So we're back to the chic retirement flat option?'

'I suppose so.'

'The TV show would get us a ton of business,' Damien chips in, never missing an opportunity to push his agenda.

Natasha yawns.

'Let's wait for the teaser,' I say. 'John, what news of the Frenchies?'

'*Je suis désolé*, but they're out. They feel the shape of London has changed with Brexit.'

'So that was a waste of time.' I know there's irritation in my voice.

'But Max, that's always the way. We either win big or we get nothing. You're always saying it.'

'Yes, I know. I'm sorry. I'm just frustrated that we can't view Billionaire's yet, nor NT's place. Damien, what have you got?'

'I've got some Hong Kong leads I'm working on.'

'And Flavia?' I turn to John.

'Still a nightmare. We've got the information back from the managing agents, but one of the owners in the building is not only suing the managing agents but his fellow residents too. It's unclear why. I think he's unhinged and bored.'

'Anything else?' I ask, trying to keep the frustration from my voice.

'Well,' says Natasha, 'I'm rather loath to put anyone forward after the Insta-Kid but we've an old family friend. Bonkers, from the deep South – Alabama, originally. She grew up in the town next door to Truman Capote and Harper Lee. Her parents knew them. She's lived here forever, having married a Brit.'

'She sounds like she's straight out of a Tennessee Williams play,' John observes.

'She is, rather,' says Natasha. 'It will be a slow burn with her, but I'll try and get something in the books for autumn. She won't be in London over summer.'

5 July 2022

I have a call from the agent selling the flat the Oscar Winner is after. We still haven't reached a deal. I know that the Oscar Winner and her partner have the 'firepower' to increase their offer, but given the level of work needed, and the already-mentioned rising costs of building, I'm reluctant for them to do so.

The agent has tried every trick in the book, talking of third viewings, of architects coming around, of how the Oscar Winner could lose it imminently, of how the sellers are getting frustrated and may withdraw it from the market. And now he tells me there's another offer. Here's the thing, though: you can use a line of intimidation once, maybe twice, but once you've used it more than that, you've lost credibility.

The agent's narrative doesn't quite stack up – you get a sixth sense for the housing truth when you've done it long enough, and, like Kate Moss, who said on *Desert Island Discs* that she could spot a 'wrong 'un', I know when I'm being played. I thank the agent for keeping me updated and promise to relay the news to my client. I'm in two minds as to whether to sit on this information or not. Part of my job is to manage stress on my clients' behalf, which often involves shielding them from it and not telling them things. It's a conundrum. After some reflection, I decide to report this supposed new 'offer' and my thoughts on it. The Oscar Winner's response: 'Max, I'm in your hands.' I'm delighted, of course, but feel the weight of responsibility. I'm trusting my gut for both NT and my Oscar Winner. These are big shoes to fill.

8 July 2022

I walk into the office and find Natasha and Damien at their desks. Natasha's eyes look red and Damien is agitated: not a look I've seen him wear before. I wonder whether to say something but reason they're adults, so the three of us sit silently at our computers.

I'd walked rather than cycled into the office this morning in an effort to calibrate my thoughts on the TV idea. Quentin hasn't been a huge help beyond suggesting I write up a pros and cons list.

Natasha takes Lord Edward for a walk. Damien and I remain in awkward silence, at our respective desks, until finally I break it:

'Is everything OK?'

'Yeah, it's all good.' He doesn't look up from his laptop.

'Natasha seemed a bit upset.'

'She shouldn't be. She's had some news, supposedly good news, and I told her I was happy for her. She didn't seem to like that.'

As I'm pondering what this means, John comes in with a fluster of apologies for being late, a linen scarf artfully draped around him.

'I've never been able to sport a summer scarf,' I say admiringly. 'You do it so naturally.'

'Well, I learned from a wonderful Italian actor, when I did a picture in Rome. There's an art to it.' With this, he comes over to my desk, beckons me to stand and loosely wraps the linen number around me twice so it falls midway down my torso in two layers. 'Think Issey Miyake,' he says. He takes hold of my shirt, which has the top button undone, and undoes the two beneath it. Natasha walks in just as he's finishing off this styling.

'What do you think?' he asks her.

'I'm tempted to say, if you're trying to look like an ageing gigolo, you're doing a . . . actually, I'm not sure whether you're doing a good or bad job.'

Ignoring her, and admiring his work once again, John muses: 'You'd make a fabulous one.'

'Now, let's talk about this teaser,' I say. 'We need to be very clear about our objectives and desires.' I get up, move to The Board and take out a marker pen. In bold letters, I write: 'PROS' and 'CONS'. 'Come on, guys, throw things at me. Let's make this a creative workshop.'

I pick up Lord Edward's ball; he barks. I throw it to Damien. 'Go.'

'Free publicity. On the back of that, we'll get a huge social media presence, which I'm happy to take charge of. We're not using Instagram or Twitter nearly as much as we should be.'

'OK. Throw the ball,' I command.

He chucks it to Natasha.

'Publicity works both ways. It could sink us,' she says.

'True.' I write 'good publicity' and 'bad publicity' in the respective PROS and CONS lists.

'You don't have the ball,' Natasha points out.

I grab it from her. 'I do now.'

She grabs it back. 'They will make you – and our clients – look ridiculous. You can just imagine the likes of Camilla Long writing a review about the waste-of-space estate agents and their spoiled, out-of-touch clients.'

I grab the ball from Natasha and throw it to John.

He says, 'It's true. But what we must show is that problems are universal. We are dealing with very wealthy people, and they don't tend to elicit sympathy.'

Fair point.

Damien, with a hint of pleading in his voice, says, 'Look guys, I'm not one to blow smoke up asses, but we're pretty good at what we do, and we're likeable. How can't this be a win?'

The ball has now been dropped and is eagerly received by Lord Edward.

'It depends how they edit us, darling,' John says, waving a hand in the air. 'I've seen terrific actors crucified by bad directors and editors.'

'But we're not actors – and T says they're not out to get us. They want to make a positive show. It's glitz, glamour and likeability. That's what she's told me.'

Natasha huffs, and John looks stage left out of the window, as if it might provide an answer. I ask Damien if he trusts T. He replies with a resounding (albeit expected): 'Yes.'

'As I've said before,' begins an irate Natasha, 'we'll lose all our existing clients. Do you think Billionaire would consider going near us . . .'

'Florentina would,' Damien interrupts.

'Well, aren't you just the honey trap?'

'I'm trying to build on something here, Tash, to help the team.'

'I bet you are. And how are you doing that, by banging Billionaire's daughter?'

I've never heard Natasha use such crude language. Before I can intervene, Damien responds, 'I guess we all use what we've got, Natasha.'

'Enough,' I demand. 'This is not personal. And nor should it be. This is about our work. And may I remind everyone that we are a supportive team who look out for each other. Please.'

'And may I say you've forgotten something rather crucial?' Although I'd much rather move on from the subject altogether, John's calming tone is something of a saving grace.

'What's that?' I ask.

'Being moderately famous is rather good fun. People tend to be nice to you; it presents lots of opportunities in many forms. Not that I want to be base.'

Seemingly unable to let it go, Natasha remarks, 'You mean Damien will get some groupies.'

'You'd be surprised. Max and I may even get a few admirers. And, Natasha, if you deigned to do it, they'd be falling over you,' John continues. 'Max, don't think I haven't spotted that you're quite a mover. I could see you wowing on *Strictly*.'

Admirers and *Strictly* – that's definitely tipped the balance towards the PROS.

12 July 2022

I call the agent for the Oscar Winner's flat.

'What's going on?' I ask.

'Are you coming up in price?' he responds.

'No. Has the other party?'

'We're considering our options. We may go to a best and final.'

'Really?'

'The sellers want this concluded.'

'So do we.' I like that I'm a *we* with the Oscar Winner.

'Well, you could make a higher offer . . .'

'Or you could accept our current one . . .'

The conversation ends as rapidly as it began.

John, who walked in while I was on the phone, says, 'That sounded fraught.'

'It's the flat for the Oscar Winner. The sellers are so unreasonable. It's driving me crazy.'

'Trust your instinct on this one, Max.'

I'm just hoping my instinct is right.

14 July 2022

I call Trisha.

'What's the time frame looking like?'

'They're starting next week. I'll be done for you by the end of the month.'

This is not good. By then, all the buyers in the right price range will be on holiday, sunning themselves in Saint-Tropez, the Hamptons or the Greek islands. The only serious money that comes into London in August is from the Middle Eastern buyers, who are keen to avoid the heat of August in their own countries.

This time frame is exactly what I didn't want.

'I know it's not ideal, Max, but what can I do? We know who we're dealing with, and I will only do this if I'm paid in advance. I'm not having my lads come to London for a month only to find Billionaire won't pay until October when he sees the work.'

'I understand.'

'Do you, Max? They're living hand-to-mouth. This is about putting food on the table, and it drives me crazy. This is the real world I'm inhabiting.'

'Trisha, I do understand.'

'I'm not cross with you. And Billionaire always pays, eventually. It's just those spoiled kids of his. They refuse to pay, and then I see them on private jets going to the Maldives or goodness knows where, and it makes my blood boil.'

'It's maddening. And I am well aware that I inhabit this ridiculous bubble that is very far detached from reality.'

'I know you're aware, Max. You're one of the good ones.'

16 July 2022

'Max, you're going to have to speak to the lawyer. I can't take it. I just can't find a way to get Flavia's deal over the line. I'm too emotionally involved.'

'Breathe, John. Breathe,' I say.

'Do you think I'm having a panic attack?' he asks.

'No, you're not,' I respond firmly.

A bad neighbour can seriously damage your life – I've seen it happen many times. And this neighbour has been so difficult that most of the building has sold out to avoid any further confrontation with him. They're on their third management company, and this one resident is still issuing an endless litany of complaints: X is walking too loudly up the stairs; he checked Y's recycling and he'd put a paper coffee cup in there, which doesn't strictly follow the rules; Z has a friend staying, who possibly could be paying rent, which is against the head lease. And so it goes on. The new management company has been appointed at great expense, as they are lawyered up, and they're attempting an injunction against this resident having any say in the running of the building. A judge has given him a heavily slapped wrist for wasting the court's time in his most recent lawsuit. He, in turn, is threatening to escalate his action and take his complaints to the European Court of Human Rights and the British High Court. This literally all started over what colour they should paint the common parts and the residents couldn't come to a consensus. I'm reminded of my Texan godmother – perhaps the wrong shade of white really can ruin your life.

I speak to both lawyers and the managing agent, then take independent advice from our own lawyer. I ask each of them, 'Has anyone actually tried to speak to this man?' The answer from each is: 'No.'

'John,' I say, 'go and chat with the man. You have charm, you have empathy. He may be so entrenched in this that he can't see a way out – unless you give it to him.'

18 July 2022

Andrew messages to say he's planning a trip to Europe and wants us to do something together. I respond saying how much I'd like that. He has been on my mind.

20 July 2022

I'm itching to get to NT's, but she's filming there so we can't. As I'm turning down High Street Kensington, I spot Natasha and Lord Edward at the junction. They're making their way to Holland Park, and I join them.

'I was just thinking about holidays,' I say. Lord Edward trots along at quite an impressive pace.

'I might have a big one coming up,' she says. We are just entering the rose garden, and Natasha takes Lord Edward off the lead – which, strictly speaking, is against the rules.

'How exciting. Where?' I ask.

'I'm not sure. I'm probably being rather old-fashioned, but I think it's dependent on the groom.'

'Hold on.' And here I give a dramatic pause and can't help but mimic Oprah as she uttered her 'Whaaattttt?' with such unnuanced incredulity when interviewing Harry and Meghan.

'Yes,' Natasha says simply, and then shouts, 'Lord Edward!' as he runs into the flowerbeds.

'You're engaged?'

'Not yet, but Piers has asked me to marry him.'

'And?'

'I'm not sure.'

'OK.' I measure myself.

'What do you think?'

'Oh Natasha, I don't know. Do you love him?'

'In a way . . . Lord Edward, come back here!' We're now walking through the more wooded part of Holland Park.

'That's not a resounding endorsement.'

'But it makes a lot of sense. I know where I am with him, and my parents would be happy.'

'And would you?'

'Yes, I think I would.'

'Well, that's a lot.' And we walk on in silence. After a moment, I can't help myself but add, 'My mother used to say, don't say yes until you can't say no.'

'Hmmm.'

22 July 2022

John took my advice and went to see the intransigent neighbour. He has, understandably, been ostracised by the building and seemingly by everyone else in his life. It turns out he really wanted someone to just listen to him. John did just that, and seems to have unlocked the injunctions. Thankfully, the lawyers can now move forward.

'You see, John,' I say smugly. 'Sometimes people just want to be heard.'

I have Natasha on my mind. I don't discuss it with John as she's asked me not to say anything, but I wish I could. He has a way of coming at things with a lateral perspective and a refreshing honesty. There's little he says that one can take offence at, as it's always meant with the best intentions. But it does allow him to say things that others wouldn't. I picture him asking Natasha, 'Are you marrying Piers just because his family own half the county?'

23 July 2022

I have a call from the selling agent of Oscar Winner's potential flat. He wants us to submit our best bids by the end of the following week and reiterates that there is competition. The shoe is on the other foot now. I'd played this game when we were selling Fortescue's, extracting the best bids – and, in fact, pushing the only serious buyer up. And now I have to get it right for the Oscar Winner. I have the weekend to contemplate the number, and I gear up the Oscar Winner and her partner by getting a letter drafted with their lawyers' details, proof of funds, their credibility as purchasers. I just leave out the space where we're going to put the magic – and, hopefully, winning – figure.

26 July 2022

It's our first day of previews at NT's house. John and I hit the M40 together so we can divide the buying agents between us, as we'd done at Fortescue's. I love the way John approaches these matters; it's a completely full-frontal performance, with no apology for not being a country agent. It's why I wanted him with me, though Damien and Natasha have chutzpah in different ways. I'm slightly more reticent in my approach, suffering from impostor syndrome.

'So, we've got Prime Purchase, Property Vision, Domby Spencer-Churchill, The Buying Solution, Strutt and Parker, Knight Frank, Katy Campbell, Savills and some Cotswold specialists too,' I tell John in the car.

'Well, you've got them all, then,' John says breezily.

'I've also got the buying agent who hunts with the Bamfords' – the Bamfords are the owners of Daylesford and reigning King and Queen of the Cotswolds – 'apparently he has a direct line to them.'

'Terrific! I told you there was nothing to worry about in taking this on. It just has to be managed seamlessly, and no one does that like you, Max.'

'Thank you, John. On top of that we've got the socialite Queen Bee of the area, supposedly . . .'

'Oh, yes, who's she?' John asks.

'She's a distant cousin of Natasha's and is *au fait* with anyone spending seriously in the county. She's married to someone eye-wateringly rich and, between us, is rather tricky.'

'Money often comes at a price. What are we offering her?'

'Apart from your charm, dear John, I've made it clear to Natasha that our introductory commission is twenty per cent of our final fee. She jumped at the idea of making money for nothing by merely mentioning it to her friends.'

'And your drinks for free?' John says.

'What?'

'Dire Straits.'

'I don't get it,' I say.

'It's a line from their song "Money for Nothing". From the iconic album. Loved by Princess Diana. You must know it,' he continues.

'I'm not sure.'

'You're not that young. My favourite is "Brothers in Arms": "These mist-covered mountains are a home now for me."'

John sings it in a husky voice and the tune is immediately recognisable.

'Ah, yes, of course. It's got that amazing melancholic melody.'

'So moving,' says John. 'And it makes me sad, as I fear that for Flavia, home is not here.'

'We haven't hit another roadblock with the flat, have we?' I ask, anxiously.

'No, it will happen. The lawyers are just crossing the t's and dotting the i's.'

'Is she back in London, though?'

'Let's not talk about it.'

'Of course,' I say, somewhat relieved.

221

The first few agents I show, crossing with John on lawns, in stables and principal bedroom suites, encourage me to feel that the booming country-house market may substantiate the strong price we've put on the property. I feel buoyed, being overly susceptible (as Quentin would point out) to the affirmation of others. When it comes to the agent who hunts with the First Family of the Cotswolds, my optimism sinks. Though he knows the price, he asks me for it repeatedly, and each time expresses incredulity. I point out the many benefits that the estate (which I insist on calling it) has to offer, one of which is that the land means the stamp duty (the purchase tax) owed to the government is six per cent rather than fifteen per cent. That's a huge saving. He feels I've overvalued the property by forty per cent, which blunts the positivity I'd felt and makes me think I should have left this viewing to John. He questions why I'm the one selling the house, asks what experience and local knowledge I have and why, of all people, NT has appointed me.

I simply thank him for his invaluable input and say how grateful I am he's spared the time to come and look around NT's house.

I regroup with John and we head for lunch to the mothership of the Cotswolds, Daylesford, which the Queen Bee informs us still holds the crown over Soho Farmhouse.

'Oh, the Farmhouse tries, but no one is seriously going to mess with Carol,' she tells us. Carol is Lady Bamford to John and me. 'She has great taste and is also smart enough to know who to employ,' Queen Bee adds blithely as we pull into Daylesford's gravelled car park, which is filled with Range Rovers and equally gluttonous cars.

The complex comprises a series of barns that house bars, cafés, wellness centres and food emporiums. These latter spaces look like the Romans have beamed down to serve us a bacchanalian extravaganza of taste and aesthetic delights. Everything looks and smells delicious. It's a cornucopia. And it's all so well staged that you think you need every single item there in your larder – the market garden kimchi, the clementine curd, the black truffle sea salt, the Kashmiri chilli. How had I previously survived without such essentials? And the people all look as if they've emerged from a Boden catalogue, with the serving staff being the most attractive.

'This place is surreal,' I say.

'I call it our local,' says Queen Bee, with a knowing wink. 'Now, let's talk buyers. And how much commission I'd make if one of my pals gets it?'

'Oh, you'd make a mint,' says John.

I give her a breakdown of what her fee would be, and she comments that it would certainly cover the cost of their rental villa in Greece, but then ponders that she may keep it as part of her escape fund, and laughs.

'There's something about this place that makes me feel rather uncomfortable. Everything is just a little bit too perfect,' John says, during a rare lull in conversation. Queen Bee is a talker.

'What's wrong with perfection?' she asks.

'Nothing,' I respond quickly.

She goes on to fill us in on all the Cotswold gossip. Names fly around, names of people I don't know personally but know of. She talks about Rebekah Brooks being back on top, whatever she knew or didn't know about phone hacking; about Jeremy Clarkson and his farm shop, Alex James and his cheese, rich-list members, affairs, wife-swapping, prenups, coke addiction, sex addiction, fetishes I've never heard of before, infidelities and scurrilous goings-on.

'Are people more risqué in the country?' I ask.

'Perhaps,' Queen Bee responds.

'Or more bored?' suggests John.

We wrap up lunch as Queen Bee greets and air-kisses various women who look remarkably like her. They all have the same blonde hair, expertly coiffed, and the same shiny, line-free foreheads. The chat is of parties, past and future, which villas they've rented in Paxos and summer plans.

Queen Bee promises to get in touch with the big hitters who might be able to afford the house. They'll need deep pockets, as apart from the asking price, it's likely that some-one will gut the place, which would be a two-year project and require at least six months of planning. And it's hard to even begin to speculate on the building costs with prices spiralling.

John and I return to the house for a final viewing. We'd worked out the best way to show it on arrival, having scoped the place previously while filming. There's a certain art to showing a house; I like to think of it as choreography. You have to start with the front door – normally, although with a country house of a certain scale there's usually more than one principal entrance. But then there's the question of where to go after the entrance. Do you head down to the basement and then up? Do you head up the stairs and start at the top and work your way down? And, crucially, where do you end the tour? You don't want to find yourself in the basement utility room, as if there's an interest in the place, the buyer will inevitably be asking questions – how long has the place been on the market, what offer might they take, why are they moving? With this in mind, I always work out the final destination, whether it be in the first-floor drawing room overlooking a garden square or in a light-filled kitchen. It also depends on the time of day and season: if it's the morning, you want east light; afternoon, west light. And obviously, if the sun is out, as it is today, John and I make sure we end our tours on the terrace of NT's house, which has sweeping views across the rolling Cotswold countryside. I make sure that I'm facing north, with my back to the front drive, while they face south, with the view. It does take a little planning and I like to test-run different routes so I get it just right.

A friend of mine who studied psychology at Oxford University told me it's all about the first and last memory. Whether it's a supper, a holiday or a meeting, people tend to remember the beginning and the end. What happens in the middle is not so important. So you want the holiday to start and end well.

If there are a few dull days in the middle, that won't matter. And I apply this theory as much as possible to the properties I sell: I try and sandwich the worst of it halfway through the viewing, while beginning and ending on a high.

As we drive back to London, John is uncharacteristically quiet. I'm comfortable in silence, but as we come closer to the city, he speaks. 'All that talk about people and who they are and what they're worth and who's sleeping with whom. Where was the talk about art? About literature? About what's going on in the wider world? There's a war in Europe and Queen Bee is cackling about someone having a bad boob job.'

'It's that scene, isn't it?'

'What scene, Max?'

'It's *The Devil Wears Prada*. When Meryl Streep and Anne Hathaway are in Paris and Anne's character says, "What if I don't want to be like that?" to which Miranda (Meryl) responds, "Don't be stupid, Andrea – everyone wants to be us."'

'Exactly,' says John. 'That's what it feels like. There's a self-satisfied smugness that I can't like.'

And I can't disagree with him.

28 July 2022

It's in. I've just got the link to the teaser. The team huddle around my desktop as I click on it.

Dramatic music blasts, and then a gravelly American-accented voice booms out: 'If you're a billionaire, a movie star, a singing sensation or a top celebrity, there is only ONE person you call when you're looking for a property in London – and his name is MAX THOMAS . . .' This is all intercut with various London properties (including, embarrassingly, Buckingham Palace) being flashed on to the screen with seven-, eight- and nine-figure numbers splashed across them. It then cuts to me walking across NT's lawn, edited to the point of no coherence – it's literally just words: 'Harry and Meghan . . . David and Victoria . . . dear friends . . . twenty million . . . not a penny less . . . no one can do what I do . . . integrity, integrity, integrity . . .' And then we see Damien flirting with Kate as they both step, fully clothed, into a rooftop hot tub that is absurdly empty. They giggle and look provocatively towards the camera. And now John is walking through Holland Park, saying in voice-over: 'The line between clients, friends and lovers can often be blurred.' It continues in this fashion with garish graphics and flashes of Brad Pitt, Madonna, Gwyneth Paltrow and various other American celebs who have lived in or profess to love London. And then we're back to the American voice again: 'So if you want an insight into the fabulous world of Max and his team . . . the rich, the famous, the romances' – and here we get a look between Kate and Damien and then, horrifyingly, one between John and me – '. . . come subscribe now to the hottest real estate show in Britain.'

There's silence in the room. I will Natasha not to speak. Finally, John breaks it: 'Well, it's clearly designed for an American audience. And I imagine it will sell. Were they suggesting there's a romance between Max and me?'

'T told me they have to present it in a certain way to get it commissioned,' Damien explains, sheepishly.

I let out a sigh and then deliver my verdict. 'I appreciate the effort that you've put in, Damien, and the relationship you've built up with T, but we can't start anything in a dishonest manner. This is a hard no. Our business would be over.'

'I can speak to her.'

'You're very welcome to, but if this is the angle they're looking for, it's simply not for us.'

Later that day, I find myself alone with Natasha.

'You're good not to gloat,' I say.

'I don't enjoy being right.'

'We all enjoy being right.'

'That's true. But I won't rub it in.' She gives me a smile, and with that our foray into the world of reality TV and my future as a *Strictly Come Dancing* contestant are over. Or so I imagine.

30 July 2022

I've been going and back and forth on what to put forward for the Oscar Winner, and decide to stick to our original offer. We could lose the place (again, I like using this 'we', though don't recall being invited to), but I feel it's a fair offer and I sense the agent is bluffing. I press send and hope for the best.

The agent calls immediately and asks me if that's 'it' in an ominous tone.

I wobble for a moment and then say, 'Yes.'

'You're sure.'

'Yes,' I say, gaining strength.

'We'll get back to you next week,' he says.

'Not that long,' I moan. 'We usually hear on the day.'

'They've got a lot to consider.'

I don't trust him.

AUGUST

1 August 2022

'I have some good news. We've exchanged on Flavia's.'

'John,' I say, jumping up, 'that's incredible. I'm so happy for you and Flavia.'

'Thank you,' he says. His whole tone is deflated and his body, normally erect from years of Pilates, is slouched.

'What's wrong?'

'Nothing, really . . . the inevitable.'

'Has Flavia gone?'

'Yes, she's in Greece for the summer. Well, between there and various boats. And I wanted her to be here for this so we could celebrate.'

'I'm sorry, John. How are you bearing up?'

'I'm OK. I think. My heart was so broken when my wife left me that I promised myself that if I was to love again, which I have, I would love freely and appreciate the moments we share together for as long as we do. Life is transitory and love is pure, and it can last forever but in different forms. I love many of my exes.'

'That sounds very healthy,' I say, while wondering about the ex-wife I never knew of.

'It is, but with Flavia, I'm not ready to let her go.'

'Well, that is a little more problematic. What are you going to do?'

'I may find a way for us to cross paths this summer. She'll be floating on the Med for most of August and I shall find myself doing the same thing.'

My summer plans, so far, involve a weekend with Kate. I have been in email chats with Andrew, and we're treading tentatively around one another, but it sounds like he's going to be in Europe in September.

3 August 2022

My instincts were right: we've got it. After three months of shenanigans and every cajoling tactic under the sun, they've taken the Oscar Winner's offer.

I don't gloat to the agent – it's better to be gracious in victory – but I can't help a tiny hint of smugness when I call the Oscar Winner, who's on Stromboli filming.

'I'm so pleased we didn't go up,' I say, rather needily.

'As are we,' she responds warmly. 'Let's have a celebratory supper in September when we're back.'

'I'd love that,' I respond honestly. June and July may have been a bust but August is looking better already.

5 August 2022

I walk into an atmosphere. No words are uttered, but Natasha is radiating anger. John barely says hello, cowering rather, and

Damien is absent. I sit down. There's a piece of paper on my desk. I pick it up and see it's a printout from a tabloid publication: a photo of Billionaire's daughter with Damien. The caption reads: 'Who's Florentina's hunk in trunks?' They're both grinning in the photo, and the body language, with them casually intertwined, suggests the relationship is very sexual. I knew he'd been in Ibiza for the weekend, but hadn't enquired as to who with.

'How did this get here?' I ask.

'I put it there,' Natasha explains. 'I thought you should see it.'

John asks whether I knew this was going on.

'No, I didn't, but I suppose I had my suspicions.'

'You know me, Max,' John says, with a wry smile. 'I'm the first one to say, "Follow one's heart." In truth, I live by it. But really, given your working relationship with Billionaire, is it wise for our young hero to be playing in this pigpen, so to speak?'

'I'd say you've chosen your words well,' says Natasha, who can't help herself.

It's not for me to determine Damien's romantic choices. But with Billionaire, it's rather different. He's massively protective of Florentina, even when he's not speaking to her – and my relationship with Billionaire is rather critical to the business. I know I'll need to have a chat with Damien but I ignore the searching eyes of Natasha and John by asking them who they may have for the Chisholms' house.

I message Damien and ask him to meet me at our local café, which we refer to as 'the boardroom'. I arrive to find him

233

looking relaxed, with a golden tan, his hair sun-kissed, three buttons of his shirt undone so I can see a new medallion hanging on his chest. He's smirking as he taps on his phone. I immediately imagine he's sexting with Florentina. The last thing I need are Damien's dick pics being forwarded to Billionaire when (because it *will* be a question of when, not if) their dalliance goes south. I've known Florentina for over a decade, and while she has a huge desire to be in a relationship, she's hard-wired to self-destruct any good ones. And Dame is a good one.

'Hey.' He greets me warmly, standing to give me a hug.

'How was your weekend?' I ask, noting to myself that I need to do some gym work after feeling his toned back.

'Yeah, terrific. I love Ibiza.'

'You look well,' I say, rather limply.

'Thanks, Max. So do you, mate.'

'Did you go with buddies?' I hate myself for asking this, as I already know the answer. I immediately regret it.

'Sort of . . .'

'I'm sorry, this is awkward and somewhat inappropriate,' I begin.

'Max, are you about to tell me you're in love with me?'

We both laugh, and it breaks the tension.

'Well, it feels like you've been trying enough, with your very public displays of exercise in the office. I suspect it's to impress Natasha, but John has his suspicions it's about him.'

'It's always about John.'

Julio, the owner, comes and takes our orders – a chicken wrap for Damien and a lentil salad for me.

I place the printout on the table between us.

'Courtesy of Natasha?' Damien asks.

'It doesn't matter where I got it, and it's none of my business personally, but it is my business in that it will affect *our* business.'

'Will it?'

'Without question.'

'For real?'

'Damien, I've known Billionaire for a long time. I know how he operates and I know his complexities. And with Florentina it's – well, it's doubly complicated, but any man who comes near her is the enemy. And . . . if I'm seen to tacitly support this relationship, it's not good. It's not about you and who you are as a person. This is all about him.'

'And if I like her?'

'Do you?'

'Mate, I can't believe we're having this conversation.'

'Honestly, Damien, neither can I.'

We both look up from our plates.

'I don't know, mate. Yes, I like her, but what are you asking me here?'

'I don't know what I'm asking you, Damien.' I fork some asparagus and take a bite. I think of the commission on the Regent's Park house. 'Tread carefully. They'll be adding things up. Not just Billionaire but Florentina.'

'What do you mean?'

'Well, how did you get to Ibiza? Did you go with Florentina on her father's plane?'

'Yeah.'

'That will be noted.'

'Really?'

'Absolutely. Damien, I'm not trying to dictate your private life . . .'

'No, you're just monitoring it with Natasha's help.'

'The point is, getting involved with Billionaire's family is dangerous. I've seen their lives, I've seen how destructive it can be. I've seen the worship of Mammon above all else, and it's an empty vessel of a life. And they are *ruthless*. When you're in, you're in, but when you're out, you're out.'

He takes a large bite of his wrap and looks at me with his twinkling blues. 'It's just a bit of fun, Max. I can handle it.'

'OK.'

'Thanks for – sort of – looking out for me.'

'Looking out for you and our relationship with Billionaire!' I say firmly. 'Look, while we're on topics that I have no right nor invitation to ask about, what's going on with you and Natasha?'

'Nothing.'

'You both seem so much happier when you like each other.'

'Well . . . that's not always easy.'

We finish our food and walk back to the office, where we're greeted by the astute glares of John and Natasha. I put on a poker face. Damien's not a gold-digger, but it's so easy to be corrupted by that level of extraordinary wealth, and it doesn't lead to happiness. Florentina, herself, is the prime example of this.

7 August 2022

Kate's found a fixer-upper in South Kensington, through a friend of a friend. It's an artist's studio, so has predominantly north-facing light with a huge double-volume window. It's on the second floor and has the air of a nineteenth-century opium den: lots of rich, dark red velvet fabrics, huge cushions on the floor, and a mist of decay, which is heightened by a lack of hygiene. Cobwebs cover the windows and beamed ceiling. Kate reports nonchalantly that it belonged to a trustafarian who sadly developed a heroin addiction and overdosed here.

'You mean he died here?' I ask.

'Yes,' she says airily.

'You could have told me that before,' I protest.

'What would you have done, Max, put on a hazmat suit?'

'I'd have, I don't know, got my head around it. No wonder this place feels like a morgue.' There is an air of gloom that hangs over the space.

The executor (his equally dissolute brother) has done nothing to enhance the flat since his sibling's passing. This is apparent from the presentation of it and the fact that he can't be bothered to hire an estate agent or anyone to clean.

'He doesn't really want to drive down from his house in the Scottish borders,' Kate tells me. 'Cities give him anxiety.'

'This flat is giving me anxiety,' I say, looking inside the sink, which has tin foil and burned spoons in it. When Kate tells me the price she's agreed, which is just under £1,000 per square foot, I have to prevent myself from squealing. How does she find these deals? I'm in the business, and I've never come across a bargain such as this one.

The metric that agents use to value property is usually pounds per square foot. South Kensington, where we are, ranges from £1,400 per square foot (and that would be for a basement flat in poor condition) to £4,000 per square foot (which would be a first-floor flat in Onslow Square). There are metrics within the metrics: condition, what floor it's on, position in the street. But this flat, despite the drug paraphernalia and cobwebbed condition, has been massively undervalued.

'Buy it right now,' I say.

'I have,' she responds, looking content. 'I didn't have to think twice about it.'

She's here to show me, meet some builders and welcome someone coming in to 'cleanse'.

'Well, it does need a thorough scrubbing,' I say.

'No, Max, I've got someone to come in and cleanse the aura. I always did it in LA, and this place has bad juju. Historically, it's had good juju and we'll reclaim that.'

'Kate, do you really believe that stuff?' I ask.

'Absolutely.'

'All right.' What else can I say?

'So.' She sits down on the sofa and a cloud of dust emerges, forcing her to stand. 'I'm thinking that we should make it an incredibly indulgent *pied-à-terre*. One fabulous master bedroom, this amazing double-volumed entertaining space, and that's it. Let's not try and squeeze in an extra bedroom and bathroom. What do you think?'

'Historically, one-bedrooms are harder to sell, but I think you're right: make it magnificent, don't compromise. It only takes one buyer, as we know.'

'Well, I'm thinking of it for me to start with. But then, you know what I'm like – I do love me a flip.'

We drive straight from there down to an Airbnb that Kate has booked for the weekend. It's in the Coln Valley, about seven miles from Cirencester, a charming market town. The area is particularly pretty, with undulating valleys and picture-perfect villages, most of them just big enough to have either a pub or a shop and nothing else.

It's good to get out of London and breathe the country air; I need to clear my head regarding Andrew but decide not to discuss it with Kate. She'll create a romantic fantasy, and the reality is it's a moment between exes who live on opposite sides of the world. We spend Saturday sitting in a shady part of the garden overlooking the River Coln, working on our pitch to Kate's Los Angeles investors. There's talk of them flying us out. I have, I think, a good instinct for property, but I'm not great with charts and data and talking with confidence about market predictions. Who can, in truth, predict the market? No one predicted COVID, we didn't expect Putin to be quite such a madman; all these bigger world events determine the market, and we're just reacting. What we can do is try and identify trends and spot which areas are on the up or are already up but set for further growth. The limited stock and ever-growing popularity of Notting Hill means it has to go up. Queen's Park is a rising star, as is Little Venice. I think Fitzrovia and those glorious Georgian squares are rather undervalued and, after my walk with Kate, I favour Highgate. But it's all speculation.

We take an early-evening walk by the river, the willows gently waving at us in the breeze.

'I mean, this is ridiculously picturesque,' says Kate. 'If I could bottle this scene, I could turn this into a blockbuster romcom. It's just perfect. You'd have to be straight, of course.'

'Of course.'

'This is why I want to get a place in the country.'

'It's glorious, Kate.'

After our evening ambulation, we have supper in the village pub.

'So Maxi Max, what's cooking?' asks Kate. 'Is the TV show happening?' She takes a sip of wine and looks around the pub. I know Kate; she's scouting for people of interest to her. She likes to join a conversation.

'No, that's axed. The teaser was horrendous. I just need to get NT's house sold and Billionaire's, and then I can focus on other things.'

'And the love life?'

'Nothing.' I almost mention Andrew but stick to my resolve.

'And the sex life?'

'Nothing, I just said.'

'Love and sex are two different things. It's great when they come together but it doesn't happen that frequently. I mean I'm having a bit of fun with someone but I'm never going to fall in love with them.'

'Who?' I say, intrigued.

'It's just a physical thing.'

'And you're not going to tell me more?' I follow Kate's eyes around the pub.

'Max, you're too hung up on sex. Look at the way you're sitting now, with your arms crossed in a defensive position. You've got to open yourself up. I did this amazing course in Topanga Canyon. People orgasmed without any clitoral or penile stimulation. It was incredible. I mean, it did take hours. But you have to be open to it.'

Kate's voice has grown louder, and our immediate neighbours are leaning in.

'I shall try to be,' I reassure her. 'What do you think are the chances of the investors coming in?' I add, in a quieter register.

'Boring!' She goes on to tell me that I must learn to hold eye contact. The rather attractive waiter has a nice line of banter; Kate suspects he may be interested and chastises me for averting my eyes when he was talking to me.

9 August 2022

The viewings at NT's have not been the flurry of frenzied competition I was hoping for. Queen Bee has produced no one. I keep reminding myself that the country-house market has less footfall than London. We showed Fortescue's house to around twenty principals, of whom three made offers, and it was at a similar price point to NT's house. But in the country, people are much more specific about requirements, and tend to have very set ideas about their dream country house. It's normally a Queen Anne or Georgian rectory with a broad lawn, swimming pool, tennis court, views, edge-of-village setting, five or six acres, and possibly a couple of stables to keep horses for little Isadora.

NT's doesn't quite fit that Jane Austen brief, as the house was built in 1910. And people are away, I remind myself. But today I've made the journey down, listening to Jeanette Winterson's autobiography, *Why Be Happy When You Could Be Normal?*, which she reads herself. I absolutely love it, her and the dry sense of humour she manages in the face of her upbringing. I can't wait to get the viewing over with so I can get back into the car and enjoy another hour and a half of listening as I return to London. But from the moment the couple arrive, on time and smiling, I sense this is different and Jeanette is temporarily forgotten. They are charming and 'get' the house, seeing all the good while not being blind to the fact that it will need updating. Even though they're being represented by a buying agent, they tell me quite openly that they're going to make an offer and want to buy it. I lap up this kind of candour, and though many would counsel against it, I think there's a lot of goodwill to be gained by being straightforward and direct – particularly with someone like NT, who, rather perfectly, was having lunch in the garden with her family, drawing a wonderful tableau to help the couple envisage their life there. Fortunately for us, they have missed out on two houses, so are super-motivated to secure one.

I drive back to London, breezing through the country lanes and singing along to Harry Styles's 'As It Was' at full volume. 'It's just us, it's just us,' I bellow tunelessly. I feel a surge of optimism. Once I've got that out of my system and I hit the M40, I revert to Jeanette.

10 August 2022

'Finally, finally, yeah, yeah, ow,' I sing, walking into the office. It must be a singing week. Three astonished faces look at me. Concern and intrigue radiate from my colleagues in equal measure.

'We can get into Billionaire's house. It is open for viewing. I'm singing the CeCe Peniston hit "Finally",' I explain.

Natasha looks blank; she's too young to remember it.

'Of course, it was in *Priscilla, Queen of the Desert*. I did a touring version of it once. Now you say it, I can hear it.'

Bless John, of course he did.

Like an excitable pup, Damien says he's got a whole list of people he thinks we should bring.

'Not so fast,' I caution. 'This is Billionaire. We're not allowed a key. We have to do it all through the cleaning lady, who will act as spy. And we need to give chapter and verse on everyone who we bring in. And I mean bank ratings, full history, inside-leg measurements, the works.'

'It's all coming back to me,' John chuckles.

I think of bursting into the Celine Dion hit of the same name but am aware the office has heard enough of my singing for one morning.

12 August 2022

We've exchanged on the Oscar Winner's flat. After all the unnecessary procrastination, once it was agreed, everything ran remarkably smoothly.

I send the Oscar Winner a message of congratulations and thank her for choosing us to help her. I get one back immediately that reads, 'No, thank YOU.'

I shall cherish that message.

15 August 2022

We're officially in quiet time. Damien is wearing shorts and polo shirts, which is an indication of how few viewings we're likely to have. Natasha is in Scotland, at Piers's family estate, and John is floating around the Med somewhere. But I'm happy to hold the fort, as I've had some good Augusts and it's possible to sweep up business when everyone else is holidaying.

18 August 2022

I have supper at Zara's house. She's made it feel like hers in the one month she's been there, which is a real talent. Some of the houses I see never achieve this, as they lack the personal. Zara has throws over sofas, artwork by friends on the wall and things from her mother's house, all brought together casually but with artistry. It's lived in and comfortable; in short, it's a home. Three of her new neighbours join us, a couple and a man, Percy, on his own; the latter being handsome, stubbled and dressed artistically in a smock and pale blue linen trousers. He's the director of a public gallery in south London. The retractable doors from her kitchen/living room are pulled back, creating a sense of flow between inside and out. We drink rosé and Zara laughs easily. Her children and the neighbours' kids alternate between the trampoline and the inflatable pool, and their dog, Enzo, splashes happily with them. It's a perfect summer evening and it warms my heart to see Zara in this new and happy environment.

As the night winds towards midnight, the couple leave and the children go to bed. Percy rolls a joint and the three of us sit in the garden and share it before Percy heads home. I stay behind and stack plates with Zara as she pours the remnants of the most recently opened rosé into our glasses.

'So . . .' she says, spooning the remains of the quinoa and prawn salad into Tupperware.

'I love what you've done with the house. You've made it feel like . . . you. Sorry, I must be a bit stoned; I haven't had weed for decades. Bravo.' I clink my glass against hers.

'Thanks,' she says, picking at a strawberry from a bowl as I finish loading the dishwasher. 'What did you think of Percy?'

'He seems great. Is there something going on between you two? Oh, I'm sorry, I should have buggered off earlier. I was getting the vibe he didn't want to leave. Forgive me, Zar.' I plonk myself at the kitchen table.

'Max, he's gay. It was a set-up for you. And I was getting that vibe too.'

'Seriously?'

'Yes, you doughnut.'

'I just thought he was metrosexual.'

'I think he liked you, Max.'

'Really?'

'Oh my goodness. No, I'm just saying it for fun. Yes, he liked you. And he's great. And interesting. I've asked him down to Devon for a weekend in September. Why don't you come along?'

'I'd like that. And what about you?'

'You know, I'm really enjoying being single, and being with the kids, and just – *being*, really.'

20 August 2022

The couple who are interested in NT's have asked for help; I've got them an appointment with the local 'starchitect', Christian. He lives in the area and specialises in the vernacular.

He has a self-effacing charm and is good-looking, with an easy demeanour. Oh, and he's a good architect too – perhaps I should have led with that. I walk him around before they arrive, and he immediately envisages an orangery off the kitchen that could create a symmetry with the drawing room and would benefit from the south-facing aspect. We both agree that the great thing about NT's house is that despite its size, it's liveable, and the main body of the house is contained; the sprawling wing could be closed off when not in use. Critically, it's not listed, so there's scope for lots of architectural adventure.

I leave Christian to chat with the couple and take a back seat. In an act of providence, I've got another viewing here, and I'm rather hoping they'll overlap, as I'd like to encourage a sense of urgency and competition.

The viewings do indeed overlap, and the second one seems encouraging too. They're a gay couple, perfectly dressed, attractive, mid-thirties, I estimate. One is in private equity and I decide the other one is in the arts. They're having a baby. I give them a tour and then leave them to wander around with their well-cut jeans, Tod's loafers and good-natured dispositions. What a charmed life they must have. I remind myself that of course one doesn't know what goes on inside these lives – but from the outside, it doesn't look bad.

22 August 2022

I have a call from both respective buying agents. As I'd hoped, the crossover of viewings has made them both declare their interest. I dare to hope.

John checks in to say the yacht he's on keeps missing Flavia's; they're literally ships in the night.

23 August 2022

Andrew messages. He's got a possible work conference at the end of next month in Athens; if it happens, how about I meet him there? Dates and times are, as yet, unconfirmed. I write back that I'd love to in theory, although, frustratingly, it will be peak work time then, whereas now we're in full lull.

With so little going on, I can avoid office admin no longer and determine to get to grips with HMRC's latest rules regarding KYC (Know Your Client) and AML (Anti-Money Laundering). I am officially our compliance officer, as everyone else has refused.

I agree with these tighter regulations, but I wish they could be handled by the lawyers. For years, huge amounts of money have filtered into London via super-prime property. Before these due-diligence checks, certain undesirables could come and spend vast sums on a townhouse in Mayfair or a country estate in Surrey. There was the Kazakh who bought Prince Andrew's former home Sunninghill Park at millions over the asking price; suddenly, he looked respectable. Not so much now, as the government has caught on and the source of funds has become a big thing. Rightly so.

I settle down to tediously plough through each sale, checking we've got certified passports, title documentation, utility bills and proof of funds, and that we've run buyers and sellers through our dedicated compliance firm.

I have several bugbears about the super-wealthy who buy in London and what the government allows. I don't approve of non-doms, and don't see why people should benefit from living in the UK and paying far less tax than those born in the country. I don't believe in the trickle-down effect argument. It's absurd that teachers, doctors, nurses and the rest are paying income tax whereas the uber-wealthy can keep their money in offshore accounts and only pay tax on the money they bring into the UK. It doesn't work morally, full-stop-the-end, as my film director friend John would say. London should believe in itself as more than an efficient tax regime for the mega-wealthy not born in Britain; we have culture, education, integration and parks, and the very civility of the city makes it hugely desirable. Despite Brexit, London is still a very international capital. If the uber-wealthy want those benefits, by all means let them enjoy them, but let them pay the same tax as the rest of us.

There are several non-doms I know who have left London and are coming close to their seven years abroad, so can now come back and reassert their non-dom status. The current law allows them do so. Why do we let this happen? One such 'entrepreneur' called me up and asked what bargains could be found in London. He proudly told me that he only buys 'distressed' sales.

'Why, particularly?' I asked.

'Because they're good value.' He responds as if I'm a four-year-old who needs educating.

'No, I understand that part. But what happens if they're just good value, but not the right property for you?'

'Oh, they are. You've seen my place in London. It's amazing.' I had, and I didn't think it was amazing; it had a busy road running right beside it with a constant throng of traffic. It felt like a pollution zone to me, but he liked it because he remembered the cut-down price he'd paid for it.

'Well, it's great that you can find the perfect thing at great value. I congratulate you.'

'I want you to look out for me. To find me a real bargain. And if you find it, I will pay you a finder's fee. But I'll keep looking myself, so you'll be incentivised to work doubly hard.'

That's not how it works, I want to scream. He's not my sort of buyer.

'Michelle' – his wife – 'always says we should look for a home whereas I always tell her, we're not looking for a home, we're looking for an *asset*.'

I know now that he is definitely not the client for me, and politely say I'll keep my eyes peeled, knowing I'll do no such thing. When I put down the phone, I think of the Oscar Wilde quote: 'A man who knows the price of everything and the value of nothing.' Didn't Oscar get that just right?

26 August 2022

I've got my first viewing at the Regent's Park house. It's required four calls to Billionaire, who has dismissed the potential buyers as 'losers', 'cheap', 'idiots' and more suited to round-the-corner Camden. They hadn't done anything wrong other than changing the time of their viewing once, as they decided to spend an extra couple of days in the South of France. This incensed Billionaire. I'm not quite sure why, as it's just the sort of thing he'd do, but I get the feeling that he's bored so is spoiling for a fight. I also hear from his cleaning lady, Svetlana, that he's not speaking to Florentina or either of his sons, and none of them are visiting him over the summer on his yacht. That's bound to put him in a bad mood.

I've begged him to relent and eventually he does, as he almost always does. We have to go through this cat-and-mouse game each time, and I wonder if he thinks I actually like it. The couple are young, moneyed, dressed in Versace (which I take as a good sign, given the style of the house) and have a driver waiting outside. They're Eastern European, but I can't quite work out exactly where they're from. It's hard to read the viewing, as they don't give much away, but they do ask the right questions. I know and trust the buying agent they're working with, and he tells me they're *bona fide*. I have a call within two minutes of their departure.

'Why do you let time-wasters into my house?'

'I don't think they are,' I plead. 'I actually think they really liked it.' I'm not sure they did but need to bluff; it's clear that

Svetlana had been instructed to call him and give a report as soon as they left.

'I don't think I want to sell. This is too much trouble. Screw them.'

I'm not sure how it's been any trouble for him or what they've done to incite such rage in Billionaire, but I can already see this is going to be the start of a long journey. We succeeded in finding a buyer quickly for Fortescue, as Natasha had hoped. I am likewise desperate to find one for Billionaire.

27 August 2022

I'm walking through Kensington Square, eating a *pain au chocolat* as I go (so much for my health kick), with an Americano in my other hand, ripping off chunks and dunking it into the coffee. I'm rather hungover from the night before, Billionaire having driven me to drink. I didn't have supper, just several glasses of wine. I turn a corner and literally bump into Slick, spilling coffee on myself but not him.

'Sorry, sorry,' I say reflexively.

'Max, what *are* you doing?' He looks at me with thinly veiled bemusement.

It's pretty apparent what I'm doing, though I'm embarrassed to be caught face-stuffing.

'How come you're in London?' I riposte.

He smiles with satisfaction, as if I've asked just the right question.

'I'm just here for twenty-four hours. I've left Therese and the family in Porto Ercole.'

'Oh,' is all I can say.

'We've just exchanged on Vera's flat. And we got such a record-breaking price, I wanted to be here for it, in case there were any hiccups.'

'I see.'

'Well, get yourself cleaned up, old boy.' He breezes past me. And then adds, 'Should I send your congratulations to Vera?'

'Yes, please do,' I say, through gritted teeth.

The gate to the square is open, and I go and sit on a bench. This should have been my sale. I found her the flat, she's my friend . . . OK, tense change – she *was* my friend. I shove the rest of the *pain au chocolat* into my mouth and look at my coffee-stained shirt and trousers. I want to scream out loud. I want to hit something.

Vera got divorced from her husband seven years ago. She's American, attractive, polished in an understated way, slender, food aware and well read. I liked her. A friend in common introduced us in the aftermath of her divorce and we clicked. It felt like she wanted a new life and a new friendship circle, and she went about looking for it proactively, in that more direct way Americans have compared to Brits. I don't know if it was, again, a peculiarly American trait or something more defined by her own character, but she had a laser focus in finding a new partner to share her life with. And I admired that. There was no pausing and smelling the roses for her; she was back on the proverbial horse, and her two teenage sons supported her. I think they'd seen their father be a low-level bully who'd undermined her. Vera played the numbers game, employing a high-end matchmaker promising the world (throwing money at the problem), joined several internet sites and downloaded all the apps. After two weeks of being on the apps, she found them depressing (they can be) and got her PA to filter through the profiles, swiping right where she thought there was a possibility and only reporting if there was a match. It meant that Vera was presented at the end of each week with a shortlist of all who had expressed interest in her and fell within the realms of suitability. I mean, genius.

I did find the notion of having a PA when you don't have a job mystifying at first. But then I witnessed the lives many of my clients lead. The more extravagant the lifestyle, the more it necessitates assistance: organising the caterers, arranging the holiday villas, dealing with the Netjet account, managing diaries, booking private tutors, maintaining multiple properties, chartering yachts – not to mention sorting out all the club memberships, drinks parties, birthday parties, yoga gurus, massage therapists and beauty regimes, from Botox to chiropodists. Then there's all the staff, and temporary staff when the main staff are on holiday. It's a lot. Believe me, I have heard many tales of woe from those living this lifestyle, usually while being informed how lucky I am to own just one property, a two-bedroom flat. 'How I dream of having such an uncomplicated life,' one client said to me.

Vera is from wealth, wealth that comes with a sense of entitlement and a notion of what her boyfriend's 'level' should be. We're all products of our environment, and hers is one that is driven by status and money. She's in that paradigm – but, let's face it, it's not a terrible one to be trapped in if you're born attractive, wealthy and bright. I'd noticed, too, that she could be ruthless about dropping people, though I never imagined I'd fall into that category.

We'd holidayed together in her family's Caribbean house. It had been one of my first glimpses into another world – one that floated above airport queues and other irritants. She'd first invited me when I'd faced a difficult moment in my life, and I'd been grateful. It was my first time on a private jet. We drove in convoy to Farnborough Airport and within five minutes were ushered on to the plane. I tried to pretend that this was all utterly normal to me, though I was given a gentle prod by the stewardess when I put myself in the seat belonging to Estelle (Vera's mother, a formidable matriarch). We landed in seven swift hours, with an official coming on board, allowing the warmth of the Caribbean air to waft on to the jet as she stamped the relevant documents. We'd come from a bleak November in London. Estelle's PA handled passports and admin, a porter handled luggage; we only had to concern ourselves with walking out of the plane and into a cavalcade of waiting cars. This was a different way to travel.

Estelle's Caribbean house was elevated above sea level with sweeping views. In the distance, specks of landmass peppered the twinkling water. The house was Balinese in style, with a series of open villas that flowed in and out with one side open. The living area was centred around a black-tiled infinity pool in which I loved to swim. Our 'picnic' lunches involved two chefs and a housekeeper preparing a sumptuous feast of salads and fish dishes that were ice-boxed and transported to the 'hut' and then styled, prepared and served for us, as we wafted to tables set up on the beach after a swim in the sea. Through my work I have come across plenty of very wealthy people, but there is an art to living well. And I don't mean 'well' as in well-being or as in living a good, honourable and decent life, both of which are more important. What I mean is using your money well. First off, the happiest super-rich people I know are the ones who give the most away, as they've worked out the ephemeral nature of our time on earth. The second most important thing to think about is how you divest your wealth amongst yourself, family and friends – some do it with style and others don't. Some share their wealth graciously and others don't. Some enjoy it, enjoy spending it and relish the pleasure it can bring to themselves and others. And the really wise ones manage, somehow, difficult as it is, to teach their children the value of money and how fortunate they are, and what joy there is to be had in giving.

My hostess hadn't managed that particular trick but she knew how to spend her money well in order to make her life comfortable and chic, and she took her family and friends along with her.

One memorable early evening, I was doing my laps in the pool, admiring the view across the sea, when a couple of guests arrived. I continued my set for another ten minutes and then decided it would be polite to get out and join the group, who were having drinks and sharing the same view across the water. I towelled myself down, somewhat self-consciously, in view of the cocktail drinkers and was grateful I'd been on a mini health regime. Kate had given me the best motivational line for staying in shape: 'Fat is very ageing.' If that wasn't a Hollywood pearl of wisdom, I'm not sure what is.

'Hello, hello,' I offered to the group as I pulled on a T-shirt and yanked my lucky chilli necklace from my back, straightening it over my chest.

'This is Fabrice,' Estelle offered. He was a model of Euro-chic: pastel linen shirt immaculately pressed with buttons undone, showing hints of a tanned torso; crisp, cream cotton shorts; and Persol sunglasses that had a 1950s retro style to them. Handsome and tall, with closely cropped dark hair, he exuded a sophistication and spoke perfect English with just a hint of a French accent. His friend, by contrast, whose name I didn't catch as the pool water had clogged my ears, looked as slobby as Fabrice was suave. He wore baggy cargo shorts that hung too low on his hips, revealing his underwear, a grey T-shirt that looked like it needed a wash, a baseball cap and oversized glasses. He had about ten days' worth of unkempt stubble on his face, and I could see the flanks of his flesh hanging out of his pants as he extended his arms and stretched. His skin was pasty compared to Fabrice's glistening tan.

Fabrice was offering a full-forced charm offensive, and it became clear he worked in the art world. Estelle was a major collector. They talked of dizzying prices, upcoming talents, which dealers they admired – not for their eye but for their ability to pick artists who were of the moment and whose prices would rocket to the stratosphere. It was more about art as an asset rather than art for art. As I sat there, I thought to myself, *Yes, this is normal for them, sitting in this island paradise, talking about selling artwork for $120 million, having flown in a private jet and living in this bubble detached from the rest of the world.* What must it feel like for this to be your reality? How glorious – and how alienating.

I remembered my manners and shifted on the sofa to sit opposite the slob in the baseball cap. He and I had not been participants in the art conversation, and I felt the need to make him feel at ease. The number of times I'd felt 'othered' in social situations makes me sensitive to people feeling out of place. Or so I told myself, in a rather self-congratulatory way, as I sidled over and said to the baseball cap, 'So, how long are you here for?'

'A few more days,' he muttered into his facial hair.

'We're so lucky,' I went on. 'This is my first time but it's a sort of surreal paradise, isn't it? I mean, particularly when you're staying with Estelle. This view.' I swept my hand theatrically, encompassing it all.

'Yeah, I guess.'

'Have you been before?'

'Yeah.'

'Lucky you. I hope I'll come again. Where are you based normally?' This was getting to be hard work.

'California.'

It's true that I was being conversationally banal, but I was getting slightly annoyed by his taciturn responses, given that I'd been gracious enough to try and engage him in chat.

'Whereabouts? I used to live in Los Angeles. I worked in *the industry*.' I sighed, reasoning he was some gaming millionaire, devoid of social skills.

He didn't respond, and I vaguely heard Fabrice talking about a project he was involved in, an ecological one. He seemed to be asking Estelle to invest.

'It's really my pal who's been leading this; he deserves the credit.' With this, Fabrice waved his arm in our direction to indicate the monosyllabic friend. 'He's passionate about the environment.'

'Umm-hmm,' said Estelle. 'How did you get here?'

'By plane,' he responded.

'Commercial or private?' There were no flies on my hostess.

'Private,' he said, but then suddenly became animated. His slouched back straightened as he talked about his passion for the environment and the real-life impact all of us could make; about the trees that he had planted to offset his carbon foot-print; about the alternative energy businesses he'd supported and invested in. He became someone else, an orator, and one I believed in. Even Estelle, a practised cynic, seemed convinced. And as his speech continued, he removed his glasses and fixed Estelle and then me with an earnest and intense gaze, with clear blue eyes of such familiarity that I realised who he was. Possibly the biggest movie star in the world – OK, maybe that's Tom Cruise, but this chap certainly is the star of his generation. The cargo shorts, the grubby oversized T-shirt, the beaten-up baseball cap, the excess flesh were all a disguise to avoid being recognised. I was watching this heartthrob and Oscar winner pitch the environment – and, according to him, the world's future – to my hostess. I couldn't bear to think about my gauche attempts to put him at his ease; I flushed scarlet at the memory of them as he was speaking. At the end of it, he gave me a firm handshake and said, 'Good to meet you, man,' with a twinkle in his eye.

What I remember vividly about those trips is sitting with Vera, glass of wine in hand, and chewing the fat of life. And feeling connected. Those memories now feel disposable – or, at least, as if they are disposable to Vera. That she could appoint Slick, knowing how he'd try to do me down, is very upsetting.

I get to the office, my shirt as stained as my friendship.

Dear Vera,

I bumped into Slick today, who told me of your sale. Congratulations: it's a great price, but then it's a great flat, so I'm not surprised. You know about the enmity between Slick and me – you've been good enough to listen to me as I've wittered on about it. I understand friendship and business cross lines, but I wish you had told me you were using someone else. You've hurt me as a friend and you've made me look lesser professionally, as people know we are close and I've helped you in the past, so you appointing Slick signals your lack of faith in me.

I am grateful for the times we've had together and the friendship you've offered me in the past, but I don't feel I would be doing that friendship justice if I didn't speak of my disappointment.

I will always wish you well,

Max

I'm aiming for a 'more in sorrow than in anger' tone.

Vera responds neutrally. She doesn't apologise, but she 'explains' that it had all been last minute: she'd bumped into Slick on the street, he said he had a buyer, she'd been flying away somewhere, our friendship was so important, blah, blah, we should have lunch when she returned.

I'm not sure what I was expecting. I remember Quentin telling me you have to think about what you want from a situation, and that clarifies how you get there. I suppose I wanted to vent my hurt.

Another Quentin thought is, 'You do you, and I'll do me.' I was doing 'me'.

30 August 2022

I am trying to cajole the two parties interested in NT's house into making an offer. They are both doing their 'due diligence':

working out the cost of the refurbishment, enquiring after the annual running expenses (two gardeners, a housekeeper, maintenance of leaking roofs, heating bills, etc.), deciding how they'd use the property and the three cottages it comes with, along with considering the potential for 'development'. I don't want them getting too bogged down with these figures and forecasts, though, as it might scare them off.

There is a real question of momentum when it comes to selling a property, and as an agent, you need to harness that and know when to push for an offer. The psychology of humans differs: some people react swiftly if they think they're going to lose something, while others resign themselves to it and therefore lose interest in a self-protective way. In general, if something rumbles along for too long, people can talk themselves out of their desire and realise they can live without it. I'm not sure now whether I'm talking about property or the early stages of a potential romance, though there's definitely a crossover.

SEPTEMBER

1 September 2022

We have another viewing at Billionaire's. It's through an agent
I don't know, so I'm somewhat suspicious – I know all the
serious players – but he's given me his buyer's credentials and
they're real. I've googled them, verified them and run them
past Billionaire, who has begrudgingly allowed the viewing
while letting us know how inconvenient it is, as his cleaner
is away. I bring Damien with me. We arrive the normal fifteen minutes early to draw curtains, turn on lights, throw
open the windows and generally imbue the place with life.
Another minion has been sent in Svetlana's place, no doubt
to keep tabs. She is pleasant but doesn't speak English, and
she flaps around us as we prepare the house. After we've done
the rounds, I sit in the window seat of the dining room, from
where I can see the front door. A collection of cars pulls up at
the appointed time: one, two, three, four, five, six, seven cars.
The doors open and people emerge. They can't be here for the
viewing, but why else would a cavalcade of cars be in Chester
Terrace, outside this specific house in practically the quietest
week of the property calendar?

I look to Damien.

'This isn't good, mate,' he states, obviously.

It's too late to hide. I step outside the front door and

Damien, who, at this point, I am very glad is with me, stands behind me, blocking entry into the property. I put my hand out in front of me with my palm facing straight ahead. 'No.' I try and identify the agent. 'I am sorry, but we can only have two people in the property; that's on the specific instructions of our client.'

The group look mystified, and there's a general chattering in Arabic. A man with an H for Hermès belt cinched too tightly around his overflowing waist steps forward. 'Hi, I'm Ravi. We all need to see the property. We're here for today only and need to buy something.'

I weigh this up. While I'm loath to lose a deal, I'm even more loath to suffer Billionaire's ire if I let some con artists in. The 'fake sheik' was active a few years ago. He appeared in a similar cavalcade of cars with a retinue of hangers-on (not entirely unusual for such clients). It's not abnormal to have people move around freely once inside properties, and one agent couldn't keep track of six people at once; while the fake sheik distracted the agent with questions, the other members of the party swiped all they could see. Jewellery, Rolex watches, drawers with cash in them: all gone. He was exposed after forty-eight hours but he'd had a good run, pulling the same trick in seven properties all worth over £20 million.

'I'm afraid it's a hard-and-fast rule,' I say. 'I'm very happy to show the principal and one other, and we can go in and out in convoy, but those are my client's instructions.'

'Why don't you call him?' Ravi suggests. 'We're on a tight schedule.'

'You may be, but I assure you, calling him won't make a difference. It's two in only or no viewing.'

We look at each other.

'Very well.' He turns to his group and speaks in Arabic, and then a lady who is almost fully covered steps forward.

'I'll stay outside,' Ravi volunteers. 'The Shaykhah and Khaled will go in.'

And so they do. Damien and I do the tour. They offer no words but follow us without deviation. It's a quick tour, and when we get out, all the cars are running. They speed away.

3 September 2022

I have finished all our compliance checks and each folder is up to date. I'm feeling a strange sense of satisfaction. I have a call from Ravi.

'They're interested,' he says.

'Great,' I respond, feeling a certain sense of surprise.

'What are you offering?'

'The asking price is eighteen million.'

'But what are you offering, fee-wise?'

I'm on a reduced fee as it's Billionaire, but I'm happy to split it. 'Zero point five per cent,' I tell him.

'That won't work.'

'What are you looking for? My client is practical and if you pay the asking price, I can certainly have a conversation.' This is true.

Ravi guffaws. 'You're not going to get the asking price. And we'd need to get £250,000.'

It's my turn to laugh. 'That's more than my fee,' I tell him.

'Have a word with your client,' he responds. 'We're cash and could move quickly.'

'I will speak to him, but as I said, it would have to be asking price.'

This is not a conversation I want to have with Billionaire.

5 September 2022

It's what the French call *la rentrée*, marking the end of summer and the return to work. I'm filled with this spirit and picture phones ringing, deals being made, action happening. It turns out to be a rather more muted affair. I'm the only one in the office, as Damien is in Ibiza with Florentina, Natasha is returning from Scotland today and John is weighing up various different transfer options: yachts, private jet, or a blissful extra week now the crowds are dissipating. It's tough facing these choices.

I brace myself, having avoided this call to date reasoning it's rude to disturb clients in August. I dial Billionaire's number.

'How are you? How was the summer?'

'Fine. All is well. What news on the house?'

'We had a very positive viewing, a Middle Eastern buyer.'

'Umm-hmm.'

'They are talking about an offer.'

'OK.'

'So, rather awkwardly – and you know this isn't the way I do business, but . . . they want a baksheesh.' I need to tackle this subject head-on.

'A what?' he says sharply. I look towards my colleagues' empty desks, as if the invisible spots they normally occupy will tell me how to explain this and, more critically, how to ask for an additional quarter of a million in commission fees.

'A backhander, a pay-off, an incentive fee, something for the middlemen. And there seem to be lots of them.' Best to get this out of the way.

'So give them one.' Billionaire is disarmingly logical at times. 'It's business.'

'The problem is, they want more than my entire fee.'

'What do you mean?'

'They want two hundred and fifty thousand.'

'It's simple. Tell them the price is eighteen and a half million, and then we all win.' Again, this seems indisputably sensical; the problem being that I've already told them it's £18,000,000, and they've already told me that's way too much. I tell Billionaire this, and he responds, 'Tell them you got it wrong.' Well, that's simple enough.

I remember my father recounting an experience he once had while working for a well-known art gallery in New York in the early 1970s. He was on the desk during lunch and a buyer came in. My father, the new kid in the gallery, launched into full charm mode, being the Brit abroad when it still carried some weight in the Big Apple. He was thrilled to sell a David Hockney drawing for $10,000. The purchaser informed him she was always offered a ten per cent discount, as she was a friend of the gallery owner. My dad willingly made the reduction, seeing the work of art had been purchased for $4,000. When the gallery owner returned from lunch, my father delightedly told him about his first sale, chest puffed, and added that he'd given the buyer her usual discount.

The owner said, 'Thomas' – our last name – 'you asshole! When someone comes in and says they're my friend, you put the price *up* twenty per cent and then you take off ten per cent. My friendship doesn't come for free.'

It was a valuable lesson to my dad. And I've learned that with various clients, Billionaire included, they won't ask whether the value is correct or not; whatever the asking price is, they'll simply want a significant discount on that figure. They have to feel they're getting a deal.

This has resulted in Billionaire buying a real turkey for one of his sons. The house is a monstrosity in St John's Wood whose 'key' feature is a swimming pool in the drawing room. Literally. It had been languishing on the market for three years, and Billionaire thought he'd got a bargain by getting thirty per cent off the listed price – a record discount for super-prime London, he told me. It was worth far less, and everyone in the business knew it. He didn't consult me, and I think, though he'll never admit it, that he knows he made a mistake. I'm pleased to say I've never allowed him to make a similar mistake and have tried to gently introduce the notion that the asking price has no correlation to the actual value. It's an approximation, and some agents and clients massively overvalue, where some are realistic. I'm there to tell the difference.

But now I'm armed with my response to Ravi's question of commission, I call him.

'Hi Ravi, I've spoken to my client. And yes, if you pay the asking price, he can offer you two hundred and fifty thousand.'

'Great,' says Ravi. 'I'll come back to you.'

'One more thing,' I offer quickly. 'Just to confirm, the asking price is eighteen and a half million.' I long just to put the phone down as soon as I say these words.

'You said eighteen million,' Ravi responds.

'I got that wrong, I'm afraid.' I deliver this in as breezy a tone as I can muster. I don't feel particularly bad about changing the goalposts, given the commission Ravi is asking for. He can earn it.

8 September 2022

Natasha and Lord Edward come in. I stand to greet them and give her a kiss on each cheek. She looks well. Her russet hair is thick and her skin glowing, as if she's just sprayed it with Evian mist. Her Celtic colouring is in bloom.

'How was Scotland?' I ask.

'It was glorious. Highland air.'

And then I notice that she's wearing an engagement ring.

She catches me clocking it. 'And yes, Piers and I are officially engaged. Keep the fourth of December free, we're going to have a winter wedding. I want my father to be there.'

There is so much information in this sentence.

'Firstly, huge congratulations. I'm thrilled for you. Secondly, how is your dad?'

'Thank you. And he's not great, but he's happy about me and Piers.'

I understand now, and I step in and give her a hug, holding on tightly. She stands rigid at first, and then puts her arms around me. I feel her head resting gently against my shoulder. She doesn't let go. When I finally release her, I pull back, place my hands squarely on her shoulders and say, 'It will be OK.' I don't know why I say it, but I will it to be so, and saying it out loud feels like I'm validating that in some way.

10 September 2022

Andrew calls now that his schedule is confirmed; he is definitely going to Athens. He proposes I meet him there and we then spend four days on Spetses, an island a couple of hours away by ferry. We've been communicating via email regularly, but speaking is different: more real, less abstract. I mumble something about the work diary and taking time off in September, and then wonder what I'm doing. What's holding me back? We agree that I'll let him know as soon as I've cleared the dates with my colleagues.

11 September 2022

I have a phone call from Damien.

'Mate, do you mind if I stay a couple of extra days in Ibiza? I'm doing some great networking with Florie's mates, there are at least two buyers here. The scene is wild.'

'Sure,' I say.

Nothing really happens until school resumes, and even then there's always a lag of a few days as people recover. There's the usual rush to Peter Jones to buy shoes and make sure the housekeepers have sewed in the nametags; then, once little Jemima and Jethro are back at their prep schools, the parents need a couple of days to breathe and recoup before they start focusing on new property. People have often mulled over their plans during the summer. All that sitting by pools or the sea, churning over what's important to them, might have them thinking of a move to the country, a bigger house in a less expensive area, or a shift of focus to their second home, as the children are going to boarding school earlier than planned. Spending a summer with their offspring often pushes forward boarding school age from thirteen to eleven – or even eight, in some cases.

12 September 2022

John is back. He comes in looking tanned and healthy, but beneath his smile I sense a sadness.

I stand to hug him. I'm not sure if this is a new thing or if we've always done it.

'*C'est fini*,' he whispers in my ear. 'But we talk later, when we're *solo*.'

Natasha is watching us. After he's done with me, he turns to her and radiates an Oscar-winning smile. 'Darling girl, I am delighted for you. Your happiness is our happiness.' He's going rather regal, but the rest of his speech is interrupted as Ravi calls.

'Maximillian Thomas, I'm going to be your new best friend,' he says. 'I have an offer, it's cash, we can move with laser-like speed. I can give you all Shaykhah's details: lawyers, bank drafts, the lot.'

'Great,' I say, looking around the room and indicating to John and Natasha that an offer has come through.

'You know we've looked at the house in Cornwall Terrace, the penthouse in Cambridge Gate, we've done our research.'

'I didn't, but that's great.' I have a slight sinking feeling – why isn't the number immediately forthcoming?

'We have, and eighteen-point-five million just doesn't make sense.'

John and Natasha are silent, standing beside my desk.

'Let's not argue about comps, which I'm happy to do at a later date. Just tell me what *is* making sense to you and your client?'

'Fourteen point five.'

'Sorry?' I hear the 'point five' but the early teen figure can't be right.

'Fourteen point five. Cash. An A-one buyer.'

John looks concerned, Natasha shrugs. She's the only one of us not intimidated by Billionaire.

'Ravi, I'm going to stop the conversation right now. If that's the figure you're at, it's simply never going to work. I would be sacked if I put that offer up to Billionaire. We can just leave it . . . or, if this is part of a negotiation, it's a strategy that's not going to work.'

John gives me a thumbs-up.

'Are you hard-balling, Maximillian?'

Natasha gives me a significant nod.

'I'm saying if your client is serious about purchasing this property, then put in your full and final offer. If I relay what you've just told me verbally, my instructions will be to never speak to you or your client again. My client does not play around.'

'I'll see what I can do,' says Ravi. 'You're not playing with me, are you?'

'I don't do that,' I say, and take a breath. Natasha looks at me, knowing my instinct will be to ramble on. She indicates for me to end the conversation by slicing her hand across her neck in a swift movement. A bit dramatic, I think.

'Bye, Ravi,' I say.

John gives a little a clap.

'That told him.'

I'm not sure it did.

14 September 2022

I have supper with Kate. She's done what I call 'a John' over the summer and hopped from Tuscany to Cap Ferret to Comporta, visiting various friends.

'Silly of you not to have been anywhere, Max. Isn't it dead in August?'

'Well, I had NT's and Billionaire's, and I felt it was best if I was present, as everyone else was away. And I may be going away later this month.'

'What? Where?'

'Greece.'

'Greece is heaven in September,' she declares. 'The crowds have gone, the sea is warm, and you have the place to yourself.' She looks at me. 'Hold on. Who are you going with?'

'We're not going to make a big thing of this, but it's Andrew.'

'Are you serious? Max, this *is* a big thing.'

'Don't get ahead of yourself. I haven't confirmed yet, just because of work timings, but I'm tempted. But Kate, can we not talk about it? I just need to sit with it for a while longer.'

'OK then. Subject change. How's the delicious Australian?'

'If you mean Damien, he's well. Back tomorrow, after an extended holiday with Billionaire's daughter.'

'Is that going to spell trouble?'

'Probably.'

'Well, send him my way when that's all over.'

'Kate . . .' I intone. 'I thought you were seeing someone?'

'I am, but I told you, it's casual. I may be living in London now but I still have an American attitude to dating. And, look, on a serious note, I've been speaking with the investors and they want us to go out to LA next month. It's a great time to be in SoCal. It's on their dime. What do you think? You know who lives in LA.'

'I think I don't have to think. I'm in.'

15 September 2022

Damien is back, looking golden and somewhat exhausted.

'It looks like you need a holiday after your holiday,' I say, after greeting him.

'I've got stamina, and we Aussies know how to drink, but they don't let up. And they don't eat. And I don't do coke. But I've got a new client. Friend of Florie's.'

'And how are things with Florie?' I ask.

'She wants me to meet her dad.'

'Well, that's big.'

'I mean, I have met him that once, but not as a boyfriend.'

'Damien, there's something I should let you know. There's no easy way to say this, but Natasha's engaged.'

'I know, mate, she told me.'

'Oh,' I say. 'Well, that's good.'

'It's not good. He's a jerk. I can't tell her, but you could.' He looks at me.

'I can't, Damien. Just like I can't warn you off Florentina.'

He did walk into that one.

16 September 2022

There's been a lot of wrangling back and forth with Ravi, and finally he's put forward an offer in writing for Chester Terrace: £16,500,000. I know Billionaire won't like it, but I am now legally obliged to put it forward. I send him a message and ask him to call me. Truth: it's not a bad offer.

19 September 2022

I spend wholesome weekend in Dorset with Zara, her children and Percy. She's bought an old fisherman's cottage on the Jurassic Coast with part of her divorce money, happily giving up the house and indoor pool they used to rent near Soho Farmhouse. The cottage is simple, rustic and charming. It has flagstone floors, painted window frames, low ceilings, a fireplace in the sitting room, and an extension with a big kitchen, armchairs and an incredible view down to the sea. There's no Wi-Fi and no TV, just an old CD player with a collection of albums. Zara plays her parents' favourites, taking us back to the seventies with Bowie, Fleetwood Mac, Renaissance's 'Northern Lights', which seems to be on repeat, and Elton of the 'Goodbye Yellow Brick Road' era.

It's one of those lovely last-throes-of-summer weekends when there's still a warmth in the air. We have gorgeous coastal walks, with the clear sea looking more Amalfi than British coast. We brave the turquoise water and swim. Percy is an incredible cook; he collects seaweed and then prepares it for us, tempura-style; he's down by the shore at 6am to chat with the fishermen and surprises us with crab linguine. He's refreshingly open and without any artifice, as if he's never built up those layers so many people have, portraying who they think they should be. Percy is, it seems, entirely himself. And that's a thoroughly interesting and interested man. We talk about the books that have meant something to us, about Marilynne Robinson and the *Gilead* trilogy, Colm Tóibín and his brilliance at capturing those repressed human emotions so vividly, and about how the repression doesn't mean there are no emotions. It's a happy time.

It occurs to me how different friends offer entries into differing worlds. I have friends with whom I talk about work (usually theirs, as I don't tend to talk about mine), others with whom I talk about family and psycho-dynamics. Some talk almost exclusively about their children or ageing parents; there are others with whom one just laughs or drinks. And then there are those with whom one finds a more existential connection. I sense with Percy that he and I could connect on a deep level. I feel a communality there: shared influences and understandings.

On the Saturday night, after the children have gone to bed, Zara tells us that Spencer has talked of reconciliation. Percy has never met Spencer, and receives the news without prejudice, pointing out the benefits: the fact that there are still remnants of love, a shared history and how it could benefit the family. I cannot be so forgiving, knowing what he's put Zara through, and knowing the inner resolve that it's taken to pick herself up and move forward, creating this new life. A life I believe will be a happier one. She has done it quickly and bravely, but I know it's cost her, and that if that level of hurt is caused again she won't have the same resilience. Besides, once trust is gone, it's very hard to come back from.

'It seems they're all realising the error of their ways,' I comment rather feebly, knowing I need to say something. On further questioning of my cryptic comment, I tell them about Andrew and that he's asked me to join him in Greece. I can see they're both taken aback. Percy says, 'And I was going to ask you to join me in bed tonight, but I can see that won't happen now.'

'Why not?' says Zara. '*Carpe diem*. And maybe Max and I should be forgetting our respective exes.'

'This is awkward,' I say. 'Jokes aside: I've loved today, but my life is a bit complicated at the moment.'

The magic of the Saturday is not repeated the following day, though it's a perfectly happy one. I message Andrew on the train home and say I'd love to meet him in Greece.

20 September 2022

I finally have a moment alone with John. He's done his best *bella figura* and kept a smile on his face while following up the new leads he's found over the summer. I remember the

keys to Flavia's flat are in the safe. I unlock them and pass
them over.

'Here they are. I sent Tina all the meter readings and utili-
ties, as I think she's doing the handover for Flavia.'

'Ah, yes, Tina. What would we do without her?'

'So, are you going to tell me what's happened? Isn't Flavia
due here any moment?'

'I suppose it was the inevitable. And she's quite right.' His
voice is mournful.

'She's sticking with the husband?'

'It's not really about him.' John looks forlorn. 'Well, it
is about him' – and now he's giving me one of his middle-
distance looks – 'and the money.'

'What do you mean?'

'I don't have a bean. Oh, that rhymes.' He gives a half-
hearted chuckle.

'But I thought *she* did. Not that that's why you're with her,'
I add quickly.

'No, she's as hopeless as me; she's spent all her own money
and that Greek so-and-so bandaged her up in a prenup like a
mummy. She won't get a drachma if she leaves him. She's such
a romantic, she says she doesn't care; she says we could live
in a Parisian garret. She even said she'd get a job! But I know
her – and I know people.'

'And?'

'And it's all very well being young and poor and in love. You
don't care about anything then, and why should you? But when
you've been used to a certain life, a certain way of living, and

you're a certain age, it's unwise to think you can live on love alone, as if it's oxygen. It's not that easy. And I can't bear to put Flavia through that. It was me that called it off, for her sake.'

'John, I think I understand what you're saying.'

'Of course you do. You know how our clients live and what they expect. Flavia may find a Ryanair flight charming once – getting up at four in the morning, taking a bus to Stansted, queueing, fighting over what classifies as hand luggage, the noise, the aesthetics of the whole experience – but when it comes to her third or fourth journey, she'd resent her choice. And eventually, she'd resent me.'

'You don't know that.' This is the woman, after all, who was a *gaucha* in Uruguay; she has a spirit that means she can roll up her sleeves and work.

'I fear that I do know. It's better, Max, truly . . . we've had a wonderful, glorious affair, and it's better it ends when it's shining as brightly as it ever can.'

'What are we going to do, John?'

'You're going to go to Greece and have a fabulous time. And *I* shall be just fine.'

In that moment, I want to say, 'I adore you, John,' but I refrain. It would probably be just a bit too much. Instead, I say, 'How I admire you,' which is also true.

22 September 2022

Billionaire and I have been playing phone-tag but finally speak. It's no bad thing, as Ravi has been calling me hourly, sweating for an answer. It makes our position stronger. What's rather more delicate is that Damien has told me that Florie has asked him to move in with her. So far, Billionaire has said nothing to me about their relationship, and I'm not sure whether he's registered that the online photo of the 'hunk in trunks' is actually Damien. He has his PA show him all press about himself and his children.

'We speak at last,' I say, as I see his name on my phone.

'Yes, I've been busy.'

'I'm sure,' I start, but he cuts me off.

'So tell me.' His economy of words is always endearing.

'OK, I'm only telling you this as they've put it in writing, so I am legally obliged to put it forward. The offer is too low, and I know the answer, but I just need to note for our records that I've heard it from you.' I'm babbling, but he makes me do this.

'Go.' He yawns.

'Sixteen and a half million.'

There is not even a beat. 'Tell them to fuck themselves and not to waste my time.'

'Absolutely, I shall. Thank you.'

'One more thing,' he says. I'm almost home free. 'Who is Damien?'

'I think you've probably met him with me. He works with me and . . .'

'He's an estate agent?'

'Yes. He's Australian. He's a good guy. He's not got money, of course, but he's decent and he will treat Florentina well.' I don't even know why I mentioned money.

'And will he treat *me* well? Flying on my plane, being paid for at hotels. Living off me. And Svetlana says he's moving in with her. So he'll be living in my house. What sort of man does that?'

I'm tempted to say 'lots', but I don't. Instead, I just repeat what I said before.

'And you introduced them?' he goes on. Suddenly he's a Chatty Cathy.

'I wouldn't say that,' I say gingerly.

'How did they meet?'

'I was at the house with Damien, and Florentina happened to be there. I didn't know she would be there.'

'So you introduced them?'

'I suppose, in a way.'

'I hold you responsible,' he says. 'Goodbye.' And he hangs up.

I have a headache and go home early to pack.

23 September 2022

I refuse Ravi's offer, and he tells me I'll regret it. I'm still cajoling both of the parties interested in NT's house to step forward. Neither wants to jump first, though I know both want it. I come closer than I've ever done to blurring ethics (in terms of making up an offer) by playing with language. I could honestly say, 'We're expecting an offer,' and leave them open to interpret that as they will.

I don't.

25 September 2022

Shit. I'm waiting for a car to take me to Heathrow when I get a call from the buying agent representing the possible buyers for the Chisholms' house.

'Don't be cross, Max. I'm cross enough for us both. My clients have just called. They're in London and can see the house in an hour. Please tell me you can make it happen.'

'I can't,' I say, looking at the time, knowing the car is five minutes away.

'Impossible?' he pleads.

I take a moment. This is the Chisholms. They've had the worst luck of anyone I've ever known in all my years in property. And these buyers are the ones I made the video for, the ones we've been pinning all our hopes on. I could send Natasha or Damien. No, I can't. I need to be here for this.

'Nothing is impossible. I will see you there in an hour.'

'You're a legend,' he says.

'And you, my friend, are making sure your clients buy this house.'

I call the Chisholms and apologise for the short notice; they are as accommodating as ever.

Now, the difficult call. Andrew is already in Greece. I dial his number.

'I can't wait to see you tonight and ravage you,' he says as he picks up.

'Andrew, I am really sorry, truly. I've had a work emergency.

I will be on the first flight tomorrow; we'll still make the after-noon ferry.'

'Are you serious?'

'I'm so sorry, I am.'

'I've booked this amazing restaurant by the Acropolis. This isn't a funny joke.'

'It's not a joke, sadly.'

'What is it that's so important?'

'It's the Chisholms – you remember them, they're my dad's best friends. I need to be there for this viewing, we've been waiting for it for six months.'

'It's a *viewing*. Are you kidding me? Get someone else to do it.'

'Andrew, I can't.'

'You're not being real.'

'I am so sorry about today. I'll be there tomorrow.'

This is becoming a circular conversation. I've discussed them with Quentin. The only way to stop is to stop, so I stay on the line.

Eventually, Andrew speaks. 'I'm so mad now, I'm going to hang up.'

'Goodbye then, I'll see you tomorrow,' I say. I add, 'I'm sorry,' as the phone clicks out.

I race to the Chisholms' house, opening shutters and blinds and making sure the lights are on. The buyers arrive on time and it all seems to go well. I think of John and *bella figura* but am seriously tempted to say, 'You may have cost me a relationship.'

I send a conciliatory WhatsApp to Andrew, saying I wish that I was with him and imploring him to make it a happy time together. The ticks go blue immediately; he's read it. He doesn't respond until the following morning, when he simply sends me a thumbs-up emoji. His brevity resembles Billionaire's.

OCTOBER

1 October 2022

Having successfully killed him with kindness, a smile soon returns to Andrew's face on my arrival.

Spetses is a sort of dream. There are no private cars and there's one town on the island, centred around the harbour. We're staying in a charmingly rustic house ten minutes' walk up the hill, which we wobble up to through cobbled streets on our Vespa. I like feeling Andrew's arms around my waist and his body leaning in against mine.

Every morning, we wake and bicycle round the island, up and down the twenty-four kilometre road. We stop, strip off and swim in coves, and feel like we've earned our breakfast of Greek yoghurt and honey on returning to the old town. We then take the Vespa out to one of the many bays dotted around the island and spend the day reading, swimming, talking, lunching at a waterfront taverna, then swimming again, returning to the house in the late afternoon, with the salt water on our skin, to shower before we walk into town for supper. And repeat.

The days follow a rhythm that is so relaxing and detached from my normal world, and I come to the obvious realisation that life continues to move forward with or without me checking my phone for the latest message. If I respond six hours later, after I'm back from the beach, it's fine – nothing implodes. I take it as a good-luck omen. When an acceptable offer on the Chisholms' is called in, I am ecstatic with the news. The delay in London paid off, I tell Andrew, and I explain the history of the bad luck the Chisholms have had and how important the deal is to me. Andrew brings me down to earth, pointing out to me, 'You're just selling expensive property, Max. This isn't cracking the vaccine code. Someone else could have shown the house.' We still celebrate, and I toast the god of property on the Greek island, asking him to make this sale plain sailing.

We talk and talk, filling in the gaps of our absence. I don't dare discuss a future, as I am loving the present, and the unreal feel of it makes it easier. On our last night, I mention Kate's investors and the prospect of building a property portfolio for them. I tell him I'll be in LA next month.

'That's it,' he says.

'What's it?' The water is lapping just feet away from us. We're in our favoured restaurant.

'How we make this work.'

A trio of singers appear at our table. Thankfully they don't offer us a rose, but they do sing a song. I thank them and give them twenty euros to send them on their way, but they take this as a sign of affirmation and give us another song.

'Don't give them any more money,' laughs Andrew, as he plays footsie with me quite obviously, moving his foot towards my groin. 'Look, come and meet these investors in LA and start doing business with them, and then set up some agency affiliations. You've got a good team in London, you could build relationships with US brokerages and be the London man in LA.'

'I'm not sure how that would work.'

'Remember your office mantra: focus on the ups. It would work. Sure, there would be logistics involved, and you'd have to get over your fear of flying. You could be part-time there and part-time here. I mean in London.'

'Andrew, what are you saying?' This doesn't seem to be the moment to stuff more pitta bread into my face.

'What do you think I'm saying? I want to give us another go. We could make this work. We really could.'

'Andrew, I just don't see how. I live in London and you live in LA. That's a big commute.'

'Max, you're the greatest love of my life. You're it. I know it. And if we feel like this still, we'll find a way to make it work.'

They were hard words to argue with.

3 October 2022

I'm not singing 'Finally' as I walk into the office this time; the offer is too low to be celebrated, but still: I have one for NT's house. It's good timing for the Monday meeting, and it's more or less the first time we've all been assembled together since summer. I report that the Chisholms' house is agreed and with lawyers. Two possible deals, two significant eight-figure offers. Things are looking good.

I then announce the work trip to LA, discussing the investors looking to build a super-prime London portfolio. I add the possibility of setting up some affiliations with US brokers. I tell them that I'll need a wing-person to work with me on presentations. Both John and Damien jump at it; my instinct tells me that Dame is more in tune with the LA way, but John – well, he has a certain magic that's unquantifiable.

'Would you like to throw your hat into the ring, Natasha?' I ask, as she's been mute through our discussion.

'Thank you, Max, but I don't think that would be fair. I suppose now is as good a time as any to tell you that I won't be here after December. Piers wants us to be based in the country. He can work remotely, I can't. But I'll be close to my father.'

No one speaks. Damien is looking straight at Natasha; John has a tear in his eye.

I begin slowly, choosing my words carefully. 'That's very sad news for us, Natasha, but if that's what makes sense for you . . . You will be deeply missed.'

There's a silence that hangs in the room for what feels like a good few minutes but must have amounted to only seconds.

John finally breaks it. 'I'm sorry. I have to say it, I do. And you know this comes from a place of love, darling girl. And you know I see you all' – he looks at all three of us significantly – 'as family. Are you making the right decision, dearest Natasha? I hate to ask, but I have to.'

I look at the floor; I can't look anywhere else.

Natasha picks up Lord Edward and leaves the office. None of us speak and then, wordless, Damien stands. He walks to the door, opens it and runs down the cobbled mews.

Go get the girl, I think – and hope.

6 October 2022

Billionaire calls.

'So, what news?'

It transpires that he's had a call from a friend who sold a place in One Hyde Park and has advised him that the market is booming (it's not) and that there should be competitive bids on Chester Terrace. I tell him that I hate to contradict his friend but we are facing challenging times. I remain cautiously optimistic that for such a unique house (it's not) we will be successful. He goes on to inform me that his friend has a terrific agent who did an amazing job for him, and I see where this conversation is going.

I get off my bicycle, realising that focus is needed, and move into a side street to avoid the noise of the road. 'May I ask who the agent is?'

'Slick, he's called Slick.'

I knew it.

'He does know about the house and is welcome to bring any of his people in. I've offered to give him a fee.' I stay calm. If it were anyone else, I'd suggest a co-brokering the deal, but I couldn't work with Slick.

There are three different ways of agency selling: a sole agency, when you are the only agent; a joint agency, when you work in collaboration with another agent and share the fee; and a multiple agency, when many agents are instructed and the successful agent takes the full fee. We usually operate on a sole-agency basis so we can be in control of the listing, manage everything and have a clear strategy that ensures the best price. I always think that listing with several agents reeks of desperation and gives the wrong signal to the market. I'm usually happy with a joint agency; it takes the pressure off a little, as you don't have the full weight of expectation on you.

But here is Slick, rearing his head again. I'd heard on the rumour mill that he's furious that we agreed the Chisholms' house, as he was hoping those buyers would purchase a listing of his. I suspect this is direct retaliation.

8 October 2022

I call both sets of lawyers regarding the Chisholm sale, just to check everything is on track. I don't want Slick to have any chance of needling his way in there. I need to cradle this deal every step of the way to exchange. I call their agent.

'Relax, Max,' he says. 'They're good buyers.'

'But,' I stumble, 'my clients have been let down several times before. We need to keep the timescale on track.'

'We will.'

I know I'm panicking, which is unlike me, but I want this done before I head Stateside.

And, on the subject of deals I'd like to get wrapped up and keep Slick away from, I call Ravi and see if his buyers are going to do anything to up their offer on Billionaire's house.

'Any news your end?' I ask, trying to keep the hint of hope/ desperation out of my voice.

'We're not budging, Max.'

'I understand. It's not a bad offer, but my client has had Slick in his ear telling him he could and should easily be achieving eighteen point five.'

'Well, why not twenty million or twenty-five, if we're just picking out arbitrary numbers? If there was a better buyer out there, you'd have sold to them by now. The market isn't looking great. You do know we're heading into a serious recession and inflation is going berserk.'

'And that's a good reason for buyers to put their money into super-prime property. It's a good hedge.' I read that in a report and have decided to back this narrative.

'If you say so. But I don't see anyone doing that. We've lost the Russians, the Chinese aren't active; you're relying on a market coming in from Hong Kong and a domestic one.'

It appears Ravi is a little more well-researched than I'd imagined.

10 October 2022

Tina and I take Fortescue to the luxury flat development for over 65s, where he's reserved an apartment.

Tina has built up a real relationship with Fortescue. They're not quite the odd couple but there's something wonderful in the way Tina is able to see the best in people and therefore bring it out. She ignores Fortescue's snapping and excuses it with the fact he's in almost constant pain; she also points out how brave he is to be leaving his home of sixty years when he himself is in his eighties. And Fortescue shows Tina an altogether different side of himself; he picks out books that he thinks she may enjoy – a collection of Katherine Mansfield short stories, the *Cazalet Chronicles* by Elizabeth Jane Howard – and is solicitous and chivalrous with her. Every time she walks into a room, he struggles painfully to his feet, despite her protestations. She brings out his old-world courtliness. The one bugbear Tina has with Fortescue is that he's cheap . . . inherently so. I'm not sure if it's living through the war or if it's just his nature.

'It's not about how much money you have, it's about your attitude towards it,' she tells me.

'Perhaps it's his age. You know how some old people are terrified of running out of money, however well off they are,' I suggest in his defence.

'No,' she says adamantly. 'He's got plenty of it, he knows it and I've told him. He's a wonderful old boy and I'd do anything for him, but you know I don't like cheap.'

As it happens, I don't either. It's like the buyers who are obsessed with spreadsheets and pound-per-square-footage analytics; they're so immersed in getting value that they're missing the bigger picture. But it's a mindset. I always feel that if someone is slow to pick up a bill or put their hand in their pocket, it's symptomatic of an attitude towards life. The person who is cheap financially despite being able to afford not to be is unlikely to be generous with their time and their spirit. They most likely lack the desire to help others, nor do they have the wish or capacity to give of themselves, in whatever form that may take.

But Tina and I overlook it in Fortescue. We go to pick him up in my car.

'I've looked at the brochure,' Tina tells me. 'It's ever so posh. I'd like to move there myself.'

Fortescue is waiting on the pavement. Thankfully, we're on time. He gets into the back seat. The property is in the same borough as his own house, Kensington and Chelsea, so it's familiar stomping ground for Fortescue and takes us five minutes to drive there.

Once parked up, Tina and I accompany him inside. He walks unsteadily, with the aid of a stick. The place is a wonder – the shared parts are like stepping into a chic five-star hotel. There's a bar area, dimly lit but stylish, a library, a private dining room, an award-winning restaurant, where we're lunching, an indoor swimming pool of fifteen metres that I'd like to take a dip in, a beauty salon, a cinema, a garden and fifty-six flats of varying sizes. We go and look at the one reserved for Fortescue, which has two bedroom suites, a sitting room, a kitchen and a small balcony to sit out on. He's been fairly silent, giving vague nods throughout the tour.

'Do you play bridge?' Tina asks when we pass the four smartly dressed women in the library.

'I can't abide cards, never have.'

'Maybe it's time to give it a go; those ladies looked rather nice.' Tina nods heavily towards them.

Fortescue grunts and we plonk ourselves down for lunch.

'What will you have, Tina?' I ask.

'Let's celebrate: champagne.' And three glasses are ordered.

'What do you think?' I venture, directing my question at Fortescue.

'Everything is very modern.'

'I love it,' says Tina, who I suspect is close to being eligible for a flat here.

'I do as well,' I say. 'I wish they'd lower the age of entry.'

'You're not going to badger me throughout lunch, are you? I've already had Natasha do that.' Fortescue hasn't lost his twinkle.

'Of course not.' Tina takes a sip of champagne. 'It's entirely your choice; I'm just saying, if I could move in here, I would.' A distinguished-looking man in his seventies walks past us, and Tina offers him a smile. 'Who knows,' she says. 'Maybe I will!'

'They all look frightfully smiley,' Fortescue says.

'Just think of all the new friends you could make,' Tina offers brightly.

'I've quite enough trouble with the friends I have already. I won't make *Brideshead*'s Charles Ryder's mistake of making too many friends on arrival and then having to gradually ditch them all.'

'Does that mean you'll move in?' I ask, taking my opening.

'It seems to be what everyone wants me to do,' he says.

'I don't want to alarm you but you may actually enjoy it here,' says Tina. 'And I'll be visiting like a bad penny; you won't be able to get rid of me.'

Fortescue lets out a smile. 'You, my dear Tina, will always be welcome.'

12 October 2022

We've got another offer on NT's from the first couple who saw it. And it's a decent offer. I have encouraged them, after their extensive due diligence, not to barter but to be as straightforward as they've always appeared to be and put their best foot forward. I call NT and she's happy. She is easy to please.

'Should we just accept it?' she asks.

'No, let's see if they'll go up a bit.'

I call their buying agent to see if we can meet somewhere between their offer and the asking price. We agree that his buyers' next offer will be their last, and he hopes to get them up. I've nudged the other interested party, but they've seen another house they're tempted by. Again, it's often a question of momentum, and I feel like we've run out of puff with them.

14 October 2022

I go and see Quentin.

'So,' I say, and then pause.

'So, you look well,' Quentin responds.

'Thank you. It was lovely to have a break and swim in the sea and feel the sun on my skin. Didn't you have a holiday?' I ask him and then remember the very nature of therapy is the one-wayness of it. He knows everything about me and I know very little of him. The social contract of give and take does not apply to our dynamic.

'Yes. Tell me how you're feeling.' He gives a reassuring head tilt.

'I'm well.'

'And what has been going on since we last saw one another?'

'Well, quite a bit. All is well with work. Andrew and I had a great time in Greece, and he's suggested I move to LA. Well, half move there and see how it goes . . .'

'That is a lot.'

'It is. I'm not sure how it would work – how it could work.'

'You are considering it, though?' Quentin reverse tilts, a new move, then examines me and makes some notes on the pad that rests on his lap.

'The idea would be that I'd develop relationships with LA brokers, create a synergy between our businesses, maybe get some co-listings. I don't know, it's sort of mad, but the only transferable skill I have is real estate. And there's a real estate market there.'

'There is. And how do you feel about this?'

'Excited, nervous. A whole gambit of emotions. And unsure . . .'

'But can you dip your toe in the water? Go there, explore possibilities, take a couple of weeks, see what real life looks like there.' His head is now almost bobbing from left to right.

'I'm going out later this month. There's some potential with a consortium who want to build a super-prime portfolio in London. And I *do* know what real life looks like there,' I add, a little too tartly.

'Max, you lived there fifteen years ago. You worked in a different business. And everything that's happened with you and Andrew recently has been fantastical: Greek islands, romantic nights in London, perhaps an idealisation of the life you had together previously. I'm not saying it's not all true and that the foundations aren't strong, but it's not reality. It's not the quotidian aspects of sharing daily life with someone.'

OK, Debbie Downer, I want to say. But instead, I say, 'Yes, I see that. And I am anxious about it and what the right decision is.'

'People show you who they are. Don't listen to their words, look at their actions. And it sounds like Andrew has shown you.'

'Yes. I know he's a good guy.'

'Yes. And an uncompromising one?'

'What do you mean?' I ask, with a hint of irritation.

'Has the option of him moving here been discussed? You have a life here and a business. Couldn't he do his work here?'

'I hadn't even thought of that, I guess. His life is so grounded in LA.'

'And yours isn't in London? Your family, your friends, your work, which you've built up over almost twenty years? That is something.'

'I suppose.' I look to the ceiling.

'There are no "supposes" about it; that's the objective truth.'

17 October 2022

The Monday meeting is in full swing.

'The summer has borne fruits,' John poetically proclaims. 'I've signed up two new clients. I've told them I may be away for ten days at the end of the month, so don't let that hinder the possibility of LA.'

'Snap,' Damien adds, markedly less poetic but equally chuffed. 'I've got a new client as well, from the summer. She wants turnkey, so I'm on the hunt. It seems my currency has gone up since I've been tagged in so many posts by Florentina and her mates.'

'And that's on your Instagram? What about the company one?' I ask.

'I haven't been focused enough on the work one. I know it's my gig but if you're on holiday with people who are so obsessed by it, it's a turn-off. They spent hours scrolling through their phones. We were in the most incredible bay and I couldn't get anyone to swim with me; they just wanted me to take photos of them. And the retouching and filtering. Jeez. It was never-ending.'

'It all sounds riveting. What a way to spend one's time.' I can tell Natasha is holding back an eye roll.

'Oh, I'm sorry, Tash,' Damien fires back. 'Did you and Piers spend the summer building a clean-water well in Uganda? Or were you just killing animals on his estate in Scotland?'

'Now, now. You know what I always say. Let's focus on the

ups. And we have an up. Tell them, Max.' John's interjection couldn't be more welcome.

'I don't want to tempt fate, but we should be exchanging on the Chisholms' by the end of this week, which would be perfect timing as we fly to the US at the weekend.'

'Who is "we"?' I can almost see Damien shift to his seat's edge.

'I have some news on that front too. The investors sent three business-class tickets. Kate has one, and we have two. I've spoken to BA and we can trade our two in for three premium-economy tickets. So if you're in, it will be the three boys heading out to LA.'

'Yeah, baby!' Damien shouts.

'The best possible solution,' agrees John, clearly delighted.

'Natasha, are you OK to hold the fort? I think we've got most things under control, but with the time change we'll need you. And I've asked Tina to be on hand.'

'I shall manage.' She looks despondent, and I gently remind her she didn't want to go.

'I would have liked to, but it wouldn't have been right.' She sighs.

18 October 2022

We've agreed NT's house. The buyers came up: not as much as I'd like, but it's a fair price and we're coming into late autumn so it's time to close. I send out the Memorandum of Sale immediately. This is basically a term sheet that puts down all the details – the lawyers, the price, the time frame, what's included and what's not. It's not legally binding – nothing is until the point of exchange (when ten per cent of the agreed price is put down and is non-returnable). This means either party can pull out right up to exchange, and there's no retribution, financial or otherwise. It's a crazy system and unlike almost any other in the world. When I was feeling like more of a crusader, I tried to speak to Grant Shapps (then Minister for Housing) on the subject, but he wouldn't take my calls. At the time, I was writing a column for a heavyweight international newspaper, so thought I may have some currency. Seemingly not.

20 October 2022

We've exchanged on the Chisholms.' There was a last-minute hiccup when the buyers forgot to transfer their full funds to their lawyers and had to be nudged. It's done at 6pm; 11am as promised would have been better, but as John says, 'Focus on the ups' – and the up is that we got there.

I race round to the Chisholms' house with a bottle of Cristal champagne that Billionaire once gave me, and we happily consume it. Their patience and good humour has defied everything. I tell them there must be something providential working, that they must be very lucky in life as their property luck has been so bad.

I go home elated and want to celebrate more. These are the moments I want to share with someone.

22 October 2022

I never pick up unknown numbers, but I do this one. I've been setting up meetings in LA with various brokers and think it may be one of them.

Instead, it's the silky-smooth voice of Slick. 'Max.' He stretches out my name. 'I hear you're having terrible problems with Billionaire's house.'

'Really? I wouldn't say that.'

'You can't seem to get an offer.' He yawns.

'We have an offer.'

'Rather a derisory one, I'd say.'

'Have you seen the house?' I prickle.

'I don't need to, I know those houses backwards. Now, look, maybe I can help?'

By stealing my instruction, I think. 'How so?' I say instead.

'Let me come and have a look, and then you, me and Billionaire can hop on a call.'

'I'm not here next week,' I say. I'm now worried that he may be in direct contact with Billionaire, but I suspect he's bluffing.

'I'm rather surprised at you being away when you have such an important property to sell. Why don't you get that actor chap to show me around?'

'I'll get Natasha to show you around,' I say quickly, thinking I don't want him to know that we're all absent from the office.

'Very well, I like her. Offered her a job once. Tell her to be there at eleven next Tuesday.' And with that, he puts the phone down.

23 October 2022

I give Natasha the brief and tell her not to give anything away to Slick, including the offer we have on the table. I hope it's still there. I can't call Ravi again. He'd have called if there was anything to say, and I don't want to sound desperate.

Kate and I have supper. She's in the midst of her refurbishment so will be spending just five days in California. John and Damien will be there for one week, while I'll be there for eleven days. We're at my Japanese restaurant, and we bump into the Oscar Winner and her partner.

Kate and I sit down, and she stage-whispers to me, 'She's so lovely. I thought she was meant to be a bit of a cold fish?'

'No, that's just some of the parts she's played.'

'And my goodness, the beauty.'

'I know. Stop staring, Kate, and tell me: will it be weird, you going back to LA?' I don't know why I'm also whispering.

She reverts to talking normally. 'No, it will be good. I'll see old friends, catch up. I have happy feelings towards the place; it was just time for me to move on. Where's your head at?'

'I don't feel it's time for me to move on from London. But I don't want to look back in ten years and think *what if?*'

'We can all look back and think *what if?* It's just we don't know whether that *what if* is going to turn out to be better or worse than the choice we made. But keep your heart open, Maxi. That's what I want for you.'

25 October 2022

Driving up La Cienga Boulevard, I open the window and marvel at the oil wells, still in operation, as if we're in a backdrop to *There Will Be Blood*. I take in that familiar Los Angeleno smell: the warmth in the afternoon air, the dust, the faint waft of the Pacific, the fumes and, most of all, the scent of possibility. I drop John and Damien at their hotel on Sunset Strip, slightly dazed and jet-lagged, and head up the canyon to Andrew's house. He's stayed in the same area but moved one canyon over, from Laurel to Nichols. The road becomes bendy and narrow as I climb the hill and look out for familiar sights. The houses change in architectural style from Victorian Gothic to Spanish hacienda to wooden clapboard and have impossibly long numbers. I'm almost at Mulholland Drive – the ridgeline of which you cross into the Valley – when I get to his house. It has a mid-century feel to it: it's wooden, with big glass panes letting in the light, and it's built on stilts into the slope, so you enter on one level, which has a big wraparound deck, and then go down to the floor below, which leads on to a tiered garden. The lowest of the three levels has a long, narrow infinity pool that almost blends into the hillside. It's upside down to a British house, as the living space is on the upper floor and has views across the city and the ocean in the distance, now covered in mist. The three bedrooms, one of which has been turned into a study, are on the floor below.

Andrew greets me in running shorts and a T-shirt, glistening with sweat. 'You made it through quickly,' he says. 'LAX is a nightmare; I thought you'd be another hour. I was going to be show-ready.'

'It's fine,' I say. 'You're great just the way you are. I love your place. This view.'

'I'll give you the full guided tour later. Why don't we get into the shower?' He has a point; I have twelve hours' worth of recycled airplane hanging on me.

27 October 2022

We retrace familiar patterns, driving out to Topanga Canyon with Andrew's dog, Rusty (another rescue mutt of sheepdog heritage). We walk to the vista point and then on, after which the trail becomes more or less deserted. Andrew has brought a picnic that we eat looking across to West Los Angeles, the Palisades and the Pacific beyond. The Getty perches on a hill not so far from us.

'This is one of my favourite views in the world,' I say.

'Mine too.'

'Are you sure you're happy to have my gang over tonight? I could easily go out for supper with them.'

'Of course I want them to come. They're your people, so they're my people. It's no sweat.'

'Were you always this nice?'

'I'm pretty sure I was the good guy in the relationship. At least, that's the narrative I'm working on.' He laughs.

'Oh my goodness, that's it. You're gaslighting me!'

'That's the plan.'

We drive back to his house in companionable silence, with the roof down on his Saab convertible, which must be eighteen-years-old now. I remember when it was new. I close my eyes and let the wind ruffle my hair. Rusty, sitting in the back, licks the side of my face, and I rest one hand on Andrew's thigh. I let myself drift into this being my life.

When we arrive back at the house, I say to Andrew, 'Thank you for today. I've had the best time.' I'm the designated tomato slicer, and he's busy mashing avocado, adding olive oil, seasoning and slicing chilli.

'Here,' he says, 'what do you think?' He spoons some guacamole into my mouth.

'Perfection,' I say. 'I still dream about your guacamole.' I'd been introduced to proper Mexican food when I lived in LA – the freshness and intensity of flavours were nothing like the version I'd had in the UK.

'Listen.' I lift myself on to his polished concrete counter, facing him. 'Don't say anything to the others. I haven't mentioned the possibility of me spending more time out here.'

'Why not?'

'Because we don't know what's going to happen, and I'm at the helm of our boat. I need to keep it steady.'

'But they know we're together?'

'Yes. They know we were in Greece and they know I'm staying with you, but I haven't gone into details. It's not really a discussion point.'

'So it's just like your parents all over again? There's a pattern to this behaviour, Max.'

'Andrew, it's nothing like that. There's no pattern here. We're just not sure what we're doing yet.'

'I'm sure,' he says, defiantly.

'You know what I mean.' I walk over and take him in my arms. 'Andrew,' I say, 'this has been a perfect day, can it remain that way?'

'Sure,' he says, breaking into a smile.

An hour later, John and Damien arrive, followed shortly by Kate.

'You are looking good, Mr Walker,' she says to Andrew. 'Why didn't we hang out after this one deserted us?'

Andrew smiles. 'Margarita, I presume?'

'Of course.' She takes a sip. 'I forgot, you make the best ones. Damien, you're driving me home. What's the secret again?'

'To what, love and fulfilment?' He tilts his head affectionately.

'Sod that, to making this margarita taste so great?'

'Mezcal and a high-quality tequila. A drop of liquid sugar. And fresh limes, always.'

'It's good.'

We eat Andrew's Mexican supper, helping ourselves to spoonfuls of food on his rustic table. He's put candles everywhere and cut flowers from his garden. We all glow in the dim light. I'm nervous at first, having three worlds collide: work, friendship and romance. But after my second margarita, I relax and let the conversation flow without trying to steer it.

We talk about the upcoming week. We've got several meetings with fellow agents, one of whom wants to explore an international reality TV show. I groan. Damien and Kate claim publicity is what it's all about; 'influencers' and 'followers' are key. At the end of supper, John asks for a tour and to see the garden, which is illuminated by white fairy lights hanging in the trees; the slate pool is also lit up. Andrew says I should show John around, and I like taking part-ownership of the house. We step into the garden. John produces a silver cigarette case and takes one out.

'You don't smoke,' I say.

'When in Rome.'

'LA is about the most anti-smoking city in the world.'

'Have a puff,' he says. 'It's not a cigarette, it's a joint.'

'Ah, I see. I'm OK.'

'Max, have a puff. It's legal here.' He passes me the joint. 'I like him.'

I inhale. 'Yup. I do too.'

'So enjoy it. Don't overthink it.'

'You sound like Kate,' I say, taking another puff.

'That's no bad thing.' He looks at me knowingly.

28 October 2022

It's our big meeting with the investors. Ironically, while most of the world has gone casual, the trio who represent the 'significant' fund are all in suits. One of them knows Kate and is aware of her success with LA property.

John's wearing a pistachio linen jacket, whereas Damien and I are in our uniform of chinos and button-down shirts. We meet Kate in a glass foyer and are then shown through to face the three suited men. They have a wall of glass behind them; beyond it is the skyline of Beverly Hills. It feels like we're in a movie, as if our livelihoods depend on this pitch.

Kate looks composed and speaks fluidly. 'Max and his team are the foremost agents in super-prime London. They are known not only for their ability to steer clients but for their foresight and total integrity. Between the team, they could firstly – and most importantly – find you super-prime property at value, then supervise its refurbishment, and finally handle the rental of it, should you wish to hold it as a long-term asset. All in-house. The dollar is strong, and London will always be a global capital city – language, history, culture, location, the world of finance. It is not just a European capital, it's an international player.'

I'm impressed and give her a nod of my head.

Damien talks of growth predictions, having compiled favourable analytics. And then I give my spiel as to why we're the best and what we can offer.

The talk is of an initial investment of $100 million to be spent over the next twenty-four months. My eyes are watering at our commission fees on the purchase, rental and eventual sale. They talk about a fee of two per cent on whatever they purchase, and a percentage of the upside, meaning we'd get a share of any profit made. It's sounding pretty good.

John is rather redundant, but there are only so many talking heads one can have. I try and include him as a chairman-type figure, a sort of *éminence grise*.

As we're leaving, one of the suits says, 'We've told you this is a long-term plan; can you confirm your commitment to London and your business?'

We assent heartily, though John rather less vociferously than normal.

29 October 2022

John has various old friends to see, and Andrew's working, so I drive Damien out to Point Dume and we have lunch at Geoffrey's overlooking the Pacific, then take a walk along the beach.

'This reminds me of Australia,' he says.

'I've never been.' I'm walking barefoot with the sand beneath my feet.

'You'd love it, mate: the nature, the hiking, the food.'

'Do you miss it?'

'I do, but I'll get back out there.'

'With Florentina?'

'I doubt it,' he says.

I think I've just seen Ryan Reynolds walking past us but feel this isn't the moment to fan-gawp. 'What's happened?' I ask.

'She sent me a message telling me to fly back tomorrow, as she wants to go to a party and wants me with her. I said I couldn't. She said she'd get her dad to talk to you, and I said if she did that, we would be over. And she said if I don't get on that plane, we *are* over, so it was my choice.'

'Ugh,' I say. 'I'm sorry.'

'You warned me.'

'It's not entirely her fault, you know. She's never had boundaries and she assumes everyone is on her payroll so should do what she says.'

'But I'm not. And though it kills me to say it, Natasha's right. Florentina's life is vacuous. She's obsessed with social media and the comments. If some rando writes something she doesn't like, she goes into a depression that can only be cured by spending. I've told her to ignore the comments or just stop posting, but it's like her life doesn't exist unless it's documented and liked by her followers.'

'It's sad, really.'

'It is, but I can't do it any more. And her ordering me back to go to some dumb party . . . I mean, can you imagine Natasha doing that?'

'No, I can't.' A wave comes up, splashing the bottom of my trousers. 'It's best you're out of it now, before you moved in.'

'I reckon,' he says.

'And you're OK?'

'I'm fine, mate. Look at us: we're in HOLLY-WOOD.'

We're not actually, we're in Malibu, but there's no need to point that out.

*

When I get back to Andrew's that evening, I relay the conversation to him as we stand out on his deck. He has a low level of interest in it and asks why I get so involved in the lives of my co-workers.

'Because I care about them. I see them as more than co-workers.'

'Well, don't care too much,' he says, putting an arm around me and handing me a drink. I take in the view and breathe in the scented air. 'This isn't so bad to come home to, is it?'

I slip a hand around the back of his neck while he places his on the small of my back and draws me in. 'No,' I say. 'It sure isn't.'

'LA has always been our place, Max. It's where we met. You said it yourself, you were happy here. Just allow yourself that.'

'I know, but London is home. Could you work there?'

'Max, come on.' He points to Rusty. 'I couldn't leave him.' And then he looks down at the pool and the view. 'I don't know London; you know LA. We work here. It makes sense for us.' He takes my glass, puts it down and then kisses me to prove the point. In that moment, he's not wrong.

30 October 2022

I drop off Kate at the airport after a follow-up meeting with the investors.

'Are you sad to be leaving?' I ask her.

'All good things come to an end. And you know, I'm excited about London. It's my next chapter.'

'Do you think we all have a next chapter?' I'm concentrating on negotiating the freeway. I'd forgotten about the weirdness of it being legal to overtake on the inside.

'If we want to, but some of us are happy not to turn the page. It's the classic stick or twist – and I guess I'm a twister.'

'You can say that again, *mademoiselle*,' I say, and we both laugh.

Damien, John and I continue our meetings with real-estate brokers. They're all possessors of sparkling, white-toothed grins and a saccharine veneer that gives very little away beyond platitudes. What is clear is that they can't get over what you pay in London for what they consider 'tear-downs'. And we can't get over what's considered 'European' taste – vast marble floors fit for a roller-skate velodrome and oversized chandeliers. That look may suit Billionaire's children but it's not the norm. The truth is I don't think there's a huge crossover in the LA/London market. Movie stars tend to rent, and London has more synergy with Palo Alto or New York than it does with LA.

31 October 2022

We have a second meeting with Mac, a broker. He set up his agency thirty years ago. He's brash and direct: less about teeth and rictus smiles, more about the deal. He tells us we should exclusively corner the LA/London market. His dress sense is Don Johnson in *Miami Vice* (a reference John has to explain to me and Damien, but once we google it, we get it) and he drives a convertible Ferrari – owned outright, he tells us, not leased.

His offices are the real deal on San Vicente Boulevard, between Beverly Hills and Brentwood. We're ushered into a large conference room by Cindy, who looks like she should be a model. Mac's second assistant, Veronica, arrives and offers us seltzer water, iced coffee, herbal teas, energy drinks and gluten-free goodies of a bewildering variety. We choose a mundane selection of iced coffee and water and await Mac. First in are Cody and Blair, Mac's social media 'team'. They have the air of *Dumb and Dumber*, dressed in a grunge style that seems antithetic to LA. They're in their twenties and look like they rarely see daylight. Just as John is beginning to make polite chat with them, we hear the booming voice of Mac, speaking into his headphones (think Madonna's *Vogue* tour): 'Close it at ten-point-six million; listen to me, you will not get this opportunity again. You get your client to accept and we celebrate. Vegas, the weekend, my corporate suite. It's yours. Get it done.' And click. He turns to us. 'Guys, great to see you again.'

He's wearing a low-cut T-shirt that shows his hairy chest (in a town that seems completely anti-hair), paired with loafers and a loose-fitting pale green suit.

We murmur our greetings.

Mac points towards Cody and Blair. 'I poached these guys from the back room of one of the hottest reality shows. Can't say which one, NDA, but they're social media makers. So, let's get to it. Max, what are your drivers?'

Me: 'Drivers?'

Mac: 'Yeah, your drivers?'

Damien jumps in: 'To simply be the best.'

Mac: 'Good answer.'

Me: 'Oh sorry, I misunderstood. I thought . . . anyway, never mind.' I can see Mac isn't listening.

Mac: 'And your legacy?'

Me: 'Umm, in terms of how I want to be remembered?'

Mac: 'Yes, you or your business.'

Me: 'I suppose as someone who looked after their clients, did a good job, behaved with integrity.' I'm floundering and take a pause. I've never considered my legacy before – should I have done? I'm an estate agent, not a nuclear physicist.

John: 'Absolutely, integrity is key to us. It's the bedrock of our business practice.'

Mac: 'He speaks. I like it, you've got a great voice. Cody, don't you think so?'

Cody: 'Yes. He could do the voice-over work.'

Mac: 'We can work on your legacy. And let's run through some mission statements too. So, here's the deal, guys. I like your energy; you know, that quirky British dithery Hugh Grant thing you've got going on. I've made some calls and I can see that you're *bona fide*.'

Me: 'That's good. It would have been an elaborate hoax not to be.'

Mac: 'The future is technology: online, social media, that's where it's all going. Am I right?'

Before I have a chance to respond, he's continued. It appears that was a rhetorical question.

'I've brought in Cody and Blair as we're going to do something national, but you guys came in and I thought . . . Why not *inter*national? Fate, Lady Luck, whatever you call it. You're my lemons, so let's make lemonade. Right? So, we should be filming you twenty-four-seven, have a live feed in the office, go multimedia.'

Me: 'That sounds very exciting . . . but . . .'

Mac: 'What?'

Me: 'It's not really how we do business. We're all about the off-market sale, not having things online or across social media. Our clients value discretion.'

Mac: 'They do?'

Me: 'Yes, so the idea of a twenty-four-seven feed isn't going to be for us.'

Mac: 'You know the way the world is going. You've heard of that little show called *Keeping up with the Kardashians*. We'll be selling houses online, auctioning online, viewing online. It's the future, Max.'

Me: 'I've never seen the Kardashians' show, but they're obviously brilliant at what they do.'

Mac: 'You see? We're on the same page already. Not so hard.'

Me: 'I have to disagree with you though, Mac. I don't think all sales will become virtual. There is a different feel in a property once you are in it, once you see the proportions yourself, the aspect, the views, how the light falls on it. And while there may be a market for online, in terms of broadening the base, I do believe people will always want to see property in the flesh.'

John: 'Hear, hear.'

Mac: 'I love this guy, don't you?' He nods towards John. 'Forget the voice-over, why not give him his own show? Listen, guys, I've got to bounce. Think about it. I think you're missing the future. He gets it.' With this, he points to Damien.

He's in and out in ten minutes and already taking a call before he's opened the door.

Cody: 'Do you want to do some test shots while you're here? Maybe we film you talking and drop it on to our Instagram stories? You could say something about Harry and Meghan.'

John: 'Absolutely not. We have another meeting to get to.' And with that, he stands up and leads us out of Mac's orbit.

I drop them off at the airport that evening with hugs goodbye.

NOVEMBER

2 November 2022

It's my last day in LA. I've gone back to see the investors for a third time to map out my proposal for the $100-million spend, spreading the portfolio from new builds to flats in Mayfair and Belgravia, to houses in Little Venice, Fitzrovia and Notting Hill.

I check in with London. Natasha reports Slick was clearly disappointed in Billionaire's house, believing everything was brand new rather than fifteen years old. Now let's see if he can get £18.5 million so easily. I've heard nothing about a call and am certainly not going to pursue it.

I take Rusty hiking in Runyon Canyon and imagine what half a life would look like here. The time change – by mid-morning London is closed – would be challenging, to say the least. The lack of my own anything here. Most of the friends I had here in the past have moved on. Kate no longer being here is particularly hard; even more so as she's in London, and I already miss the idea of her.

At night Andrew takes me to the birthday party of one of his closest friends. He promises we won't stay late, as tomorrow I want us to have as full a day together as possible before I get on the plane. He's suggested Christmas in Palm Springs and New Year skiing in Big Bear. *Pas mal*, as the French say. Brad (the friend) has a house in West Hollywood, on a street running between Sunset and Santa Monica Boulevard, which takes me back to the first apartment I had. I remember the jacaranda trees flowering in late spring; I'd thought the fragrance and colour the most beautiful thing.

'This looks charming,' I say, as we walk up the wooden steps.

'Don't worry, we'll be in and out.'

'It's fine,' I say. 'We can stay as long as you like. I'm relaxed.'

'Relax, Max,' Andrew sings, in the style of Shania Twain. The song 'Don't Be Stupid (You Know I Love You)' had been a hit when we were together, and Andrew always enjoyed the lyric 'Relax, Max'. He used to sing it, and the rest of the song, frequently. I returned the favour on his thirtieth birthday, when I surprised everyone (including myself) by giving a barnstorming karaoke performance of Shania's 'You're Still the One'. When I say barnstorming, I mean the literal Collins Dictionary definition: 'full of energy and exciting to watch'. It was also a train crash vocally, but I felt my enthusiasm could counter that. I was pleased to see Shania singing the same song at Coachella with Harry Styles, although when I looked at Harry, I wondered whether I could have done an equally good job.

We walk into a party in full swing; I forgot they always start early in LA. There are about thirty people there: attractive, toned and well dressed, just as you'd expect from affluent metropolitan gays and a handful of their female friends.

Andrew introduces me to Brad, and is then pulled in another direction, so I go and help myself to a drink. As I'm pouring some wine, a voice says, 'So, you're Andrew's Brit.'

I turn around and put out my hand, saying, 'I'm Max.'

'Stephen,' he says. He's blond, good-looking, five foot nine, in the uniform of fitted T-shirt and jeans that many of the other men seem to be wearing. He gives me a critical gaze, as if assessing me and making mental notes.

'How do you know Andrew?' I ask, taking a sip of my wine.

'We used to date.'

I spit out my mouthful. 'Oh, right.' I'm not really sure where to go from here.

'So, what's your deal?'

I play with attempting something pithy but can't think of anything, so end up being anodyne. 'Well, I'm here visiting and exploring some potential affiliations.'

At that point, Andrew comes over and nods at Stephen. 'There you are,' he says to me, slipping his hand around the small of my back. He works that move well. 'I want you to meet Brad properly; you disappeared.'

'You know me and alcohol.' I attempt a humorous voice. 'We can't be parted for long. Nice to meet you, Stephen,' I add, as Andrew steers me away.

I launch myself into various groups and chat away. I see this as some sort of test in which I should show that I can be socially independent and not cling to Andrew's side. Generally, I like the people I chat with. I gravitate towards a couple of women, Lachelle and Heidi. They know Andrew and speak of him warmly; they'd all holidayed together for a long weekend just over the border in Mexico, in the wine region.

'He's a cutie,' Lachelle informs me. 'And a catch.'

'I know, I need to lock him down,' I joke.

'You do, seriously,' Heidi says earnestly. 'If he was straight and mine, I wouldn't let him out of my sight.'

I'm happy to see Andrew has this tight-knit group of friends, and I try to see them as my friends. Instinctively, I find the men too quick-witted, too fast to deploy one-line put-downs and too fond of making in-jokes that are exclusionary. Andrew used to have a much more serious cohort, intent on making the world a better place. I thought I'd be inhabiting that space, not this more flippant one.

I remember being with a wonderful American client whose best friend is Candice Bergen. Candice had been making a film with Jane Fonda, and a third party enquired excitedly: 'Do you know Jane? I bet she's the most marvellous fun.'

The client had responded: 'I've known Jane for forty years. She's admirable and passionate, but I'd say Jane is a serious person.'

I'd thought of Andrew in the same way: as a serious person. But seeing him with this group of friends, he's more light-hearted. We end up being the last ones there and I find myself sitting in the backyard with Brad when Andrew goes to the bathroom.

'It's so great to meet you, Brad. And thanks so much for including me in the party,' I say, slurping back more wine.

'You're welcome, man. I'm really happy you're here. And I like seeing my bro happy.'

'Thanks.' I blush.

'When are you moving over? I tell you, he's a hot commodity in LA. They all want a piece of Andrew.'

'Does he pay you do his PR?' I laugh.

'Of course I do,' says Andrew, coming to sit beside me. I put my arm around him.

'I'm just telling the truth, man.'

'No, I'm sure.' I turn to look at Andrew 'He is a catch. If I didn't know it already, I've heard it several times tonight.'

'I paid them all.' Andrew laughs.

'You don't by any chance have a joint?' I ask, surprising myself. 'It's my last night, and . . .'

'Are you sure?' asks Andrew.

'Yes, I think so,' I say, taking his hand in mine.

'You're the love of my life, Max Thomas,' Andrew says, squeezing my hand.

'I'll go and get that spliff before this gets too heavy.' Brad gets up.

'I would,' I say. As he heads inside, I turn and look at Andrew. 'Do you mean that?'

'Absolutely. And you?'

I move my hand around to the back of his neck. 'I love you. I've loved being here with you, but I'm still stuck as to how we make this work.'

'Let's not do this now.' He echoes my gesture, placing his hand around the back of my neck, our faces close to touching. 'Do you really want a joint? On top of all that booze?'

'It's my last night. Come on,' I say. 'Have a puff too.' I take my hand away from his neck and stroke his face.

Brad comes out with a lit joint and passes it to me. I inhale hard.

'So what do you again?' he asks. 'Is it insurance?'

'He sells houses to his rich friends,' Andrew responds for me, and laughs. 'So we need to introduce him to all our rich friends so he can do the same here.'

'Yeah,' I say and inhale hard again. I take one more puff and wash it down with a last swig of wine.

We are both quiet on the way back to Andrew's house. It's a different quiet from that drive back from the beach.

3 November 2022

I have a message on landing that simply says, 'I miss you like crazy. Let's make this work.' A less agreeable item in my inbox is from Slick, informing me that he's set up a Zoom call with Billionaire – and it's happening in one hour. I'm jet-lagged and looking dishevelled; the plan had been to go home, freshen up and then head into the office. That isn't an option now. As I jump into a taxi, I wonder, again, if this is going to be the nature of my new life. Admittedly, it makes me feel somewhat important and high-powered. The dynamic agent making deals across two continents, permanently on a transatlantic flight, with the appropriate flying status to show for it. And then I nod off, jolted awake as the taxi arrives on the cobbles of the mews.

'Hello all, I've got a call with Billionaire and Slick in five minutes.' I burst into the office, *AbFab* style, in a state of high commotion.

'Take a breath. And again . . .' John looks at me with a slight sense of horror. 'We need to straighten you out.'

'That's going to take some doing!' Natasha exclaims.

Damien chuckles.

'This isn't the time for jokes.' John whips out an ebony-handled comb and walks over to me, pressing down my errant hair down, spitting on his hand and then applying it to my scalp. 'Do you have any Touche Éclat, Natasha?'

'No.'

'I've got some concealer,' Damien offers.

'Suitably metrosexual. Pass it over, dear boy.' John dabs it beneath my eyes and blends it in with his fingers. Then he pinches my cheeks. 'Just for some colour, that's better, and you've got that lovely base tan, which covers a multitude of sins.'

'Thanks, John.' I'm not sure what's just happened, but I open my laptop. John is still fussing around me, putting my computer on a pile of books and checking what the backdrop looks like with the camera on. I pull off my sweatshirt and realise there's a T-shirt beneath it.

'Here.' Damien passes me a shirt he has hanging up. 'Take this, mate.'

I button up the very fitted shirt, squeezing into it, leaving the last two buttons undone so my neck isn't strangulated. And, ping, I connect. I see Slick's face on the screen.

'Max,' he drawls. 'Nice of you to join us.' There's no 'us'; it's just him on the Zoom so far. 'What an interesting shirt . . . do you want the name of my tailor?'

Natasha waves at me.

'Just one moment, Slick.' I put him on mute.

'He's such an arse. You know he offered me a job . . . again. I told him we had some serious interest in the place and I have a ton of viewings lined up.'

'Do you?'

'Of course not. I did show another agent, who thinks he might have someone.'

'OK, thanks for the intel, and for keeping up appearances. Ugh, I don't feel good about this.'

I see now that Billionaire has joined the call, so I click off the mute button.

He's already talking. '. . . I cannot understand how such a property hasn't sold. And people want property now more than ever. Everyone I know wants to buy something that's the top; it's a marker against inflation.'

'I couldn't agree with you more, Billionaire.' Slick's using his best Uriah Heep tone, totally unctuous. 'I'm finding there are a lot of serious buyers about who appreciate a house of this quality. It's baffling to me that it hasn't gone.'

'Agreed,' Billionaire says in his usual staccato.

'And what a good job you've done in decorating the house,' Slick continues to oil.

I literally cannot believe what I'm hearing. Despite Trish's best endeavours to neutralise the house, there's no getting away from the fact that it needs a gut job.

'That was not me, it was my son.'

'Well, may I compliment your son on his taste.' There's no stopping Slick.

Billionaire says nothing. I know he doesn't agree with this assessment.

It's time for me to chime in. 'It is disappointing that we haven't found a buyer at the right price yet. But I believe we're close, and I haven't given up on the Shaykhah.'

'I don't want to sell to them. They've pissed me off.'

'I think it's the people around her who are stalling; I know the principal loves the house and really wants it.' I try and keep the desperation out of my voice and wave at John to keep silent; he is talking to someone in the background.

'Then tell her to get rid of her advisors.' Billionaire's actually picking his nose as he says this.

'If I may say, a fresh approach is needed, one to energise the property and give it the currency it deserves; we have a wonderful photographer and could get him in, get a brochure, get it on to the internet – in a high-end way, of course.' Slick's back on the offensive.

'No,' Billionaire states emphatically.

I see Natasha suppress a laugh; I'm not using headphones as I want to allow full office participation. Slick hasn't done his homework. Billionaire won't have photographs taken of any of his properties. Privacy is tantamount to him. That's the primary reason he likes us; we are experts in the off-market sale.

'Well, absolutely . . .' Slick struggles. I remain silent as he rallies. 'As you know, we would love to be involved in whatever way you see fit. We've sold many houses in Regent's Park.'

'Which ones?' asks Billionaire.

I happen to know from the central London database that he's sold only two; granted, that's one more than me.

'I don't want to bog you down with details,' Slick wafts.

'Tell me,' Billionaire insists.

'Well, we sold number 24 Chester Terrace for a record price at the time,' Slick states with confidence.

It's time for me to come back in. 'When was that?'

'And we sold 61, in terrible condition,' Slick continues, ignoring me.

'When, and for how much? Both properties.'

Go Billionaire, I think.

'We sold 61 in 2013 for eleven million.' He has to come clean.

'And the other?' Billionaire isn't going to let it go.

'Well, that must have been back in . . . I don't have it to hand.'

Luckily, I have the information and can jump in. 'According to Lonres' – the central London database – 'you sold it in 1994 for six-point-five million. Does that sound right?'

'What you have is a terrific asset that needs to be handled with professionalism and skill, and I believe we can do that,' Slick says.

He's such a politician: refusing to answer the questions he's asked but rather making the statements he wants to make. I send Billionaire a WhatsApp; I know his phone is surgically attached to his right hand.

'What buyers do you have for it?' he asks.

'Oh, a whole host of buyers whom I'd love to show it to.'

'I need to take another call,' Billionaire says. 'Slick, send me a named list of the buyers you have. Then we talk again.' He clicks out.

Billionaire had read my message and asked the only question worth asking of Slick. Let's see if, like Meryl Streep in *The Devil Wears Prada*, he really does have 'the list' – in this case, it would be made up of suitable buyers. I'm fairly confident that we've already had everyone serious in.

5 November 2022

I go and see Quentin.

'You have a lot think about,' he says, after I give him a brief update.

'I'll say.'

'And where are you in that process?' With this, I receive a particularly slow and meaningful head tilt.

'Realistically, the work side is going to be a challenge. I just don't think there's an LA/London real estate synergy. And, ironically, if I get this contract with the LA investors, I'll need to be present in London and buying on their behalf.'

'And are there other credible things you could do in LA?'

'I don't think I can launch myself as a broker there. I've just not got the right temperament. I could get to grips with the property and understand the neighbourhoods – I'm a pretty quick read on that front. But the vibe there is just not *me*. I have a reputation here, and credibility. And I've worked at getting that. I have clients, referrals and recommendations. I'm nothing in LA – no track record, no infrastructure. *Nada*.'

'And what about writing?'

'Yes, I could sit in Andrew's house, enjoy the view, take the dog for walks, procrastinate generally, map out a script. But it all feels like a fantasy world. And I don't want to live off him.'

'So, work-wise it will be difficult to establish yourself, and it's not an environment you'd naturally thrive in. Would that be a fair assessment?'

'It would,' I say, looking beyond Quentin at the range of titles on his bookshelf. James Joyce's *Ulysses* is a definite nod to his intellectual side.

'And putting work aside, what about for you personally?'

'That part of me is desperate to go. Well, the romantic side of me. I like loving and feeling loved. I've missed that. I want to share what you so accurately described as the quotidian with someone, to have those text conversations about who's picking up dinner and whether we'll watch a movie, if we'll eat in or out, or just chat. And having briefly had that back makes me realise I want it again.'

'And that's not possible here?'

'It is, of course, but I haven't found it. I'm not sure why. As my Texan godmother used to say to me' – and here I put on her accent – '"Honey, the older you get, the more picky and less desirable you become, and that's not a great equation."'

Quentin doesn't laugh but simply takes a beat and then says: 'And yet?'

'And yet, my life is here. California is great: the weather, the lifestyle, the outdoorsiness of it, the fact you can be skiing in a couple of hours or in the desert, or go to the vineyards. All that works, but I'm established here. And it's more than work: it's my friendships, my family, my everything really. My dad. And there's Kate. I love having her back here, and what we have together. It's a lot to say goodbye to and leave a twelve-hour flight behind.'

'I know we've discussed this before – but could Andrew not move?'

'Seemingly not. His dog, his work, his life.'

'So rather the same as you?'

'Yes, but we met in California and he says it's our place. I've touched on it with him and it's a no-go. I've lived there before, so it's familiar to me, whereas London is alien to him. And he won't put Rusty in quarantine. I do see it.'

'So, you are at an impasse.' Quentin scribbles something in his notepad.

'You know, that's where I often find myself in a property deal. In fact, I'm fond of using that word. But I always tell myself there is a way through.'

'And so maybe there is.'

'Maybe.'

8 November 2022

Damien and I go to show Billionaire's house to a cousin of Shaykhah's. I'm concerned there will be an entourage, so take Dame along as security. I needn't have feared, as the man –

courteous, polite and urbane – arrives on time and on his own. He doesn't give much away, but given how well he's dressed and how pleasant his manners are, I can't think that he'll like the house. As we're heading back to the office, I ask Damien for a Florentina update.

'It's over,' he tells me.

'All because you didn't fly back early for a party?'

'More or less.'

'How ridiculous . . . of her, I mean.'

'I wouldn't jump to attention. She thinks she wants someone independent but she doesn't.'

'I'm sorry, Dame.'

'I'm not; I'm relieved.'

And that's the thing about relationships. When they end and they're not right, it is just that: a relief, as well as a loss. I never had that relief with Andrew – it was always a regret, as geography took us apart.

'Does Natasha know?'

'Sure. I haven't hidden it.'

10 November 2022

After months of conversations, Natasha takes me to meet Lucy-Anne, her eccentric family friend. She has a charming house tucked behind a gate in what's officially still Belgravia. It really should be labelled Pimlico, but for financial reasons they cling to their postcode, reasoning that it adds value to the home, which it does.

We pass through what's part-conservatory, part-garage; it has a stone-paved floor with a glass-and-plastic roof leading to double doors. A lady, mid-sixties with jet-black dyed hair, sporting a 1950s-style pinny, answers the door with an air of weariness.

'Madame is upstairs,' she says.

'She prefers to receive in her bedroom,' Natasha says. 'Rather like I imagine a dowager countess would have done in the 1920s; she's old school.'

We walk up the stairs, which are cluttered with piles of books, while paintings cover almost every available inch of the walls. We pass through a first-floor drawing room, rich with fabrics and throws. We reach a door and Natasha taps gingerly saying, 'Lucy-Anne, Lucy-Anne?'

'*Entrez*,' comes the response in French, heavily accented with a Southern drawl. We enter her 'boudoir', which is thick with the scent of marijuana. She's sitting up on a mass of cushions, draped in a kaftan, with an ashtray beside her.

'Lucy-Anne, this is Max. Max, Lucy-Anne.'

'Oh my daarrrrling, you are so divine to come. Come and sit beside me. And still as beautiful as ever.' She strokes Natasha's cheek as she sits down. Lucy-Anne's accent is Jerry Hall on speed, with a hint of Scarlett O'Hara, made raspier after years of smoking. John was spot on when he said that she could be straight out of a Tennessee Williams play.

'It's so nice to meet you, and your house is just, just, beyond charming.' I clasp my hands together.

'You are a doll. Now, did Celeste offer you something? I've

just discovered this wonderful drink called a negroni. Shall I have her fix you one?'

I politely decline on the grounds it's a little early for me. It's 10am.

'Is it ever too early?' Lucy-Anne says archly.

Natasha raises an eyebrow at me.

It transpires Lucy-Anne bought the house thirty-five years ago, and she still has a property in her native Alabama, though she hasn't visited it in over fifteen years. She tells us that she can't bear seeing the place for fear it will have gone to 'rack and ruin' – which, inevitably, it will have done in fifteen years. Her nieces and nephews are trying to persuade her to down-size in London, as it appears that the various trusts she's lived off are 'running dry'.

'I can't think why,' she wheezes. 'I mean, I live like a nun. I just have a little marijuana, which is medicinal, and momma always taught me to pour drinks – that's why I need Celeste. It's what we call Southern hospitality. My nephew says there's no money; Daddy used to say it grew on trees. But my nephew works in *banking*.' This last word is proclaimed with total disgust.

The conversation continues in this vein, travels in Italy, the villa she rented in Ravenna, her love-affairs and friendships with Paul Bowles, Truman Capote and Gore Vidal.

'Those were the days. Life is so conventional now, there are so few people with style. I remember a party we had at the Cockatoo Club . . .' And as she launches herself into another anecdote, and we're now an hour into our visit, I excuse myself, claiming a need for the bathroom. Lucy-Anne seems oblivious to my departure, as she has an audience of one remaining. Once out of the room, I give myself a tour of the house. It needs gutting, but it has a wonderful secret garden as well as parking, and it's so tucked away you'd never know it existed.

'I just love that the house is *cachée*,' she'd told us, again slipping in a French word. I imagine a celebrity buying it – maybe Harry Styles. It would be good to meet him and get him on our books, I muse. And this could be the house to lure him in. I smile at Celeste as I pass her on the stairs and she follows me into the garden, whispering to me, 'She hates the nephew, but he's a nice boy. She has no more money. She hasn't paid me for three months. She needs to sell.'

'Does she have any of her own children?' I ask.

'No, and the nephew, he's a good boy. He looks after her.'

I finish my tour and knock on the door to Lucy-Anne's 'boudoir', where I offer my thanks and then apologise for dragging Natasha away, which I insist upon.

'That was the longest loo break in history,' Natasha says as we walk up Pimlico Road.

'I was having a look around. Does she actually want to sell?' I ask.

'Clearly not, but I suppose her nephew is making her. He sounds like a shit.'

'I'm not so sure; I buy the innocent Southern belle act up to a point, but I suspect she's more of a steel magnolia. She probably has a better idea of her finances than she lets on and simply doesn't want to move.'

'You could be right,' Natasha concedes.

12 November 2022

We exchange on NT's house. I am delighted, as is she. I go out and buy a couple of bottles of champagne, as I've decided this should be our new routine every time a big deal is done.

Damien and John are out with clients as I return, so it's just Natasha and me in the office.

'We did it.' I pop the cork and pour two glasses.

'You did it, Max. And this is a double celebration.'

'Tell me?'

'My dad's operation was a success. They've got the tumour out, and if the radiation takes, which they think it will, the outlook is good.'

'Natasha, this is the best news ever.'

I go over and give her a hug, and she collapses into me, her body shaking and heaving with tears.

'Oh, Natasha, it's OK. It's OK. It's OK.' I repeat it over and over, stroking the back of her head with my hand. We stay like that for several minutes, and I think of the comfort that can be given and found by simply holding someone.

'I'm so sorry. I don't know where that came from.'

'I do. You've been keeping strong for your dad, and it's just your body letting go and releasing all the emotions.'

'Thank you, Max.'

'I didn't do anything.'

'But you would have done. And that meant the world to me.'

13 November 2022

I'm on a call with Andrew as I drive home to my flat. It's raining, so not a bicycle day, and I've just put the heated seats on; he tells me it's sunny, with temperatures in the mid-seventies.

'Have you booked your ticket for Christmas yet?' he asks.

'No, not yet, I need to work on things here. And there's also my dad. I haven't talked about anything with him yet.'

'Things don't change,' he says, exasperated.

'They do, Andrew. But he's almost eighty and I'm not going to say anything until I know what's going on. I thought we'd agreed not to discuss this?'

'We did, but it's been almost two weeks now.'

'And it may take me two months, Andrew. Look, I've got to go, there's a call I need to take coming in. Have a great day.' And before he can say anything, I put the phone down. I imagine he knows I'm lying. I think of the Californian sunshine as the rain starts to bucket down and I increase the wiper speed. It's 5pm and already pitch black.

14 November 2022

All has been surprisingly quiet on the Slick front. I don't trust him, and I'm wary of him having calls with Billionaire. Equally, if nothing is going on, I don't want to mention Slick to Billion-aire, for fear of putting him in his mind. I am hoping that the Shaykhah's cousin might give a positive report.

NT calls and books in a celebratory supper, which puts me in a good mood. These are things that I'd miss if I was part-time in California.

15 November 2022

Flavia is in town meeting her decorator. She's asked John to recommend someone, and our Rolodex is full of the right people. We select one who gets Flavia and her Euro-chic style. John makes the introduction and returns to the office looking forlorn.

'Are you OK?'

'I'm rather flattered to be honest, Max.' He slumps into his chair.

'I'm sorry, John. It must be hard seeing Flavia.'

'It is. I know that I've done the right thing, but when there's something there, and you both feel it, it's hard.'

Tell me about, I think.

16 November 2022

I wake up to an email from Andrew.

> I don't want to pressure you, Max, but I'm unclear what
> the hold-up is. You of all people know that life can be fragile.
> I want us to be together.

He's referring to the heart attack I had – three years ago to the day. He's such a lawyer, remembering dates and details. I'd actually forgotten this is the anniversary of what I refer to as 'the incident'.

That day had started as any normal working day does: John did the morning coffee run; I felt a slight shortness of breath but reckoned I'd overdone it at my 7am boot camp. Natasha, John and I headed off to view a top-floor flat – the brochure promised the world, the agency selling it being inclined to use flowery language to differentiate themselves. The reality never quite lived up to the hyperbole.

'This lift feels dangerously rickety,' said Natasha as it creaked to a halt in the shabby common parts.

'And looks frighteningly claustrophobic,' added John, as the shaking doors opened to reveal a coffin-like space. 'Let's walk up . . . CARDIO!' he sang.

And off we climbed, though halfway between the first and second floor, I found myself winded – had I downed my doppio espresso too swiftly? Or just overdone the burpees and failed to accept I was soon to hit forty?

'I've got to take this call,' I said, waving my phone at them. 'You go on, I'll catch up.'

They both stopped and looked at me.

'It's Billionaire's lawyer.' That was enough to get them moving. I inhaled slowly and deliberately while sitting, down trying to remember the mantra I'd been given on a weekend meditation course some years ago. It had been offered to me like a precious gift, whispered into my ear so softly and respectfully that I didn't dare ask my shaman to repeat or spell it, so it had morphed into my own interpretation of whatever it should have been. I'd figured at the time that it wasn't really the point to create an exact facsimile of it, but in that moment I wanted to say it out loud, precisely, as if my previous distortions had invalidated the process somehow. Five minutes of deep breathing and nonsensical word-muttering later, I heard chortles from several floors above and the RP enunciation of John.

'What happened to you?' he asked, on seeing me still sitting on the stairs. 'We were worried. It could work for Dominic.' Dominic was our client. 'It's overpriced at three and a half, but you'll be able to get that down. Are you OK?' He finally noticed that I wasn't.

'I don't feel great,' I said feebly.

'You're as a white as a sheet,' Natasha said, concerned.

That's when I got worried. With her impeccable aristocratic pedigree, she doesn't really 'do' concern unless it's properly justified.

'I'm OK, just feeling a bit queasy,' I said.

'Go home, have a hot bath and lie down. Listen to your body,' John directed in his best doctor's voice. 'And Natasha's right; you look like you've seen a ghost.'

John hailed a taxi on the street, fussing over me, patting my knee and generally treating me like an octogenarian. I couldn't even chortle inwardly; every speed bump was an assault on my body, each lurch of the accelerator or heave of the brake induced a grimace. I felt a fragility I'd never known before.

Once home, I ran a bath, but an overriding sense of discomfort had me pick up the phone to my dad.

'What's wrong?' he said immediately.

'I don't feel great. I'm finding it hard to breathe.'

'Call an ambulance,' he responded, followed by: 'Do you think it could be trapped wind?'

'Umm, I doubt it,' I said, supressing annoyance. 'I can't help thinking of Mum.' She was healthy and in her sixties when she died from a heart attack.

I went through my emails as the bath filled, but I still chased for breath. Eventually, I overrode my British instinct not to fuss and called an ambulance just as the steaming bath was ready for entry. The ambulance crew arrived almost immediately, and I felt better as my blood pressure and an ECG were taken and sympathetic words offered. My breathing returned to normal and I felt a wave of embarrassment as I was told there were no signs of any heart issues – though, as I had a family history, I should be checked. On arrival at St Mary's, the same tests were repeated and I was told the same thing. I messaged my dad and told him everything was fine.

And that's where the timeline blurred but the pressure in my chest became overwhelming, as if something was weighing down on me. I positioned myself on all fours, somehow imagining it would release the impact on my heart, which felt like it was searing into me. I remember saying to the nurse who'd walked in to check on me, 'I'm going.' And true to my word, I did.

I only discovered this in retrospect, for the next thing I remember is being asked, 'Do you know where you are?' The questioner's dark hair fell neatly, framing her face like curtains.

'The hospital,' I said tentatively, taking in the scene. I was lying on a gurney with tubes coming out of me, connected to a drip. I scanned the room; pricks and aches not wholly identified jostled me into clearer consciousness.

'You've had a severe cardiac arrest. You were out for six minutes. There's a surgical team prepped at Hammersmith. Our cardiac unit is depleted, but we've got an ambulance standing by to take you there. Any questions?'

'Am I going to be OK?'

'We hope so.'

It wasn't the assurance I'd hoped for.

'You'll need to sign a release form.'

'OK,' I said, digesting it all. I cast a glance over words and signed with a squiggle, a deliberately half-hearted attempt at my signature, as if that invalidated it in some way.

'Who is your next of kin?' she asked.

'Uh, my father,' I said, awkwardly.

'We'll call him and let him know.' Two nurses unlocked the wheels of the gurney.

'Good luck,' she continued.

My stomach plunged.

The operation was a success. I was moved to the Hammersmith, and a surgical team fitted me with two stents. I spent a week in hospital in recovery, and now I have biannual checkups, take various pills and inject myself twice a month with a wonder-drug to control cholesterol. And I don't think about it, as I don't want to feel frail or vulnerable. I'd told Andrew about it when were in Spetses. He was shocked I hadn't been in touch when it happened.

Since then, I've learned not to sweat the small stuff. Moving part-time to LA counts as big stuff.

I respond to Andrew's email with a holding one.

17 November 2022

I walk into the office to find Natasha and Damien in close conversation. This is broken off when they see me, and Natasha tells me that Lucy-Anne wants to see us again. I can't do it tomorrow, as Kate has requested we spend the day together, but agree to the following day.

'Is John OK?' Natasha asks.

'He's a little flat,' I respond.

'He's in a rut,' Natasha states. 'He needs a change of scene.'

'Well, let's not go too far.'

'No, I can tell,' she says, authoritatively.

18 November 2022

Kate picks me up with *pain au chocolat* and coffee.

'This is very spoiling,' I say, sinking into the leather passenger seat.

'And why not? Nothing wrong with a bit of spoiling.'

'Where, may I ask, are we going?'

'To the Cotswolds,' she says, pulling on to the Westway and putting her foot on the accelerator. I feel the surge of electric power.

'Why?'

'I've found a place. Don't ask questions, let's just go and look at it.'

And so we do. The cottage is just outside the village where we'd been earlier in the summer. It needs a lick of paint, some general 'tarting up' and a new bathroom, but Kate's negotiated a peppercorn rent for three years in return for doing this and making it look fabulous (her word). It's late Victorian, so although it's not architecturally pretty, it has good ceiling heights and a glass-to-stone ratio that lets in lots of light. It faces south and has a sloping garden that meanders down to a stream in a valley. I can see the potential. It has three bedrooms, two of a decent size and one just big enough for a double bed. There's a bathroom and a shower room, a large kitchen with doors on to the garden, a boot room and a sitting room with an inglenook fireplace.

'It's pretty perfect, isn't it?'

'It could be,' I say. 'And you will make it perfect.'

'I want us to get it together. It will be our sanctuary.'

'Kate, I'm – well, I love the idea, but you know what's going on. I could be in LA.'

'I know, but I want you to feel that you have options. That this is a place that you and Andrew could come to. And if things don't work with Andrew . . .'

'You are a good pal,' I say and then turn away. I'm ridiculously sentimental at times, and it's when people offer me kindness that I really crack.

'Oh, sidebar news: the LA deal has come through. They're on board for us to start investing. They're starting with fifty million.'

'WHAAAATTTT?' I go full Oprah.

'I'm serious. We've got the gig. You and I are now business partners. And I thought this could be our retreat: somewhere to strategise and make property magic. A working country office.'

'I love it,' I say.

'You see, Max, it's the audacity of hope. You didn't think we could pull this off, and we have.'

19 November 2022

Natasha and I visit Lucy-Anne a second time, as she's curious to hear how we'd sell her house – and what for. I have a figure in my head, but I'm pretty sure she's a reluctant seller. From experience, these are ones you don't want to deal with.

'Can we chat after this?' Natasha asks as we cross the road to the gated entrance.

'Of course,' I say.

Celeste lets us in and we're shown into the 'boudoir', where Lucy-Anne awaits us.

'*Bienvenue, mes* cherries.' The first two words are pronounced in French, the third in English with a Southern drawl.

'Celeste, will you fix us a drink? How about a Buck's fizz? Don't you just love that quote from Madame Bollinger about drinking champagne?'

I confess I don't know it; Celeste heads for the kitchen.

'Oh, it goes something like, "I drink champagne when I'm alone or in company, happy or sad, day or night." It's something I've always lived by.'

'What's the update with the house?' Natasha asks.

'My beastly nephew is saying I must move. I hate the idea, but he's telling me *The Trust* insists and that it's necessary. But if I am to go, I need to get a decent price for this house. I've never been in a London house I'd rather live in. Have you?'

I tell her it's a wonderful house and that she's decorated it with great charm.

'Thank you. And could you sell it without having to actually bring people inside? I hate being disturbed. This is my sanctuary, you see.'

'That wouldn't be possible.'

'But don't people trust you? I presume you have a reputation.'

'I do, but a buyer would still want to see inside the house.'

'Well, that could be very tiresome. But I suppose for the right price . . . what were you thinking?'

'Well, we'd need to get a floor plan and know the exact square footage, and then run the comps.'

'Comps? What are they?'

Celeste comes into the room with a bottle and a jug of freshly squeezed orange juice.

Natasha explains that comps are houses similar to Lucy-Anne's that have sold recently.

'But my house is unique,' she protests.

'Quite right,' I say. 'We'd factor that in, but seeing what else has sold in the area will help us.'

'I'm not sure how, as I'm so different from the rest. But you must have a figure in mind.' Lucy-Anne pats her hands on some cushions and plays with an earring. I knew she was shrewder than this fey persona that appeared to be beyond money.

There's no point in delaying this. I've learned it's better to rip off the band-aid and tell people the truth. If you overvalue, you're simply left with something you can't sell. 'I suspect around the five million mark.'

Lucy-Anne chortles and receives a glass of Buck's fizz from Celeste. 'I think it would have to begin with a seven. David Bowie came to the house once and said he'd pay anything for it.'

Natasha reveals that Mr Bowie is, in fact, dead. I take a glass too. I think I'm going to need it.

There's a piercing cry. I think she must have been unaware of the sad demise of David Bowie. We sit in silence and Natasha reaches out, taking Lucy-Anne's hand in hers.

'I'm sorry,' Natasha says. 'You didn't know?'

'Of course I knew about David. This is cava. Do you see what my nephew is doing to me? He's a torturer. I don't expect Bollinger in my Buck's fizz but to have *cava*! This is what I'm fighting against. And now you tell me this beautiful house is

347

worth five million? I'm sorry, I need to be alone for a while. My nerves are shattered.'

Natasha and I take our relieved cue and head to a local coffee shop, where we sit down for our chat.

'Well, she's a character,' I say.

'She is. Max, I want to keep my job. I don't want to leave.'

'Of course, Natasha, I'm delighted! Has Piers decided he's happy to live in London rather than Northamptonshire?'

'Not quite.'

'Oh?' I take a sip of coffee.

'I've broken it off.'

I take a beat. 'You have?'

'Piers isn't as bad as you all think; it's really an act. But part of me was marrying him for my family, and when I spoke to my father in hospital, I told him that I wanted to give him the money Fortescue had given me from the sale of Victoria Road. He refused to take it. I told him that I wouldn't need it because of marrying Piers, and I knew how happy he was about that. He said he was only happy because he thought *I* was, and that if I wasn't completely committed, I shouldn't go through with it. And that the money didn't matter, as Fortescue has given him a big whack too.'

'Good old Fortescue,' I say.

'And good old Dad. He even asked me about Damien.' She smiles up at me.

'Well?'

'That ship has sailed.'

'Does he know you've broken it off with Piers?'

'I wanted to tell you first.'

22 November 2022

Ravi calls me. It seems the Shaykhah's cousin approved of the house, and their offer has increased to £17.5 million. Ravi tells me that this is it, and there's another option in Hampstead. I know the house he means, and frankly I'd take it over Billionaire's. I'm suitably threatened and call him.

'They have given us their full and final. It's seventeen-point-five million.'

There's a silence. I don't fill it.

'Is that it?' he finally says.

'I believe it is.'

'And you want your commission and don't want me to give it to Slick, so you think I should take it?'

'I think you should take it because I believe it's a good price and the market is turning. We haven't had a request for a viewing in two months.'

'Why aren't you getting me a better price?'

'Billionaire, I have tried. I've done everything, and I do believe this is a good price. I will carry on going . . . if you want . . . but I feel this could be as good as it's going to get.'

'I'll think about it.'

I come off the phone, and John looks at me expectantly.

'He'll think about it,' I say.

'We all have things to think about,' John offers cryptically, but I'm not in the right headspace to take the bait.

24 November 2022

I can't put it off any longer. It's been hanging over me, this sense that this is my last chance to find romantic happiness: that if I turn down Andrew, I'm turning down this possibility forever. Generally speaking, my approach to life is one of cautious optimism, so I'm not sure why I feel this way, but I do. Quentin and I haven't managed to unearth the reason. There's a lot I love about Andrew, and if he lived in London or I lived in LA, we'd definitely be together. But when I dig deep into my emotional core, I don't want to leave home. Maybe I'll never love anyone enough; maybe I'm not capable of it. I think I am, though. The love that I've been questioning is hard to define, because it's intangible. Yes, I get butterflies when I see him, and the chemistry is as strong as it ever was. But there's also still the dynamic of Andrew, ever so microscopically perceptible, knowing just a little bit more than me; this sense that I'm someone who fits into his world, rather than the other way round. And while I know there's never 100 per cent equality in any relationship, there are all sorts of nuances at play here. I'm the one who is having to give up a lot for him, not the other way round.

I try and explain this all to Andrew, focusing on the impossibility of the geography. He tries persuasion at first, talking of all that is good. Which is a lot. I don't falter, as I can't leave him twice. The same problem is still there. When he realises I won't change my mind, he switches to anger, suggesting I've led him on. Somehow, this makes it easier for me. It's a bruising call, and I feel utter despair on ending it, knowing that I've closed the door on this potential life. But I also know, deep down, that it is the right decision. I think again of my mother and her credo: *Don't say yes until you can't say no.*

25 November 2022

Ravi calls. He needs an answer from me. I send Billionaire a polite WhatsApp aide-memoire. He sees it and doesn't respond. I know from experience that if I push him, he'll simply walk away. And on this day, I really don't care any more. Billionaire can eff and blind as much as he likes, and he can give the house to Slick if he wants to. In fact, a part of me would like to see Slick having to deal with Billionaire.

26 November 2022

John comes in singing 'Californian Dreamin'. I don't point out this is rather insensitive, as he has no idea of what's happened. Then he doubles down, saying, 'Wouldn't it be nice to be in that Californian sun?'

'Rather than dark nights, rain and soaring heating bills? No, much better to be here, John.'

28 November 2022

I have supper with Kate.

'Well, thank God for that. I mean, it was totally ridiculous. You couldn't go and live in LA.'

'Why didn't you tell me?' I ask. We're back at our favourite sushi place.

'You had to figure that out on your own. But I was amazed you were even contemplating it.'

'I'm pleased that you and Quentin were the only people I told about it.'

'So am I. Anyone else would have thought you insane. So, the cottage is a go? Before you answer, I'll do everything: organise the redecoration, get it looking perfect.'

'There's not much for me to think about. I'm in. And thank you, Kate. You being here this year has made my life so much happier.'

30 November 2022

Natasha, Tina and I go and have lunch with Fortescue. He's moved into the flat, and we want it to be a cheering occasion. We've made it clear that it's our treat – or rather, my treat.

It's quite a contrast to his former home, with the smell of expensive candles wafting through the foyer and the chicly dressed clientele, who look ready for an upmarket Saga holiday. Fortescue is waiting in the library and chatting to two ladies when we arrive, but he pulls himself up and leads us into the dining room without introducing us to them.

'So, Uncle F, this isn't bad.' Natasha examines the menu.

'I've had to give away so many of my books.'

Tina raises an eyebrow. 'We did talk about this. And you've turned the second bedroom into a library.'

'But still.'

'You did only really live in two rooms in Victoria Road – your study and bedroom,' Natasha says gently.

'But the other rooms were there.'

We're all keen to know how he's getting on with the other residents.

'I've done my best to avoid them. They are all worryingly friendly. I can't think what's wrong with them.' There's a glint in his eye as he reports this.

'Do you eat here a lot?' Tina asks.

'Certainly not, it's far too expensive. I buy a sandwich at Pret a Manger or totter down to Marks and Sparks to get something for the microwave. You know, I've never had one before. They're rather marvellous things.'

'Well, Uncle F, I am very grateful that you've been so generous to me and the parentals. It means so much that Mum and Dad don't need to sell the farm now.'

'You'll have to keep me alive for seven years to make sure it's all tax-free.'

'You'll outlive us all,' Tina laughs.

Fortescue relents after a sherry and admits that he's rather enjoying the movie nights and having twenty-four-hour hot water and heating. He even lets slip that he's letting a dowager viscountess give him bridge lessons.

DECEMBER

1 December 2022

Natasha receives a call from Celeste. The report is that Lucy-Anne will reluctantly sell at £7 million. My suggestion of £5 million was a push, so this is hardly a win. I'm tempted just to say we won't do it. The situation with Andrew means I'm feeling less tolerant of ridiculous clients. I tell Natasha that we'll review it in the new year as there's no point in even 'placing' it on the market until mid-January.

Ravi calls again and I tell him that I've heard nothing from Billionaire. I know the nature of the beast, and I can't push it. I ask Ravi if there's any chance they will go up again and he gives me a categorical no. If we ask for more, he assures me they'll walk away. By now, I feel that I've got the measure of Ravi and know when he's bullshitting and when he's not. In my game, you have to trust your instincts, and mine tend to guide me well in business.

3 December 2022

Billionaire calls me. I knew it would happen eventually.

'What news?' he asks.

'Well, they're eager to hear your thoughts.'

'And they haven't gone up?'

'No.'

'I might sell.'

'Great,' I say quickly. 'I think that's the smart decision.'

'But this price they're offering. I don't like it.'

'I really think that's it. I wish it wasn't. And you know I would always be honest with you. I believe seventeen point five is a good offer.'

'They should give me a hundred thousand more, though. As a gesture. That would make me feel better.'

I'm sure it would, I think.

'I really don't think they will.'

'Well, there's no deal then.' his voice hardens.

'Wait, we're so close. It's such a small percentage of the total sum.'

'So why won't they go up?'

'They feel it's a good price. And while, of course, I have been presenting an argument for them paying more . . .' I tail off. There's nothing more to say.

'I'll keep it. It's a good house. I don't need the money.'

'You're right, it is. Keep it,' I say. I'm exhausted by it all.

Billionaire stays silent. And so do I.

'I hate London,' he says eventually.

There's nothing for me to say to this.

'I will sell, on the condition they move quickly and are exchanged and completed in ten working days.'

'That will be tough.'

'That's the deal. Take it or leave it.'

'I'll make it work.' I credit myself with more power than I

actually have, but I've out-pokered Billionaire so am feeling invincible.

I call Ravi immediately and tell him the terms, letting him know that he won't be getting his £250,000, but that I'll share my commission with him. I think he knows me well enough now to know this is true. He wants it as much as I do. The ball is in Shaykhah's court now.

5 December 2022

Lucy-Anne tells me how disappointed she is in my valuation and that I should give it a go at £7 million. I tell her, again, that I'm not the right agent for her, that I'd be delighted to be proved wrong, but that I can't put it on at £7 million. She harrumphs and flusters, and finally we agree that we'll try it at £5.5 million. A compromise of half a mil on my part but this new, slightly tougher version of me seems to be working.

I report this to Natasha and she promises that she'll be the principal in handling Lucy-Anne. I've been treading around her cautiously, as her wedding to Piers was to have been this weekend. She seems completely steady. When I ask her what she's up to, she tells me a friend is taking her away to a country-house hotel in Sussex.

7 December 2022

I receive a long email from Andrew. He's not happy about how things have panned out and wants us to talk. He suggests we spend New Year in Palm Springs. But I feel it wouldn't be right to go into the new year with him, much as I'd like to. What is there left to say?

I have supper with my dad. He has an extraordinary ability for insight, despite not often seeming to listen.

'Darling,' he says to me. 'Andrew sounds like a very nice chap, but your life is here. It always has been, and it always will be. And my goodness, you're a Thomas; the only reason you don't have a partner who adores you is because you don't want one. There will be other Andrews, should you wish.'

I write back to Andrew post-supper, reiterating how heart-broken I am, that geography is cruel, that I wish things could be different but the hard truth is that they are not.

8 December 2022

I show Lucy-Anne's house to a couple of buying agents. They get the house but not the price. Celeste hovers over us like a Mrs Danvers figure. To be honest, she proves rather a distraction as I try to talk up the value of the house.

I walk back to the office earlier than planned and open the door to find Natasha and Damien in an embrace. There's nothing to say, though the awkwardness is apparent.

'I'm just getting my laptop, guys,' I say, grabbing it from my desk and walking down the mews. I am elated; there is a bounce in my step and a smile on my face. I just sense they'll be happy together.

Damien runs after me. 'Mate, mate, wait up,' he says.

I turn to face him. 'It's fine, Damien, you don't need to say anything to me.'

'But I want to. I'm pretty sure Tash and I are the real deal. For me, it's always been her. And, well, she says the same about me. I took her away the weekend she was going to marry Piers and it all came out: how we really feel about each other.'

'It's—' I start.

'I love her, mate.' He cuts me off with those few words that confirm everything I need to know.

'Oh Dame,' I say. 'Come here,' I put my arms around him and give him a big squeeze. We hold each other for some moments. 'I am so happy for you both.'

10 December 2022

Kate and I go down to the country cottage. To 'our' country cottage. I can't quite believe that this is part of my life: that I have a cottage, and I'm sharing it with Kate. And that it's so close to where I grew up, and my dad. She's already made huge progress in the few weeks we've had it. She's found, at record-speed, a local builder she likes and trusts. The place has already been painted, and a new bathroom is being installed.

'How is it,' I ask Kate, 'that while everyone else is suffering from Brexit stagnation, COVID backlog and impossible building delays, you are able to mobilise so quickly?'

'I don't know, Max. I want us to have our first Christmas here – and you know when I decide on something, I tend to get it done.'

How lucky am I to be sharing a place with her?

11 December 2022

I call the Schulenburgers. Florence, like me, is a lover of property, and I often send her links on our 'property porn' WhatsApp group. I don't really 'do' WhatsApp groups, but this is an exception: membership is determined by the love of beautiful houses. A glass box in Bariloche, overlooking the lakes; a Frank Lloyd-Wright house in Montana, Big Sky Country; a Balinese villa of exquisite simplicity; or a modest eighteenth-century cottage in the Lake District. All recent postings to the group. I realise that, for me, most of the beauty in this architecture is in the setting. A house without a view doesn't have the same allure. As my mother used to say, nature trumps everything. Once, when my father put a vase of peonies in front of a painting he was trying to sell at an art fair, she advised him not to. The simple beauty of the flowers topped the Kandinsky they were in front of.

I've found a house that is beyond the Schulenburgers' usual patch. They've lived in the borough of Kensington and Chelsea for thirty-five years. In all that time, Florence has been going to the same greengrocer and fishmonger, the same hardware store and butcher. Aleco still shops at John Sandoe's bookshop. They frequent the same local Italian restaurant, Riccardo's, that they've been going to for three decades. So plucking them away from there will take a truly special house.

The one I've found is Queen Anne, tucked up a pedestrian cobbled street, opposite a National Trust house in Hampstead. It's literally a Hollywood producer's fantasy of romantic London: perfect for a Richard Curtis rom-com. In fact, Curtis and his long-standing partner, who did so much to 'make' Notting Hill, have since left it for Hampstead, and I wonder if this will become a trend for the more 'creative' types.

The house is wide and mainly on two floors. It has a ground-floor kitchen, which is a necessity for Florence. It is approached via a front garden, and the cobbled street has no car access so it's country-quiet. I spot the Schulenburgers walking spryly up the steep incline towards the house. They are holding hands and I think it's one of the most romantic things I've ever seen. After forty years of marriage. It seems that everywhere I turn, love is in the air, almost like I'm observing my own version of the Christmas hit *Love Actually*.

I know Florence will love the house – and she does. We go to a pub around the corner and talk about the possibilities of moving here. She's enthused. Aleco, more practical, talks about their children and friends who live near where they do now. He's right, of course, but it's fun to have these *Sliding Doors* moments.

I come away, as I always do, with a warm feeling from having been in their company. And I think how lucky I am to have the job I do.

This hazy winter glow, the equivalent of basking by a log fire, is punctured by a call from Billionaire. He's thinking of pulling out of the sale and suggests, again, that we're underselling it. I tell him everything is on track and that the house will be one less headache for him to worry about.

I feel exhausted by the shenanigans, and I remind myself it's simply Billionaire's way to make things complicated – but I do wonder why he does this. I'm usually so emotionally exhausted by the end of a deal with him that it loses any joy when it's complete. It's a pity.

14 December 2022

I have a celebratory supper with NT and her husband. It's a happy occasion and reminds me how simple and straightforward things can be. NT is a life force and a great example of looking forward. In her eight decades, she has had, as one would imagine, knocks and sadness, but she looks at the positive and enjoys life to the full. She balances work, marriage, parenthood, grandparenthood, friendships and an intellectual life. She is a can-doer. Many of us have ideas and thoughts, but often they remain just that: things in the abstract. NT gets things done.

16 December 2022

Kate and I start looking at properties for the fund. I'm sitting in the office, working on numbers with a calculator, when John enters with a meaningful sigh. With all that's been going on, I haven't been fully conscious of him.

'How are things, John? I don't feel that we've caught up properly for an age.'

'I've made a decision, Max. And it has been thought through. You know what you mean to me . . .' There's a catch in his voice.

'You're making me nervous, John. I hope you know what you mean to me too.'

'There's no easy way to say this . . .'

I wait, but John is inhaling deeply, as if he's doing a breathing exercise.

'Please tell me, John . . . when you're ready.'

'I'm taking a sabbatical. I'm moving to California to do a touring production of *My Fair Lady*. I'll be playing Professor Henry Higgins.'

Should I laugh? I pause for a moment, but his expression is deadly serious.

'Oh, John, I don't know what to say. I'm very happy for you if that's what you want, but desperately sad for us.'

'It's for six months. But I need it. I need to sing and be creative and be on the stage and be out of Europe, just for now. It's my *cri de coeur*.'

I'm not sure he's using the French correctly, but what would John be without a foreign malapropism?

I tell him if that's what he needs, that's precisely what he must do.

'You are family, Max. You know that.'

'That's just what I feel too,' I say.

17 December 2022

I suggest we have drinks to celebrate John. I feel that's the right word. He's declared that he's not one for long good-byes, and I rather agree with him. But I feel a bit of a salute is appropriate.

We're assured it's very much an *'au revoir'* rather than an *'adieu'*.

'It's been quite the year: *Love's Labour's Lost*, I should call it. Flavia, Florentina, Piers – though, forgive me, Natasha, I am relieved on that front. And Max, I presume your handsome Californian friend Andrew is no longer part of your romantic tapestry?' John is in a reflective mood.

'That's right,' I confirm.

'I think we should tell you that while some love may have been lost, it's also been found.' Damien looks to Natasha and continues. 'Max knows, and we want you to know too, John. Well, Tash and I are—'

'I knew it. I knew it! And I'm thrilled for you both. And I can't say I'm surprised.' John claps his hand together glee-fully.

Natasha looks at me and I give her my warmest smiling eyes, saying without words, *You know how happy I am for you. For Damien.*

John asks them to promise him one thing. They chorus their

yeses and he goes on: 'Always be kind to each other. Whatever happens. Always be kind. And remember this moment.'

We make a toast to kindness, clinking our glasses together.

18 December 2022

John doesn't come in after his farewell, but we create a WhatsApp group to receive regular updates from California.

I am chasing Billionaire's lawyer, as the exchange date is rapidly approaching. We didn't get the full documentation to them until three days after the agreement, so I let Billionaire know that they're still within their time frame. He's skiing at his chalet in Verbier and there's been an early snow dump, so he's blissfully distracted. Probably bargaining with the heli-ski companies to secure the best rate.

19 December 2022

I go to see Quentin. As I'm walking along Earl's Court Road on a well-trodden path, I realise that I'm going for my *adieu*. I first came to him so I could deal with the grief of my mother's death and navigate a life without her in it. She was the anchor of who I was, the better part of me, the person I wanted to make proud, though she never asked that of me. I think of the letter she wrote to me when I moved to Los Angeles, part of which said: 'I shall miss you dreadfully, but I can bear that all as long as you are happy.' And so happy I should try and be.

Quentin has helped me, but principally he's been the

bedrock in supporting me so I can support my father. And in supporting him, I helped myself. And my dad has come back from our loss. He has such strength. As a client of mine, the famous Russian film director Andrei Konchalovsky, said of him, 'Your father, he is Shakespearean; he is *big*.' In truth, he's part-Mafia Don and part-Jewish mother, and very un-British. He's given me and my brothers an absolute unconditional love: a sense that wherever we are, we have a heavyweight in our corner. I think of this, of my incredible good fortune in the parent I have and the one I had. And I know my time with Quentin is done.

I thank him for everything.

'And what now, Max?' This comes with the inevitable head tilt. I'll miss it.

'You've given me the tools, Quentin. Andrew is on the other side of the world and, at the moment, he's not terribly fond of me, so there's a communication embargo. I am sad, but I will be fine. I'll obviously be sickeningly jealous of the love bomb between Natasha and Damien.' I laugh, to indicate this is a joke and he doesn't have to make notes in his book about my green-eyed nature. I go on: 'And I shall miss John. But he'll be back. There is the cottage in the country with Kate; there are work opportunities to be excited by. And I'm going to start scribbling more, using that MFA I have in creative writing.'

'I like the sound of all of that. And I wish you well, Max.'

It feels like a hug sort of moment, but I suspect there are therapist/client boundaries, so we nod at each other meaning-fully and I turn and leave his consulting rooms.

20 December 2022

We're ready to exchange on Billionaire's. I can hardly believe it. The purchaser's lawyers are in funds, but our lawyer can't get hold of Billionaire and asks me to help.

I call Billionaire and it goes to voicemail. I follow it up with a WhatsApp, letting him know we're ready to go and are awaiting his authorisation. An agonising two hours later, I hear from him; he's having lunch and has clearly had a couple of glasses.

'Do it.'

'Are you sure?' I ask, and actually hit myself for asking that.

'Yes, yes, it's a good price . . . you agree?'

'I do.'

'Get it done. And well done, Max. You showed that Slick.'

I am loving this side of Billionaire. I tell our lawyer to message Billionaire *now* to get authorisation before he changes his mind.

She pings me five minutes later and tells me it's done. What a Christmas present.

21 December 2022

I love that Zara is continuing her Christmas party tradition but in a way that reflects her new life. In truth, I'd rather dreaded her parties of old, as they were full of people who looked you up and down, assessed you and calculated whether you had any potential value to them. Inevitably, I didn't. It was never a *simpatico* group. The staff ratio was too high; the spaces became cramped, and not in a good way. I went because I like

Zara, and I liked Spencer back then, but I always made sure I arrived punctually, gave them five minutes face time and then slipped away after half an hour.

This party is completely different. There's a warmth and friendliness as soon as the door is opened, by Zara's children rather than a hired butler. Friends mingle, pouring potent cocktails and passing around nibbles. Everyone plays their part. The open-plan room holds a group of forty or so. There are a couple of people smoking in the garden, which lets in a nice shot of cool air. Zara looks relaxed and happy and very pretty. I go to greet her.

'I'm loving this party vibe,' I say. 'And you look great. Really great.'

'Thanks, Max. It's a new mix this year, new neighbours, old friends. Spencer's even here.' She nods her head in his direction.

'With the Pilates instructor?'

'No, that seems to have fizzled out.' Zara waves a greeting to someone across the room.

'And have you two fizzled back together? No, that doesn't really work, does it? I can never do word play.'

'I don't know, Max. He wants to and there's a part of me that wants to, more for the children, but . . .'

'A soufflé never rises twice,' I say, taking a quail's egg from a child who is handing them around.

'Something like that.'

Spencer's looking at us as we chat, and comes over. 'Hi, Max, good to see you.' He offers his hand.

'Hi, Spencer,' I say, in the flattest voice I can manage.

Zara excuses herself. I'm not sure what else to say. I felt hurt by Spencer choosing Slick, but at least it's clearly defined the lines of friendship. And I'm really angry with him on Zara's behalf.

He breaks the silence. 'So, well done on finding Zara this house. She seems to love it.'

'Yes, she does. And, along with her many other talents, she's made it a home. In the best sense of the word. A place of warmth and happiness.'

'Point taken.' He looks around the room.

I don't say anything and nor does he. At that moment, an arm touches my shoulder and I turn to see Percy.

A few hours later, there are ten or so people left at the party, and Percy and I are sitting on a sofa, chatting. He's telling me about a new exhibition he's curating that will travel across Europe. In a pause, I go to fetch us both a glass of water. The cocktails have done their work.

'So what happened in Los Angeles?' he asks, holding my eye and facing me on the sofa.

'It was a good trip. We secured a terrific new work contract.'

'Congrats. But that wasn't really what I was asking about.'

I take a swig of water and decide there's no point in being coy. 'It didn't work out with me and Andrew.'

'I can't pretend to be sorry.' And for a moment I think he's going to lean in and kiss me, which would be suitably dramatic – and would certainly wrap up the Christmas party satisfactorily. Instead, he says, 'I'm desperate for a pee, hold my seat.'

I'm not sure it's the line Richard Curtis would have written.

Zara comes and sits beside me. 'So, New Year's resolutions, Maxi?'

'Hmm, I haven't thought about it.'

'Well, come on. Think about it now.'

'What are the four life corners of the square again – work, family, friendships, romantic love?'

'And what about fulfilment? Giving back? Altruism?'

'Well, that too, obviously.'

She passes me her glass. 'Have a sip.' I do.

'I'll do gratitude for now. I am so lucky to have you in my life, Zar.' I lean in and kiss her on the cheek.

Percy stands over us. I give Zara a seated hug and then get up. It's time for my exit, stage left, or rather through the front door.

Percy walks with me. 'I'm having a New Year's Eve party. Will you come?' he asks.

'I'd love to,' I say and kiss him goodbye on the lips. He may not have had the Richard Curtis line, but I'm taking the filmic moment.

I walk home to my flat. I feel happy and optimistic.

30 December 2022

Christmas is spent with my dad and family. Kate and I meet at the cottage on Boxing Day and spend the following days titivating it, keeping the fire going almost constantly, taking muddy walks through fields and being the best sort of non-romantic couple. We sit and talk in the evenings with glasses of red wine by the fire and reflect on the past year and the one to come. There's a lot of laughter and self-deprecation, two elements that have always bonded us together and I believe always will.

Life rarely follows the plot of a Jane Austen novel, with everything neatly tied up by the last page, but this year has ended with much falling into place. Fortescue's settled and as happy as I think he's inclined to be; Billionaire's house is sold. Zara is well and resilient, and ready for wherever life takes her. Damien and Natasha are in love and spending the holidays together. John is in Montecito, staying with friends before rehearsals start in early January. He's been keeping us updated. And I am where I am. Happy to be with Kate. The new year will bring new adventures: the LA fund, Lucy-Anne and a flash of Tennessee William's theatrics, no doubt some shenanigans with Billionaire and a few adversarial bouts with Slick. The wheel continues to turn.

The thing with property is that it reflects life: you never know what's around the corner. But homes – finding them, making them your own, sharing them – say so much about us.

I think of the quote I have plastered above my desk: 'It's never too late to be who you might have been.'

And I believe in the mantra. It sounds about right to me.

Acknowledgements

There are many people to thank for seeing this book come to fruition. Way back when my friend Joanna van der Borgh encouraged me to do a creative writing MA, my tutor, Hanif Kureishi, taught me to search for authenticity and supported and cajoled in perfect balance. Alison Beard took a chance on me and commissioned me to write a weekly column in the *Financial Times*, 'The Secret Agent', for many years.

My clients have been, as this book attests, on the whole a pleasure to work with and many have become friends. And for that I am very grateful. The trickier ones have all taught me something – usually patience!

My colleagues make it a joy to come into work every day. Without them, my working life would be far duller. A particular thanks to my F.

Sarah Emsley at Headline believed in the book from the get-go. Holly Purdham's expert editing has only improved the book.

In seeing the book become a reality, I owe the biggest debt to Charlotte Merritt of ANA. She steered the ship with utter professionalism, dedication and calm perseverance. It wouldn't be here without Charlotte. Thank you.

THE SECRET AGENT

There are too many friends to name but my father and Saffron Wace allowed me sanctuaries of beauty to edit and write in. The triumvirate of Yanna Stewart, Simon Hombersley and Jane Thompson have in their ways been bedrocks of love and support that will always be reciprocated.

Finally, my dear friend John Huddles has – for nearly a quarter of a century – encouraged, improved, edited and been a greater stalwart than I could ever have hoped for.